KAMMY

About the Author

Chris Kamara, known to millions as 'Kammy', is one of Britain's best-loved television presenters. A former professional football player and manager, he worked as a pundit and football analyst at Sky Sports for twenty-three years, achieving cult status for his off-the-wall catchphrases and lively banter with Jeff Stelling and the team. In 2022, he left his post at Sky Sports after being diagnosed with the neurological condition apraxia, which impacts his speech. He continues to present a number of television programmes and podcasts, including *Ninja Warrior UK*, *Cash in the Attic* and *Kammy & Ben's Proper Football*.

He joined the Royal Navy at the age of sixteen, before signing with Portsmouth FC in 1974. He went on to represent several other clubs, including Swindon Town, Brentford, Leeds United, Middlesbrough, Stoke City, Luton Town, Sheffield United and Bradford City, until he finally hung up his boots in the mid-1990s. Following his retirement from playing, Kamara became a manager, first at Bradford City and then for a brief spell at Stoke City.

In March 2023, he was awarded an MBE for services to football, charity and anti-racism.

CHRIS KAMARA

KAMMY

MY
UNBELIEVABLE
LIFE

MACMILLAN

First published 2023 by Macmillan
an imprint of Pan Macmillan
The Smithson, 6 Briset Street, London EC1M 5NR
EU representative: Macmillan Publishers Ireland Ltd, 1st Floor,
The Liffey Trust Centre, 117–126 Sheriff Street Upper,
Dublin 1, D01 YC43
Associated companies throughout the world
www.panmacmillan.com

ISBN 978-1-0350-2384-4 HB
ISBN 978-1-0350-3665-3 TPB

5 7 9 8 6 4

A CIP catalogue record for this book is available from the British Library.

Typeset in Fairfield by Jouve (UK), Milton Keynes
Printed and bound by CPI Group (UK) Ltd, Croydon, CR0 4YY

Visit **www.panmacmillan.com** to read more about all our books
and to buy them. You will also find features, author interviews and
news of any author events, and you can sign up for e-newsletters
so that you're always first to hear about our new releases.

Contents

Foreword by Ben Shephard		vii
Introduction		1
1	Speechless	7
2	In My Defence	15
3	The Home Front	31
4	Falling	35
5	Kick-Off	47
6	Secrets	61
7	On the Move	65
8	Out	71
9	Growing Up	73
10	Ups and Downs	83
11	Moving On Up	91

12 Feeling the Love   95

13 Leeds United   103

14 Enter the Dragon   119

15 Boro   121

16 Lost at Leeds   125

17 Gary   129

18 Kammy the Gaffer   135

19 Lost for Words   151

20 Sky Calling   157

21 I Don't Know, Jeff   165

22 *Soccer AM*   173

23 *Goals on Sunday*   179

24 Shep and Steph   197

25 Be Yourself   203

26 Hollywood   215

27 Crooner   223

28 Brazil   251

29 Animals   271

30 Royalty   279

31 Giving Back   295

32 A Mountain to Climb   307

33 Mexico   319

34 Extra Time   335

Acknowledgements   337

Picture Acknowledgements   339

Foreword

August 2010
World Cup, England v. USA
Rustenburg, South Africa

You never forget the first time you meet Kammy.

For me, it was in South Africa at the 2010 World Cup. England versus USA – not the greatest game of football, and not the greatest atmosphere either. The whole World Cup in South Africa was blighted by the presence of the vuvuzela, an instrument that single-handedly sucked away, suppressed and generally destroyed the atmosphere of any stadium it was allowed into.

Fortunately, I had something very special to distract me – a shining light of joy, laughter and teeth (so many teeth!) in the form of Kammy.

'Heeeeeeyyyyyyyy Shep!!!' He's a bit like a northern Fonz, just without the thumbs and with a bigger, broader, beaming smile.

'Hi Kammy, how you doing?' I smiled back.

'Ahhh, never better!'

It's an exchange that would become familiar to me over the years. To this day, whatever he's going through, regardless of how serious or tough life is – and, in the coming pages, you'll read just how tough it has been – his response is always the same, and he never wavers: 'Ahhh, never better!'

That first meeting was just a few weeks before we started working together at Sky Sports on *Goals on Sunday*. Kammy didn't know it at the time but, after that first meeting, I just couldn't wait to get started. Kammy was a confirmed legend in the world of football and had been hosting the show since the early 2000s. I was the new boy from a completely different world of broadcasting, and to say he welcomed me with open arms would be an understatement; there was always a fresh pint or two available at the rugby club behind Sky right after the show.

My time with Kammy on *Goals on Sunday* was one of the most enjoyably instructive, challenging and brilliant experiences of my career. Of course, I learned so much from him about football – his fascination and joy in exploring the detail analysing any incident is endless. But one of the most telling things I learned from him was the importance of not taking yourself too seriously. Kammy was always the first to laugh at something unfortunate that he or I might have said – of which there were plenty! The shirts he wore in those first few seasons were notoriously loud; so loud, in fact, that the man who sold them to Kammy was thrilled they were leaving his shop, and only sold them to him as long as he didn't tell anyone where he'd bought them. But, despite this laid-back approach, he never compromised on work. He took immense pride in what he did, what we were discussing and his analysis. No one worked harder or wanted to deliver a better show.

Over the years, I've taken great joy in witnessing Kammy's work move from the world of sports broadcasting to the world of light entertainment. A world of stylists and make-up artists to help you look your best/younger/less tired self (this is a part of TV he's really embraced!) – all the glitz and glamour that Kammy was made for.

We got the chance to work together again, alongside Rochelle Humes, on *Ninja Warrior*. The show is filmed in Manchester over two weeks each summer. As Roch always says, 'It's like our summer school trip,' the three of us acting as ringmasters to this remarkable circus of incredibly physically fit and nimble men and woman as they take on the world's toughest assault course. The fact that Kammy, Roch and I didn't quite measure up to some of the physical specimens on show was never lost on us. We would struggle to climb the stairs to our commentary tower, let alone swing from ropes, fly through the air or try to 'beat the wall'. This was illustrated vividly one evening when the three of us had to walk down a staircase together, in front of the live audience of hundreds of people, to our start positions and introduce the show.

Everything was set: the director queued the theme music; the audience were screaming and shouting; and the voice-over announced, 'Please welcome your hosts, Ben Shephard, Rochelle Humes and Chris Kamara!', to even louder cheering. It was at this point we started descending the stairs . . . only to reach the bottom and realize that Kammy, who had been distractedly high-fiving kids in the audience, had missed a step and ended up rolling down the final few stairs to settle in a heap on our start position. Although it wasn't the most ninja-like manoeuvre, in typical Kammy fashion, he styled it out beautifully – with a broad grin and of course a huge laugh. The audience loved it, and we still laugh about it when the three of us are together now. In fact, I don't think I've ever laughed as much as when we were filming *Ninja Warrior*. We were so lucky to work with such a great team on the commentary, and they really let Kammy and me bounce off each other.

You can't begin to know how loved and recognizable Kammy is until you go out on the street with him. Honestly, it's like going out with Justin Bieber. Everyone wants to say 'hi' and have a picture taken and, Kammy being Kammy, he never says no. As a young boy, he once waited for hours for an autograph from a footballer who, when they eventually emerged from the stadium, just walked past him. This stayed with Kammy and he promised himself that, if he ever became famous and was asked for an autograph, he would never say 'no', because he knows what that feels like to the fan.

It really speaks to who he is and what's important to him that he stays true to that ethos to this day. It can get a little frustrating, however, when we are already late and he's stopping for every single person in the street to have a picture and shout 'Unbelievable!' What is unbelievable is that we ever manage to get anywhere on time!

In the past few years, Kammy's health has really affected him and his TV work. For someone whose career has been built around spontaneity, quickness of wit, pace and energy, to be suddenly robbed of that for seemingly no reason has been really tough. His confidence took a huge hit. Even though, for me, Kammy firing on one cylinder rather than eight is still better than the average person firing on ten, me saying that and him believing me are two very different things.

As you'll read in the pages that follow, Kammy came to a serious crossroads in his professional life. We discussed him stopping broadcasting entirely as, in his own words, he suddenly 'felt like a fraud'. It was something I was always convinced was not the right thing to do, but Kammy needed to come to his own conclusion, so I was very honoured when he trusted me and my production company to make a documentary about his diagnosis, *Chris Kamara: Lost for Words*. The documentary set out to share what he was going through, the treatment, other cases, and the journey that would hopefully allow him to make a decision about his future broadcasting career.

Kammy's frankness about how apraxia has affected him made the programme immensely powerful. We have both seen the positive impact of his honesty on children, teenagers and adults – and their family members – who have the same or similar conditions. We were in Lake Como, recording our podcast for BBC Sounds, when a couple approached us. There we were, in Italy, miles from home, and these people came up, excited to meet Kammy and thank him for the documentary. They had a family member with apraxia and the documentary had really struck a chord with them; they said it would make a massive difference to the understanding and awareness of the condition. This was a really moving moment for both of us, and one of the many signals that helped Kammy realize the public that love him don't want him to stop broadcasting – despite what he's battling. Crucially, he concluded that he really doesn't want to stop either. He spent his footballing career taking on the trickiest opposition and never giving an inch. Apraxia may be his toughest opponent to tackle yet, but his journey and battle to do that could well be the most important match of his life.

Kammy is unique. Professionally, it's been a dream (and occasionally a nightmare) to work with him; I've learned so much from him. Personally, it's an absolute privilege to call him a dear friend, and a true pleasure to see how becoming a grandad has filled him with as much joy as he creates in others.

Everyone feels that they know Kammy – and, to a certain extent, you do – but once you've read his story and got to understand what makes him tick, what makes him smile and what makes him laugh, you'll not only know him better but you'll love him all the more – maybe even nearly as much as I do.

Ben Shephard
September 2023

Introduction

THERE WERE TIMES WHEN I'D WONDER WHERE HE'D GONE. Kammy, that is. You know Kammy? Always there with a quick quip. Happy grin. Making Jeff Stelling laugh, wince, or weep on *Soccer Saturday*. You must know Kammy – 'Unbelievable Jeff!' and all that.

I used to know Kammy too. But then he disappeared. I've spent the past three years trying to find him again.

Don't get me wrong, there is a Kammy out there, but recently he hasn't felt like the real one. He's felt like an embarrassment. A fraud.

He's been slowed down, like someone's put an old 45 on the record player and then realized they're listening to it at 33.

At the same time, words have become muddled, or even sometimes totally impossible to say.

When he woke up, the first thing Kammy used to think was, 'What did I say last night?' Now it's, 'Am I going to be able say anything today?'

1

Somewhere between brain and mouth, the Kammy that everyone knows had been lost in translation.

That's not great. For Kammy, the voice is everything. For good or bad – mostly good, I hope! – millions of people know him the minute he opens his mouth. His voice is his trademark.

Sounding like someone completely different is no use to him. He sees it as the death knell to the life he's come to love. If his voice isn't working, how can he carry on?

Slowly, creepingly, apraxia, a rare neurological disorder, has arrived at Kammy's door. It doesn't only affect speech. It affects balance, dexterity and strength. Away from the cameras, Kammy has been falling down a lot. He's changed the way he dresses so doesn't have to deal with button-up shirts. His laces are so loose a little kid might as well have tied them. He's stopped eating things that mean having to unscrew lids off jars.

To be honest, Kammy would live with the odd stumble, a bit of difficulty with a button, for the rest of his days if it meant getting his voice back to normal. The voice would make every-thing fine again.

Kammy, you might recall, was someone who used to talk at a million miles an hour, pretty much saying whatever came into his head. In fact, until now, the only problem Kammy's ever had with his mouth is how often he'd put his foot in it.

Then he became the complete opposite, clamming up because he couldn't keep up with the conversation, let alone add anything off the cuff. A bit of banter would be in his head but by the time it reached the tip of his tongue the moment had gone.

It felt like he'd gone for a run with friends only to find they were permanently fifty yards up the road. In the end, he'd just sit there and say nothing. The only conversation was with himself: 'How has this happened? What did I do?'

People are very nice. They say that 25 per cent Kammy is good enough, but he doesn't want to be half, let alone a quarter of what he was. He wants to be the complete Kammy. That's why he's been ready to walk away from it all. Simply disappear from public life. Maybe even disappear from life altogether. If he can't be Kammy, what's the point?

That's why Kammy, ex-footballer, bit old school, kept his fears to himself, made out he was just a bit tired and overworking. Professionally, he became very good at covering up the problem. To get through performances on screen, short words and even shorter sentences helped to disguise the issue. I know better than most how Kammy thinks, and his attitude was very much 'I don't want it to be there, so I'm going to pretend it's not there.' I know also that wearing a blindfold is only going to lead to a collision with a brick wall. Getting away with it? The only person Kammy was kidding was himself.

Kammy has no idea why apraxia has come to visit his brain. Was it all those years heading a ball? Maybe. Or perhaps it's totally random. Either way, he's come to see that asking 'Why?' is utterly pointless. No one can provide the definitive answer. The more relevant question is 'How?' – how can it be fixed? He hopes there's something out there that can help him in the long run. In fact, he's travelled the world to find a solution.

Those are the lengths he'll go to in search of the person he was before. The one who could walk into any situation – showbiz, sport, audience with royalty – and not worry. Who had a natural confidence about him. Whose life-embracing motto was, 'What's the worst that can happen?'

Kammy's had enough of feeling trapped, of being stuck inside someone he doesn't want to be.

He wants to get back to being me.

*

Being me has been fun. I might be struggling to speak at the speed I used to but I still have plenty of tales to tell. And that's what you'll find here as well: stories, memories, incidents – many of them as daft as you might imagine – that reflect the person I am.

A lot of them come from the life of a footballer, which I always knew I was lucky to have. I sometimes played with a grimace on my face but every time I was smiling on the inside. To be a professional footballer was simply, well, WOW!

Then when finally I left the game I enjoyed a TV career that was again – yes, I'm going to say it – unbelievable. I became part of some of the biggest landmark football shows around, met some of the greatest names in sport, and had the most amazing time while doing so. If that wasn't enough, I was welcomed into mainstream TV and even recorded a couple of albums!

All this for a lad from Middlesbrough.

I never stopped long enough to think of myself as an inspiration, but people tell me I am. The only time I've ever really paused to consider anything like that was when Prince William gave me my MBE.

At a moment like that, you really do think about the road you've been on. If you don't mind, I'd like to take you down that road too. It's a bit like the one outside my house. Smooth in sections, a couple of blind bends, and the occasional pothole!

Together I think we'll enjoy the ride.

Chris Kamara, August 2023

1

Speechless

My heart felt like it was beating out of my chest. I was gripped by palpitations.

I'd been doing live match reports on Sky for more than twenty years. My appearances on *Soccer Saturday* are what I'm known for more than anything. I'd actually been the instigator of this kind of on-the-spot reporting. And yet now, facing Jeff down the camera, my tongue felt as if it had swelled to double its size, as if it was hanging out of my mouth. The famous Kammy smile had disappeared. I was also sweating profusely. Hot prickly heat spread up my back. If no one had been around, I'd have been pulling at the neck of my shirt, trying to get some air in. But of course there were plenty of people around – including an audience of thousands staring at me on their TV screens. All I could think about was getting through what had become an awful and terrifying ordeal.

I'd noticed a change in myself, as if someone had taken

over my voice box. Like someone else was talking through my mouth – someone with a slow and increasingly croaky voice. Each morning I'd taken to shutting myself in the bathroom and talking to myself in the mirror to see how quickly I was speaking and if I sounded 'normal'. At first, it seemed to have no pattern to it. One day it was there and the next day it wasn't. Or I'd have three days on the bounce when I was suffering and then it would disappear. Other times, I'd feel happy with what I was hearing in the bathroom, but then by the time I got downstairs and started talking to my wife, Anne, I'd sound totally different. If she asked, I'd wheel out the 'I'm fine – just a bit tired' excuse. It became a catchphrase, I'd use it so much over the next couple of years.

Of course, in reality 'fine' was the last thing I was. The fear that my vocal problems would trip me up, hold me back or be noticed by the *Soccer Saturday* team would lead to off-the-scale anxiety. When I'd hear that Jeff was coming over to me for the first time, I'd feel properly scared, like something really awful was about to happen – a creeping presence, slowly grabbing hold of my mind until I was barely able to function. Panic is not something I've ever experienced. This is me. Kammy. Speak first, think afterwards. Never fazed by anything. And yet nothing – my experience, know-how, nothing – could prevent the onset of a truly horrible feeling of dread that would only get worse and worse. This was something I'd been doing for years – and now the thought of doing it was making me feel seriously ill.

When the cue finally came, all too often I could hear how slowly I was talking. How words weren't coming out clearly. How I had no power or personality in my delivery. It was beyond devastating. *Soccer Saturday* meant so much to me, as did my relationship with Jeff, and now I was letting him down – at least that's what it felt like. Having spent so many years working to such high standards, I was devastated I couldn't reach those same levels every week.

After one game at Doncaster where I'd clearly struggled with a couple of names, Jeff rang me to check I was OK.

'I'm just tired,' (the catchphrase) I told him. 'It's not easy covering players you're not familiar with. I'm looking at my notes, the match programme, the game and the camera all at the same time.' I wanted to believe that was true, but deep down I knew the truth. My words weren't flowing properly. What had once seemed so easy was becoming increasingly hard work.

I noticed also that people were starting to comment on Twitter after games. After I had reported on a match at Rotherham, one person asked, 'What's up with Kammy? Is he drunk?'

'Has he had a stroke?' wondered another. I hoped no one at Sky was reading those tweets.

Of course, my work extends way beyond *Soccer Saturday*. After a particularly tough day filming an advert on the famous Transporter Bridge in Middlesbrough, I asked for the footage to be sent to my agent for approval – he responded by asking the production team to speed up my voice in the final edit. I was horrified that it had reached the point where some kind of technical intervention was needed to make me sound normal.

Elsewhere, my first appearance on Channel 4's daily lifestyle show *Steph's Packed Lunch* turned out to be a disaster for me. It was a job which I really wanted to succeed, especially since it meant appearing alongside fellow Teessider Steph McGovern. Filmed live, I really struggled with the autocue when I had to read out the news of the day. After the show, I noticed a tweet – 'Before getting Chris Kamara to read the autocue, somebody should have checked if he can read or not.'

Again, I was shocked – the audience had noticed that something wasn't right. The TV company certainly had too. When I did the show the following week, they changed my role so I didn't have to read from the autocue. I also incorporated a routine – two Red Bulls and a large bottle of Lucozade at nine in the morning before I arrived on the *Packed Lunch* set, and then keep topping up with more Red Bull before and during the show. I didn't want my caffeine and sugar intake to give me wings, so long as it gave me words. In the very short term it seemed to work but in reality it was a sticking plaster on an open wound.

As ever, if anyone asked how I was, I'd insist I was OK. And actually every now and again a good day would come along to fool me that I was worrying unduly – everything was going to be all right. Although it was out of my comfort zone, when I was a guest pundit for a rugby league match between Castleford and St Helens I was completely comfortable, my old self, utterly unfazed at being in an unfamiliar environment. I felt the same when appearing on Michael McIntyre's primetime quiz show *The Wheel*. Everything went perfectly and for once I drove home happy.

A few days later, however, I was back on the floor. I covered Huddersfield versus Bristol City, with my son Jack, who does a lot of work for Sky, on the camera. While I love working with Jack, that day was probably the worst I'd felt. My reports really weren't up to scratch – slow, no energy – but nobody said anything, not even Jack.

As I reached the top of the gantry steps, which I'd walked down literally hundreds of times, I was gripped by a feeling I was going to fall down the fifty or so concrete steps before me. My balance seemed to have gone completely and I negotiated them very gingerly. As I reached the last one, I saw a steward looking at me. 'Watching you come down the steps reminded me of my old man,' he joked. He wasn't to know, but it was the last thing I wanted to hear.

'I know,' I replied, 'you can't be too careful. I've slipped over before.' I hadn't, at least not here – I was making excuses.

On the way home, I had a call from my long-time Sky colleague and pal, the former Fulham and West Ham defender Tony Gale. 'Are you OK, Kammy? You don't seem your normal self.'

I made a joke that it must be my age. But I knew Galey was right to worry and people were starting to cotton on. We talked all the way from Huddersfield until I was nearly home. He finished off the conversation by saying, 'Don't work too hard, mate.' It would be a while before I listened.

Matters came to a head when, after adding an unexpectedly successful singing element to my job description, I went on *The One Show* to promote my second Christmas album. 'Right, tell us about the album,' said presenter Michael Ball. I just looked at him. There was literally nothing in my head. I couldn't think of the name of the album, and I couldn't think of any of the songs. I was talking, mumbling, but had no real idea what I was saying. He then set me up to reveal that Roy Wood was a surprise guest on the record. Again it was gone. 'What's his name?' I said. 'You know him, he's an absolute legend.'

Finally, Alex Jones put me out of my misery – 'It's Roy Wood.'

'Oh yeah,' I said, barely audible, 'That's him.'

Michael must have got a word in his ear to finish the interview quickly. 'And a Happy New Year is Chris Kamara's second album, and it's available to buy now.' And that was that.

I went into the green room, where Adam, the record producer, was sitting. 'I've gone, mate,' I told him.

'What do you mean, you've gone?' he asked.

'I couldn't remember anything. I can hardly speak.'

Usually in a green room there'll be people in and out all the time. This time, nobody came to speak to me. I was worried they might have thought I'd been drinking. I felt I'd spoiled the show. I'm normally a glass-half-full type of guy, but now it was definitely glass-half-empty. Adam did his best to change that by buying me two miniature rosé wines before I boarded my train back to Wakefield.

'Hi, Kammy, how you doing?' It was the conductor – after twenty years as a regular on the service, I'd got to know all the staff. I'd just started to reply, when he interrupted – 'Oh, you've had one or two, I'll leave you alone.'

It was another shock. 'Hang on,' I thought, 'I've had two miniatures and he thinks I'm drunk!' All I could think about for the rest of the journey that night was packing it all in.

When I got to Wakefield station, Anne was waiting for me in the car. 'Oh my God,' she said, 'you came walking out of there like an old man with the weight of the world on your shoulders.' Those two words again: 'old man'.

Anne had watched the programme herself and so had witnessed my abject performance. 'What's the matter with you?' she asked.

It was the perfect moment to let it all out, to finally unburden myself and allow her to help. And of course I didn't take it. 'All this travelling is catching up with me,' I replied. 'I'm just exhausted, not sleeping properly.' Still hiding. Still in denial.

I thought that because Anne was with me so much, the changes in me would have appeared gradual and not so notice-able. Of course, the truth was she'd been watching my decline with as much concern as anyone else. She'd noticed the loosely tied laces. Also that I was becoming increasingly unsteady on my feet – which I shrugged off by saying I was having trouble with my back. She was giving me that chance to talk but, stupidly, I was determined to fight whatever was happening to me on my own. I didn't kid her. I didn't kid anyone close to me. The only person I was kidding was myself. I chose to pretend I was still the same Kammy as ever. When I woke up the next day I talked to myself in the mirror and sounded OK. All good then. Except of course it wasn't.

Another low point came with a live New Year's Eve party for the BBC. Fellow guest Shirley Ballas thought I was drunk on the show – I'd only had water all night. She wasn't alone. One tweet I read later said, 'Did you see Kammy? He was funny but he was three sheets to the wind.'

To be honest, I didn't mind. It was better than people think-ing there was something medically wrong with me. And not all my audiences were so critical. I read a children's story on Zoom for my grandson Solomon's nursery school and didn't see any negative tweets all afternoon!

That aside, I knew, reluctantly, that the point had come where I couldn't go on hoping my problems would simply go away. This wasn't like being a footballer where you feel a niggle but stay on the pitch in the hope of 'running it off'. This issue, whatever it was, wasn't going to miraculously disappear. This time, life wouldn't work out like that. I was in trouble. A deep dark pit of trouble. Scrabbling at the sides wasn't going to get me out. If I was going to see daylight again I needed a helping hand.

By the time I reached the conclusion that I needed to act, I'd spent a year keeping my fears to myself. When I should have been sharing my worries I simply kept bottling them up. When I did take the lid off I was ready to explode. Fear and lack of knowledge eat away at you. Is there something seriously wrong with me? Is this dementia? Alzheimer's? There'd been several high-profile cases of footballers of my era now paying the price for repeatedly heading a football. Could that be what had happened to me? I tried to put those thoughts aside. But it's like having lions sleeping at the bottom of your bed. You're just waiting for them to bite.

2

In My Defence

BLOKES ARE RARELY ANY GOOD AT SHARING THEIR PROBLEMS, and unfortunately for me I'm one of the best examples. In fighting that battle on my own, all I'd done was heap a whole lot more stress on myself.

But that was me – just get on with it. Once, as a player, I broke my cheekbone on the Saturday and still played on the Tuesday night. It hurts breaking your cheekbone, but it's a great way of winning over a new set of fans. That was my second game for Stoke City. When I turned out to play on that Tuesday they knew they had a player who was never going to give anything other than his absolute all. At the end of the season, they voted me supporters' Player of the Year!

★

If those fans had been able to time travel back to early 1960s Middlesbrough, they'd have seen why I had that attitude. Not

15

so much because I wanted to. More because I had to. Middlesbrough wasn't the easiest place to be at that point – and being a black kid made it particularly difficult. We were the only black family on our estate, and my dad was one of only a handful of black men in the town.

Dad was christened Alimamy Kindo Kamara but changed his name to Albert, possibly after the huge old sign for Albert Road that he'd have seen as his train pulled into the station that first time. There's also an Emily Street and a Vulcan Street, so it could have been worse.

Dad was from Sierra Leone. He told me he was brought up in a mud hut, without basic facilities and electricity. He escaped to the Navy as soon as he was old enough. Sierra Leone was part of the British Empire at that time, and he originally signed up during the Second World War to do his bit. After the war, his ship docked in Liverpool, and he jumped on a train to Middlesbrough. Knowing the trains up north, it was probably the hardest part of his travels! That was in 1949, and it's about as much information as I have. I love nothing more than interviewing players and managers for Sky, but never quizzed my dad about his life growing up in Africa. He never talked about it and I never felt comfortable trying to break down that wall of silence.

Our family consisted of my dad, my mum Irene, my older brother and sister, George and Maria, and me. Dad's working life was spent in the blast furnaces at British Steel and chemical paints department at the ICI plant near Redcar – two dangerous jobs in industries that dominated the town back in the day.

Dad often got into fights in town. Racism was rife and he was a target. Dad was never going to take prejudice and aggression lying down. He stood up for himself and his family. If anything happened on the Park End Estate where we lived, when the police were called, inevitably he was the one who was arrested.

I lost count of the number of times the police knocked on our door and took Dad away. Sherlock Holmes they were not. A crime had been committed and Dad fitted the bill. He'd get cleared, come home furious, and a few days later the whole process would start again. Neighbours would shout, 'It's that black family there causing all the problems,' whereas Mum and Dad simply wanted to get on with their lives and be left in peace. If pushed, though, Dad wasn't going to sit there and not defend himself.

Funny thing was he drove it into me and George that we should turn the other cheek to racist abuse and never react. 'Take it on the chin and ride through it,' he'd say. 'I'm saying this for you, and you'll benefit.'

That wasn't always easy. Sometimes it would seem like, apart from my close mates, the whole town was racist. Forget the keyboard warriors of nowadays, back then people were quite happy to deliver their hatred straight to your face. And because nobody had any sympathy or empathy for what I was experiencing, they got away with it. If I had confronted someone, it would have been me whose behaviour was deemed unacceptable. I was well and truly on my own.

I'll never forget the first time I encountered racism. I was eight and, as often happened, had been sent to the corner shop to buy cigarettes – ten Woodbines for Mum, twenty Full Strength Capstan for Dad. I'd just given the note to the shopkeeper – I was way too timid to ask – when a woman pushed in front of me and asked for a pint of milk and a loaf of bread.

'I'm serving this young man here,' the grocer pointed out.

She looked at me. 'His lot should go back to where they came from,' she said.

'I live five doors away from you,' I thought. 'I'm not from somewhere else.'

The shopkeeper stood his ground: 'No, no, I'm serving him.'

She stormed out – 'These blacks shouldn't be here.'

I took the cigarettes and went home, her words still ringing in my ears.

I've tried to blank such incidents from my mind – carrying that weight of negativity around in life isn't useful – and have largely succeeded in doing so. But there will always be times that bring moments of prejudice springing to the front of my mind.

A couple of years ago, for instance, I was honoured to switch on the Christmas lights in Wetherby, thrilled to see more than 3,000 people turn out on that chilly night. As I prepared to press the button, compere Bryn Law, my former Sky Sports colleague, did a little interview with me and asked about my recollections of visiting the market town over the years. I cryptically replied that I had many great memories 'and one not so great'. I didn't elaborate, as I wanted to keep the mood light, but it's fair to say I had received a very different 'welcome' on my first visit in 1976.

Wetherby was the traditional stopping point for teams coming back from games in the north-east. It was the last day of the 1975–6 season, and my Portsmouth side had just been relegated from the then Second Division, losing to Sunderland, who went up as champions. In the mood to drown our sorrows before the long journey home, we stopped in Wetherby, placed our order for the chippy with our club physio and headed to the pub opposite for a couple of pints.

Straight away, the barman spotted me among the lads – 'We don't serve his type in here.' I'd been going to pubs for a couple of years by then and would occasionally be refused entry because I was 'wearing jeans' or if 'the place was full', but I always knew the real reason why I wasn't welcome.

It was the first time many of the lads had witnessed such blatant discrimination. 'Do you get that often?' one of them asked.

'Occasionally,' I replied. 'It's part of life. You get on with it.' It bothered my teammates more than it bothered me, but I had grown up as a black lad and was used to it. In those days, when Leeds were at home, Alan Ingledew sometimes took me and his son Jason to Elland Road. It was part of the agreement for me joining Alan's Sunday team at Beechwood Youth Club and playing for them in the Teesside Junior Alliance, one of the biggest youth leagues in the world. It was frightening walking to the Leeds ground. I was just a skinny young kid from Middlesbrough and couldn't understand the hatred that was directed at me. I'd sometimes get racist abuse at Middlesbrough games too, but I was usually with my mates so I could handle it and block it out.

In Leeds, the taunts were relentless when we got near the stadium. Even though I was with Alan and Jason, who were white, and had my white, blue and yellow scarf on, people stared and spat abuse. Alan treated me like his own son and held me close at all times. 'Keep your head down, son,' he'd say. 'Just ignore them.' It was intimidating, but I felt safe with Alan. I never let the ignorance of a few affect my love for football and for Leeds United and that team. And every time Alan took me, I imagined the day I would play at Elland Road, which is why I'll always treasure my time at the club.

The good memories will always outweigh the bad. On the same day that the barman refused to serve me in Wetherby, I remember Sunderland's captain Bobby Moncur finding me after that end-of-season game. 'I can't believe you're only seventeen, son,' he told me. 'You're going to be a good player – keep working hard.' It was also my first taste of champagne – courtesy of Bobby and the Sunderland players, who sent a few bottles to the away dressing room as they celebrated winning the title.

It's hard to explain the emotion I felt when the request came through to switch on the lights in Wetherby. On the evening, everyone was lovely, the mayor and dignitaries couldn't have been nicer, and I thoroughly enjoyed the event, sharing in everybody's anticipation of a 'normal' Christmas after many months of disruption due to the Covid lockdowns. The only downside for me was that I was not having a good day with my speech, so I had to limit my words. The next day, I headed to my Twitter account to celebrate the good time had by all. But I also shared my early Wetherby memory and received overwhelming support in return. Many people could hardly believe what had happened all those years earlier, and I made a point of saying that attitudes have changed since the mid-seventies and the world is a better place for it, even though there is still work to be done.

★

Two decades after that Wetherby pub ban and too many years to count since abuse was hurled at me outside Elland Road, I got involved with Show Racism the Red Card. The charity was established that year thanks to then Newcastle keeper Shaka Hislop, who'd recently started to play for the club when he stopped for petrol near St James's Park with his pregnant wife Desha. Four youths shouted racist abuse at him as he paid, but when one of them recognized him, they went over to ask for his autograph. The experience had a profound effect on Shaka, who realized the power of football to educate young people. The incident also coincided with a letter sent to Newcastle United players from founder Ged Grebby on behalf of an organization called Youth Against Racism in Europe. Shaka was the only player to reply and sent a £50 cheque and a letter outlining his idea to educate kids. Ged teamed up with his fellow Newcastle fan and activist Kevin Miles to form Show Racism the Red Card, along with Shaka and Viv Anderson, who was then Bryan Robson's assistant at Middlesbrough, and the first black man to play a full international for England.

They started with the big three clubs in the north-east – Newcastle, Sunderland and my hometown Middlesbrough – talking to schoolkids around that football-mad region. This was the era of Kevin Keegan's 'Entertainers', so when Ged and Shaka brought Newcastle players like Les Ferdinand to the schools, the kids went crazy. And they listened. I was Bradford City manager at the time, and Ged contacted me and asked if they could bring their workshops to the club. I of course welcomed them with open arms and soon started doing a few talks myself around the primary schools in West Yorkshire. It was never heavy stuff, simply the truth about my experiences over the years.

The aim of Show Racism the Red Card is to educate people at a young age and teach them about the effects of racism and how to speak out. This is hugely important. Anti-racism must also be taught at home, but by educating children in schools we can encourage that age group to pass on their knowledge to their elders, some of whom, unfortunately, either remain ignorant or part of the problem. It's about teaching kids when they're young, because when they're older it's harder to break down barriers. Kids soak up information so well at a young age – that's the time to guide and teach them.

Kids don't see colour. I'm a different colour to my sons Ben and Jack, but to their kids, my grandkids, I'm just Grandad. When they paint pictures of me, they paint me brown, because that's what I am. I'm not different – I'm Grandad. No one is born a racist, so advising young people what is right and wrong gives them a fantastic chance to be themselves and say, 'That's not right,' or, 'I don't want to be part of that, and I am going to walk away.' Show Racism the Red Card has made a huge difference over its twenty-five-plus years, but there is still, sadly, much work to do.

When the charity launched a new magazine at Middlesbrough's Riverside Stadium in October 1996, a small group of players and managers got involved, and only a handful of media turned up for the press conference. But slowly, over time, interest in the organization and its cause increased hugely. In fact, it wasn't long before Show Racism the Red Card was attracting a number of high-profile players as supporters. In 1996, as well as signing up Shaka, Viv and me, Peter Reid, Kevin Keegan, John Beresford, Les Ferdinand, Gary Bennett, David Kelly, Dariusz Kubicki, Curtis Fleming and Glenn Hoddle all came on board. The following year, another sixty high-profile managers and players signed up, including Bryan Robson, Paul Merson, Kenny Dalglish, Eric Cantona, Sol Campbell, Paul Ince, David Ginola, Dennis Bergkamp and John Barnes. Today, of course, I'm glad to say virtually every player and every club supports the campaign.

When I got the sack from Stoke City, of which more later,

Ged and his assistant Gavin invited me to join them on my first trip with the charity – around the schools of Ireland – and I became a patron of the organization later that year. There were just the three of us with a box of leaflets driving round Ireland in a car back then. Today the charity has grown to more than forty staff, with offices in Newcastle, Manchester, Glasgow, Cardiff and Southend, and they have educated more than one million kids in their workshops since 1996. In 2022, 440,000 took part in the annual Wear Red Day, which shows the charity has never been more relevant and supported. I've done a number of events over the years and contributed to debates in parliamentary committees. I've even given a speech at Oxford University.

I was also among 170 footballers, managers, rugby players, basketball players, celebrities and dignitaries invited by the then Prime Minister Gordon Brown to a garden party at Number 10 on behalf of Show Racism the Red Card. Chelsea manager Avram Grant also turned up, even though it was the week of his team's Champions League final match with Manchester United in Moscow. Reading chairman John Madejski was there to support Shaka just a day after his team had been relegated from the Premier League, and the big keeper was hobbling around the garden on crutches after breaking his ankle a few weeks earlier. I knew the PM was a Raith Rovers fan, so when I was introduced, I made sure to quiz him about his team, who were flying high in the Scottish Second Division at the time (I'd done my homework). But I wasn't the only one. Gordon said he was a huge fan of mine and had followed my football and management career and watched me on *Soccer Saturday*. Before I knew it, he was leading me back into Number 10 and taking me on a personal tour of the building, including the famous staircase and the pictures of the former prime ministers on the wall. If I couldn't believe it, I am not sure many of the other guests could either.

In early 2023, I went along to a Show Racism the Red Card event at Huddersfield Town's John Smith's Stadium just after the charity had engaged more than one million people in their anti-racism educational programme since 1996. It's a fantastic achievement. It wasn't only me and Ged this time. John Beresford came along as a fellow patron. Bez was with Shaka for the charity's first presentation at a school in Newcastle and has been awarded an MBE for his services to anti-racism. And, like me, Bez has watched up close the growth of the charity from those early days, and how much it has become an integral part of the game and seen the difference it has made. I gave a little talk with Bez, and we were joined by former Town forward Fraizer Campbell, and academy players Tom Iorpenda, Cian Philpott and Fope Deru, for a question-and-answer session. Frazier's from Lowerhouses, Huddersfield, and he certainly brightened up the day for the kids from Field Lane Junior Infant and Nursery in Batley, and Moldgreen Community Primary School, Huddersfield. We all did our best and simply hoped they got the message. The workshops we presented to clubs in the late 1990s were a first for the Football League, and we only had a few magazines, stickers, leaflets and CD-ROMs. There are now videos with dozens of world and Premier League stars backing the campaign – a million miles away from those early days and that trip to Ireland.

When I go into schools, I tell the kids about the racism I've suffered, and say to them that I hope they will never have to go through what I went through growing up and playing football. The N-word was prevalent when and where I grew up, and

throughout my football career. But, like when Shaka was recognized by his abusers, I haven't heard it since I started going
on TV and the 'Kammy' character evolved. Of course it is still
happening, and kids should not have to put up with racist abuse
today. It has certainly improved, though. When I was at school,
people said racist things to your face, and we all accepted it –
nowadays, they hide behind social media accounts.

★

Rightly or wrongly, I blanked it out back then. My mates remember the abuse I got more than I do, and they were more likely
to deal with it on my behalf. As much as Dad fought back when
he was arrested, and after becoming number one suspect when
anything untoward occurred in our area, he always told me and
my brother never to fight back.

I would hear racist abuse all the time playing junior and
school football. It wouldn't take much for a player or parent to
scream something at me if I committed a foul or scored a goal.
I ignored all of that on the football pitch and never let it bother
me, which was just as well, because when I joined Portsmouth,
I played alongside one or two teammates who were not comfortable with my colour.

There was only a handful of black players in English football
when I broke into the Pompey first team, so I was a rarity to
fellow players and supporters. The home dressing room at Fratton Park had a huge communal bath, and when I jumped in, one
or two players would immediately get out – it wasn't a coincidence. There were a lot of racist 'jokes' told within earshot – and
people would say, 'Hey, Chris, you don't mind, do you?' I didn't
really have any choice, so I tried my best to laugh along with

them. No black player would have ever dreamed of speaking out about it back then; I just had to swallow it. If you were black and wanted to be a professional footballer, you were expected to get on with it, because abuse was part of the game. On the odd occasion I challenged it, I'd be told it was a bit of fun and I should shake that chip off my shoulder; I put my head down and played.

Certain other incidents stand out, like the day a banana was thrown at me at Millwall. The Den was a tough place for any visiting footballer – it could even be a tough place for their own players – but it was especially so for a young black lad in the mid-seventies. I made the mistake of going over to take a throw-in and was met with a volley of abuse and monkey chants. Then, suddenly, the back of my shirt was covered in spit and a banana landed at my feet. I never took a throw-in at the Den again. Millwall had two black players: Trevor Lee and Phil Walker. I could only feel for them, having to witness that sort of abuse by their own fans.

When I was a manager, there were a couple of incidents involving the opposition crowd which I'd like to think would not happen today – or would be dealt with differently. I was managing Bradford at Oxford United when I was called a 'black b******' by a home fan who was sitting behind the dugout with his young child. He had been abusing me all game whenever I got up to remonstrate with referee Steve Baines, an ex-Bradford player who, in my opinion, wasn't having a very good game. The fan suddenly let loose with a volley of abuse and the racist slur, and I had to be held back from jumping into the crowd like Eric Cantona by my assistant Paul Jewell, who was appalled by what he was hearing. I might have heard it all before, but this was new territory for him. Fortunately, a police officer stepped in and escorted the individual from the ground with his son. I decided not to press charges and said I only wanted a letter of apology. Oxford threatened to ban him unless he sent the letter, but nothing came of it. I hope he was banned. Oxford United couldn't have been sorrier on his behalf.

The language was very similar when I was in charge of Bradford City at Port Vale. As I was walking down the tunnel to the dressing rooms at half-time, a Port Vale supporter came from nowhere and started having a go at me, calling me every name under the sun, preceded by the word black. I needed to get to our dressing room for my team talk but made sure to tell the stewards about the incident and the individual in question. You can imagine how furious and disappointed I was when the same person was still in his seat after the half-time break. I tried to get the stewards to throw him out, but they simply refused. I later discovered that he had been thrown out but the club had decided to let him back in because he'd claimed I'd started it. There was an FA investigation into that claim – and the incident – but I wasn't surprised to hear that nothing came of that either.

Ironically, in 1989, while captain of Stoke, we lined up against our nearest rivals, Port Vale, who had Robbie Earle as their captain. It was the first time two black captains had faced each other in a Potteries derby. We shared the spoils that day in front of 27,000 locals.

During my time at Bradford, chairman Geoffrey Richmond occasionally insisted that I go up to the boardroom after the game, home or away, and meet the opposing directors. There were some boardrooms where I felt people weren't comfortable in my presence. It's a look they give you, something in their demeanour or how they treat you. It's strange but you grow up to recognize that look of disdain. And, of course, in those days there were no black faces among the directors, same as there were few female executives either.

I'm pretty sure that day at Port Vale was the last time I was racially abused to my face. I don't think I heard it working as a pundit or reporter at games for Sky, and I certainly haven't heard it filming programmes like *Ninja Warrior* or *Cash in the Attic*. When I first started going round the grounds for Sky, I think there was some scepticism – but that was more to do with my ability and lack of media training, rather than the colour of my skin.

The most blatant racism I've encountered in the years since my playing and managerial years was when making the simple journey to Tenerife. I quite often travelled to the island on a Sunday afternoon, via Madrid, after recording *Goals on Sunday*. The direct flights had all departed by the time the show finished, but I liked flying to Madrid and getting the connection to land in Tenerife in the early hours of Monday morning, rather than losing half a day travelling the next day. I always flew with only hand luggage, and I always travelled in the front rows to get a quick getaway when we landed. I must have made that journey more than fifty times, yet on a couple of occasions, the last one being about ten years ago, I was pulled in for questioning by airport security staff with guns and taken to a room with a one-way mirror and strip-searched. I had done nothing wrong. The second time it happened I knew why they had stopped me, but it was still terrifying. And humiliating. After being questioned – and clearly giving the right answers about my identity and reasons for travelling – they still stripped me completely. I have since spoken to a few of the Senegalese lads who sell their goods on the island – some of whom are now Spanish citizens – and they've told me they have been subjected to that treatment on countless journeys to and from the island.

Those incidents gave me a real insight into how they are treated. It only happened to me on the internal Spanish flights, and not once on the hundreds of occasions I have flown from the UK. It is a horrible experience. It makes you feel dirty, and although I wanted to be rude to the officers and object to the treatment, I knew it might make the situation much worse.

Thankfully, my experiences when I have been picked out at British airports have been much more pleasant. Anne and I had once flown into East Midlands Airport, when I was approached by two serious-looking armed police officers as we stood in the passport control queue. They addressed me by name and asked me and Anne to follow them. Our hearts sank – we were both concerned that something was terribly wrong at home. They didn't say a word as we walked off, and we had no idea where they were taking us or why. They took us into an interrogation room round the corner, put their guns down on the table and said, 'Can we have a selfie?'

★

People told me when I was a kid that I would find it hard to play football professionally because of my colour. I did it. People told me I would find it hard to become a manager when I retired from playing because of my colour. I did it. Then people said it would be hard for me to go into the media. I did it. Then people said it would be hard going into mainstream TV. I did it.

I was driven, regardless of my colour. I never used it as an excuse. It meant nothing to me – I carried on regardless because I wanted to prove myself. I never thought what I was doing was to improve diversity – it was simply my determination to succeed and prove myself. I had that work ethic, to do my job and be conscientious, and hope that would get me through.

As I said to Steven Bartlett on *The Diary of a CEO* podcast, I never regarded myself as a trailblazer when I started to work for Sky Sports. I didn't think at any stage that I was a role model for future generations, but I now realize that maybe I *was* an inspiration. Just seeing me on screen, I have been told, has spurred people on in the hope that they can take the same path as me – and this is from those who are now enjoying their own very successful careers.

The opportunities in the media for people of colour have improved so much in recent years. Look at the number of black people working in TV compared to the 1980s or 1990s, or when I was growing up in the 1960s. There is more equality, but I know it is not the same everywhere. Racism is still there, and I will be there to fight it for as long as I am needed.

3

The Home Front

HOME WAS SOMEWHERE NOBODY COULD TOUCH US. BUT IT didn't always feel comfortable. Dad's presence dominated. For instance, only he was allowed in the front room. We had to stay in the kitchen when he came in from work. Mum would give him his tea and he'd go in there, put the radio on, and sit and eat. When finally we got a telly he'd sit on his own until he went to the pub, while we sat in the kitchen.

Dad was always cold, so the coal fire in the front room had to be lit when he walked through the front door. I was eight when I learned that trick – pages of the *Evening Gazette* on the bottom, layer of coal on top, another sheet, then coal, like a fuel lasagne – not that there was a lot of lasagne around in Middlesbrough in the 1960s! The fire had to be kept going so Dad could sit in front of it when he came back from the pub. The absence of central heating meant the rest of us were in the kitchen relying on heat from the oven. No wonder that while he was out we'd nip into the front room, switch on the TV and enjoy a cop show or *Match of the Day*. All was good so long as we scarpered upstairs before his hand was on the doorknob.

Dad ruled his house with an iron fist. I loved him because he was my dad, but his volatile temperament, which often spilled over into violence, could make life difficult. Only later did I realize this wasn't how all homes worked. Despite everything, my mum was the most loyal wife you could imagine.

She was also absolutely everything you could want in a mother. My main protector, she'd do anything for me – I don't think my dad saw my school report from the age of five until I left school at sixteen! – she was my world.

Mum looked after me and the rest of the family as well as she possibly could. On Thursdays, despite thrombosis in her legs, she'd walk ten miles to the ICI plant to meet Dad at the factory gates and make sure he didn't take his pay straight to the bookies. In later years, she trekked to the British Steel works in Grangetown, near Redcar, and they'd go straight to the pub from there while the three of us sat outside, each with a bag of crisps and a bottle of pop. We spent hours outside pubs waiting for them to come out when we were younger. Then, once George had reached eight or nine, we'd wait alone at home. Sometimes I'd be out playing football until about ten o'clock and nip indoors when I heard the bus bringing Mum and Dad home. Little food and all that exercise – it's no wonder I was as skinny as a rake.

If money did run out, Mum had a couple of neighbours she could call upon to borrow milk and bread. She had to do that so we could eat. She often got turned away, but she persevered because she needed to see her kids were OK.

Years later, I told Dad that the way he'd behaved towards

Kammy

Mum had been wrong. But he wouldn't accept what he'd done. He'd mellowed tremendously in his old age and probably erased much of his past from his memory. Yet here I was, exposing it all. It was a mistake. I should have kept it to myself. I have very few regrets in life, but that is definitely one.

4

Falling

MY CHILDHOOD, AND THE BATTLES IT CONTAINED, SEEMS A very long time ago. Right now, I feel more like an old man than I ever have before. A few weeks ago, for instance, I found myself on the floor at Dallas Fort Worth Airport, where me and Anne were changing planes on our way from Heathrow to Mexico. It seemed a simple task: to take ourselves from one part of the airport to another. Unfortunately, though, as happens in so many airports, it was about a half-mile walk to the departure gate, and after a few hundred yards my body began to seize up. Eventually I quite simply fell to the floor. My knee took the brunt of the fall and I needed assistance to get me back on my feet. I was embarrassed more than anything – the only thing that had been hurt was my pride. What hit home was the look on Anne's face: totally horrified that my situation had come to this.

I'd like to say this fall was a one-off. It wasn't. It was just the most public. In fact, I'd fallen on numerous occasions, once actually into a wheelbarrow full of manure – I might be getting on a bit but I still like to do things in style! This wasn't at a country show or the middle of a garden centre, I'd like to point out: we have a few animals – sheep and a couple of horses – on the land at the back of our house. I'd shared the manure incident with Anne. I thought it was a lucky landing – the wheelbarrow, with me perched on top, somehow managed to stay upright – but Anne was more concerned than amused. To suddenly start falling is a pretty good indication of all not being well. And now here I was on the deck in the airport too. I was busy resisting the offer of wheelchair assistance – the ultimate humiliation, in my mind. As I hobbled the rest of the way it was more confirmation for her that this journey we'd embarked upon was more than justified. After all else had failed with my apraxia, we'd travelled to Mexico for one last throw of the dice.

★

The internal struggle of dealing with the good days and the bad, talking to myself in the mirror to jump-start the day, and then saying nothing to anyone else had continued until early 2021 when, finally, I bit the bullet and made an appointment to see my doctor. I walked into his room, sat down, and it was like an avalanche – everything I'd been going through for the past twelve months came crashing down on the poor bloke.

When I got home, Anne commented on how long I'd been at the surgery, not surprising really – I'd told her I was going for my bad back. The time had come to be honest and so we sat down together while I revealed exactly what had been going on. First the doctor, now Anne, and eventually my entire family, it felt like a whole weight had been lifted from my shoulders. Everyone said

I'd done exactly the right thing – I'd opened up and sought help. There was shared hope that I'd be back to my old self before long.

Blood tests showed I had an underactive thyroid. I felt my prayers had been answered. 'Underactive' – that explained everything. I felt I'd been switched to a slower speed, after all. They'd give me a few tablets to get my thyroid back to normal activity and that would be it. All good.

My thyroxine levels were raised with a hormone-replacement tablet. The dose needed to be increased gradually. My thinking was that when finally the balance was right, my problems would be solved. It was a slow process, involving lots of blood tests to monitor the levels, and plenty of patience. So many people reported that the medication had changed their lives for the better that, to me anyway, my own recovery was never in doubt. I'd be my old chipper self in no time. From then on, the only problems in my life would be the pure unadulterated Kammy cock-ups that everyone was used to.

At that point I also decided to talk about my health problems on *Steph's Packed Lunch*. It was a relief to admit publicly that I wasn't a sandwich short of a picnic, that I had, indeed, been struggling but that it was down to an underactive thyroid. A specialist came on the programme to explain that the earlier the thyroid condition was detected the better.

'If you had gone to the doctor initially when you first had problems,' he told me, 'it might have saved your thyroid. Your thyroid doesn't work any more.' It was a good lesson for anyone out there watching to get themselves checked out early.

Steph told me she'd been worried about me for a few months and that it had crossed her mind that perhaps my slurring was down to booze. The only drinking I was hiding from her was the gallons of energy drinks I was consuming to get through the live shows. More than once I talked openly on *Packed Lunch* whenever the conversation took us that way, and Steph always took time to have a conversation before the show and to ask how I was feeling.

Reaching the correct level of medication did settle things down a bit but didn't make as significant a difference as I'd hoped. Disastrously, because this was what bothered me more than anything, the struggles with my voice continued. At the same time I started getting horrific headaches, brain fog and pains in the back of my neck, particularly when it was cold. And, believe me, it's rarely warm on a TV gantry. There was clearly something else going on. It was time to admit that there really was something wrong.

Mindful of the publicity at that time surrounding head injuries, in particular with ex-footballers, I couldn't help but think back to the time I'd nearly come a cropper on a fishing trip with my boys Ben and Jack near Barcelona in 2017. We had three fantastic days and even managed to catch a few catfish (we put them back after the customary photos, of course).

Ben does enjoy trying to find a bargain when he plans our itineraries, and there's no chance of five-star luxury when he's in charge of the accommodation. On this occasion we were booked into an Airbnb with bedrooms upstairs and a toilet and shower room on the ground floor. After a great first day, a lovely meal and a few beers, I unfortunately woke in the middle of the night in need of the loo. That meant negotiating the stairs, which for some reason split halfway – right to continue the journey down or left for four feet of open space and a concrete floor. In my hazy state, I went left and landed on my forehead. The commotion woke the boys, who flew the correct way down the stairs to find me lying in a heap with blood pouring from my ear and from a graze on my head. Although at first we were all convinced I had a serious injury, and my sons had a terrible fright, after a while we realized it wasn't too bad and I persuaded them to go back to bed. I was still shook up and in a bit of pain, but I'd been lucky. I really had banged my head fiercely.

The fall was definitely in my mind when my GP arranged a brain scan. Thankfully, the result was clear – no sign of dementia or other brain disorders. That was a huge relief. The thought of suffering dementia, and knowing heading a football and playing the game I love might have been the cause, had hung over me for more than a year. I'd seen first-hand how desperate the condition could be, for instance with my good friend, the now sadly departed Manchester United and Scotland legend Gordon McQueen.

That's not to say heading a ball – something I must have done literally tens of thousands of times – couldn't be a contributing factor in my issue. No one can ever be sure, and there are growing numbers of examples, in rugby league especially, of players suffering from neurological issues later in life. It's just difficult to pinpoint the link right now.

While the brain specialist told us there was no visible evidence of a problem, my GP continued to investigate other potential causes. In the meantime, there were some good days and some terrible ones. I never felt I was getting on top of the condition. I would lie awake at night worrying about my ability to do any kind of TV work and if it was worth me putting myself through the agony of performing, even for pre-recorded shows. The commitment that particularly terrified me was hosting *UK's*

Strongest Man for Channel 5, something which, after much umming and ahhing, I'd agreed to do after being approached by former strongman champion Glenn Ross, whose baby the show was. The request had put me in a dilemma. It was a great opportunity to take on something different, while presenting as the main anchorman. But it wouldn't only be the strongmen carrying a burden – I didn't want my speech to fail me and make a total hash of the programme.

Initially, I'd tried to put Glenn and his producer off, but they were having none of it. They wanted me and that was that. After a chat, they offered me a three-year deal.

'Don't you want to try one year and see if it works?' I asked.

'Not at all,' they said. 'We want you for the full three years.'

I'd tried to stand down, but they really wanted to take a chance with me. I think they knew I would always be trying my very best to deliver, but, as I was discovering, wanting to and being able to were two very different things. The result was weeks of fretting, to the extent that the night before we started filming in Milton Keynes, I could hardly sleep. I knew I was taking on a lot, what with having to explain the challenges and introduce the competitors. On the other hand, I wanted to show people, myself included, that I could actually do it. Three stressful days ensued. Luckily, the show wasn't live, so we could do as many takes as we needed. I got through it with multiple cans of Red Bull from the supermarket next door – 'Carry Kammy's shopping' could have been a strongman challenge in itself. While the contest itself was fantastic and I loved every minute of it, I knew I wasn't great and felt guilty not being able to give my usual 100 per cent.

Straight after filming *UK's Strongest Man*, I went down to

Devon for some much-needed rest and relaxation with the family. It was a relief to be away from work and have the opportunity to try to get my head round what had been going on. I did a lot of thinking on that trip and reached the conclusion that I would give up my TV career. I couldn't put myself through the stress and the worry any more.

I did cut back on the work that summer, enjoying England's journey to the final of the European Football Championship, simply as a fan. But as soon as the domestic season loomed into view, I cast aside ideas about giving it all up and decided to go back to covering games for *Soccer Saturday*. I'd see how it went. I was fooling myself that one day everything would miraculously come right and I'd be able to continue doing the job I loved in the same way I had for years.

I also continued to turn up for *Steph's Packed Lunch*, finding a way to speak in soundbites, so that long conversations were avoided. The show was nominated at the Television and Radio Industries Club Awards at the Grosvenor House hotel in London, and although we didn't win, it was a great night – my first ceremony where I was involved with a nominated programme. I was invited to present the Best Entertainment Programme award to the *Gogglebox* mob, but when my moment came I was overcome by a familiar fear, terrified I wouldn't be able to get up the steps to the stage. They were really narrow and there was no handrail. I asked an assistant to help me up, struck by how much of a fragile old man I must have looked to the audience. Later, one award winner did actually fall down the steps. While it wasn't a great look, I was glad I'd asked for help.

★

In his quest to help me further, my GP recommended a visit to Leeds-based neurosurgeon, Dr Oliver Lily. Virtually the minute I walked through his door, he delivered his diagnosis. For the first time I heard the word that has come to dominate my life since – apraxia. Even before testing my reflexes and balance, and after I'd only said a few words to him, he was adamant that apraxia was my problem. His verdict was straight – it could get worse, would probably not get any better, but could be managed with speech therapy. When I got home the first thing I did, of course, was scour the internet for anything apraxia related, but there was very little. And, surely, my symptoms weren't the same.

I soldiered on, doing some speech therapy, but little changed. My speech seemed the same and the endless mix of good days and bad days continued. Dr Lily recommended I go for a further test, a DaTSCAN, which involves injecting a radioactive substance into the bloodstream to scan for neurological conditions. I had come this far in my search for answers, so I agreed, hoping that it would reveal something, anything, that was physically wrong with me.

It was a tense time waiting, but Dr Lily announced that the scan was clear.

'I know you were hoping we would find something,' he said, 'but trust me, you really didn't want us to.' Anne and I left the hospital feeling relieved.

Despite the apraxia diagnosis, I was soon back in the swing of things with *Soccer Saturday* and various other shows. You can't say no to Ant and Dec, who invited me back on for a slot on *Saturday Night Takeaway* at the turn of 2022. Thankfully, I didn't have to say a lot and I got through it OK. In all honesty, those two were more interested in the latest gossip about Newcastle

United, who'd recently been taken over by Saudi investors, and were delighted when my mate Kieron Trippier became one of their first signings. A *Question of Sport* was different. I wasn't very sharp and host Paddy McGuinness asked me after filming if everything was all right. I told him about the underactive thyroid, and that I was – yes – fine.

Again, though, I was feeling more and more embarrassed about myself. I saved one of my worst performances for a pilot of a show called *Smile*, hosted by my great buddy Ben Shephard. He later said the decision not to go ahead was nothing to do with me, but I'm not sure about that. I can't really remember the premise of the programme, but it's a good job Frankie Bridge, Anthony Cotton, Joe Swash and Josie Gibson were there too because I offered nothing. Sitting there dumbstruck was another huge moment – a gut-wrenchingly hideous realization that the spontaneous wit and sharpness that had made my name as a broadcaster was no more. Even when I did open my mouth, I was slow and lumbering. They might as well have used a life-size cardboard cutout. It would have added the same amount as me.

I apologized to Shep straight away, but he said I was fine. 'You're only saying that because it's me and I'm your friend,' I replied.

'Believe me, mate, simply having you on there was great. You were all right, honestly.'

But I wasn't happy at all. It was a real wake-up call. I knew I couldn't do it any more. I wasn't 'Kammy', so what was the point?

★

I'm going to admit something now, something I've never mentioned before. It's hard for me to talk about, so bear with me.

As I was gripped by apraxia, and the apparent hopelessness
of my future, I'd been escaping more and more down to the animals at the back of the house. Hidden away, that smallholding
became my refuge. Animals don't judge. You look after them and
in return they show you unconditional love. I would talk to them
as I stood there. I'd let all my innermost feelings tumble out. I
didn't need to worry about them noticing my slowed speech or
my compromised stability. It seems silly to say they 'listened', but
in those moments that's how it felt.

Going down there allowed me to unravel my thoughts. And
I'll be honest, some of those thoughts could be dark. I worried
about where I was going to end up. Would my physical and
neurological deterioration just keep going and going? And I worried more about the effect it would have on those around me.
I'm a man who has always wanted to help, to provide, to love
and nurture those around me. And now I could only see myself
as a burden. A shell of the man I used to be that they would
be left to look after. Seeing myself like that was like staring into
an abyss. I could never reconcile that image in my head. It was
unthinkable. And it's at that point I'd think, 'They'd be better
off without me.'

The death of Gary Speed had affected me deeply. It's something I have never been able to understand, and probably never
will. To me, Gary had everything. Beautiful family, successful
career, and people who loved him dearly. And yet this amazing
young man had taken his own life. I thought of Gary and then
I thought of my own position – a man in his mid-sixties, whose
best days, because of a brain condition, were gone, struggling

on while becoming a weight on all around him. Whose wife and children would be left to deal with whatever I became. I didn't want that for Anne and the boys. So how do you prevent it from happening? You take yourself out of the picture.

There were times when I definitely thought that was a way out. If you're stuck in a maze, with no sign of an escape route, eventually you'll try something extreme. Especially if you have chosen to wander that maze alone.

And that really is the key. When finally I did start to share my problems, I began to see that the future might not be so bleak. That a world could exist with me in it. Hopefully a me who was better, but nevertheless a version of me who I could live with.

It's hard to look back on those dark times. To the outside world I know how irrational those thought patterns must seem. But when the walls are closing in it's easy to feel differently. By being honest and talking about it, I want to help others see that there is always another way out. There is always hope. You just have to let other people help you see it.

5

Kick-Off

AT THE START, YOU NEVER THINK ABOUT THE END.

All I knew as a kid setting out in life was that I didn't much fancy going down the route that had apparently been set out for me. The Teesside steelworks dominated the south bank of the River Tees from Middlesbrough to Redcar. Dad didn't want me to end up working there every day of my life either. In my late teens he took me to see what it was like working in a foundry to make sure I understood what a hard and unforgiving environment it was. I'll be honest, it frightened the life out of me. Sparks flying everywhere, a constant din of clanging metal, blokes throwing everything they had at smouldering bars of steel. I couldn't wait to get out of there. That's not to say that I'm not proud of the area's steelmaking heritage, as pretty much every Teessider is. Years later, I was honoured to back Middlesbrough's fight to keep the steelworks open, but sadly the British Steel foundry where my dad worked so hard for so long couldn't be saved. I returned a week before it was demolished with a documentary crew. It was poignant to look at it, bleak and neglected, with memories of that visit with my dad. And then the whole lot was erased from Middlesbrough's skyline.

*

While Dad might not have wanted me to go into heavy industry, neither did he indulge his increasingly football-mad son's dreams of becoming a sportsman.

Dad had no interest in football, which didn't exactly help him to bond with his footie-crazy boy, and so we had next to nothing to talk about. In fact, while I played as much as I possibly could, he only came to watch me once. I can still picture him on his bike at the town's Clareville Stadium when I was fifteen and playing for Boro Boys.

When I was a youngster, forget the three Rs. It was the three Fs – football, football, football. Mind you, if I'd taken any exams, I'd have probably got three Fs in them as well. I didn't pay a lot of attention in lessons. Instead I'd be waiting for the bell to ring so I could go off and do what I did best. If I didn't have a football to kick, I'd kick a stone – school shoes were always quickly scuffed-up and ruined.

I also played on the field near our house, and by the age of twelve was taking on grown men who wanted to kick lumps out of me because, despite my age, I was already as good as they were. That stood me in good stead when I got my chance later on. I wasn't afraid of anyone and knew how to look after myself.

The first big match I went to was at Middlesbrough's Ayresome Park in 1966 – an infamous World Cup tie in which Italy were beaten by North Korea. Being only eight, I didn't take in that I'd witnessed what is still one of the biggest upsets in the tournament's history. Walking into the stadium, seeing the players close-to and listening to the crowd blew my mind. I was hooked and from then on was desperate to see Middlesbrough as much as possible. Me and my pals would sneak in for home games if we could, and Eric McMordie, the Northern Ireland international, was my favourite player. Naturally, my big ambition when I was a kid was to play for Middlesbrough. Then, when I saw Leeds United on *Match of the Day* at a mate's house, the dream changed to play for them.

Boro Boys came into my life when I was fifteen. Their manager Dave Richardson, who now works for the Premier League, asked me along. He'd built a good side, including Bill Athey — who'd go on to play cricket for Yorkshire and England — as well as Ted Coleman, Micky Taylor and Lee Cattermole's dad, Barry, all very good players who became apprentice footballers at Middlesbrough. As for me, Dave told my dad on a visit to our house that there was a very good chance I too would be offered terms. Dad wouldn't have it. He didn't see football as a career option for me. He had no interest in the game and no interest in my football obsession.

That season, Boro Boys beat every team to win the Teesside Junior Alliance League and reach the national Youth Cup final. When I didn't turn up for that game, held for some reason at a prison a mile from our house, Dave had no idea why.

Truth is, within days of Dave's visit, Dad had announced I was joining the Navy and marched me down to the recruitment office to sign on the dotted line. My brother George had joined the Army four years earlier and had become a very good soldier in the Green Howards infantry regiment. Dad thought my best

49

place was in the Navy. It was never up for discussion with either of us.

I left for the south coast on the eve of the big match. I didn't even have a chance to finish school and do my exams. I could have rebelled, but I respected and trusted my dad's judgement so simply did what I was told. That was that. At least Boro Boys went on to win the cup.

One person who did get to work with his hometown club – and, boy, has he worked hard – is my brother from another mother, Steve Gibson. Steve is my oldest and best friend. He lived about a quarter of a mile from my house in Aldridge Road on the Park End Estate, but we didn't meet until our first day at St Pius Roman Catholic School, where he became part of the close circle of friends who had my back then – and have my back now. I've been lucky enough to meet royalty, football superstars, world-class managers, Hollywood actors and pop stars, but the most important people I've ever met were my school pals. Steve, along with Michael O'Neil, Peter Conley, Bernie Wilkinson, Denis Alderson, Jimmy Wattis and the late Dennis Newsome, knew how hard it was for me growing up and befriended me, protected me and made my life comfortable. They were always there on my side at a time when plenty of people were trying to make my life a misery.

We're still in touch and manage to meet up from time to time, like last year when I was honoured to receive the North-East Football Writers' Association Personality of the Year award, presented in association with the Sir Bobby Robson Foundation to recognize those who use their position in football to benefit the wider community. I was thrilled to pick up the prize, but it was made even more special that my oldest mates were able to share the evening with me, even if none of us are quite as mobile as when we played football in the park at the end of the street. We would be there nearly every night, pretending to be our heroes, in my case Eric McMordie or Johnny Giles, and in Gibbo's the striker John Hickton. Steve went on to become the Labour councillor for the Park End ward. As my dad, who was a staunch Labour voter put it, 'Your old mate is going to be my MP.' Not quite, but Steve was always ambitious, and would go on to do an unimaginable amount for the town.

Mine and Steve's paths would cross in ways we could have never imagined, but for now, as teenage lads, we'd be going our separate ways.

Unlikely as it might sound, joining the Navy was actually the best thing that could have happened to me. I didn't think it at the time, mind, but then I didn't really have any say in the matter. Dad thought if I stayed in Middlesbrough I'd get into bother, drink too much and waste my life. If I was going to get into fights, he reasoned, best to do it with 16-inch guns on my side. He'd applied the same reasoning to George, worried, from his own experience of discrimination, that even if it wasn't our fault we'd still be targeted by the police.

Overnight, I went from the backstreets of Middlesbrough to Torpoint in Cornwall. I was posted to HMS *Raleigh*, not a ship but a training establishment where from day one I embraced the regime of discipline and physical exercise – up at 6 a.m., spend the day working, cleaning and exercising, and then play football until eight or nine at night.

After a few days, my dad received a letter.

Dear Mr Kamara,

Now that your son has arrived at HMS RALEIGH to begin his training in the Royal Navy, I expect that you will be wondering what his life here will be like during the next few weeks. He will spend some four months here with a class of about twenty young men in the charge of a Petty Officer who has been specially selected for training duties. On average, three or four classes are grouped into a Division under the supervision of a Divisional Officer who is my representative for the welfare of the men in his Division. Unless you hear from me to the contrary you can assume that he is getting on well, and that there is no need to worry about his well-being. Slight homesickness is naturally not uncommon at first, but we find that the vast majority overcome it with sympathy and, best of all, encouragement from home.

The Captain
HMS Raleigh

I guess all parents got that letter but, still, it was a letter from the captain. And it wasn't because I'd broken anything.

Luckily for me, the Navy football team trained at Torpoint and I asked the coach if I could join in. He said no. 'For three reasons,' he explained. 'One, you're still on your six-month trial and you can't play until that's over. Two, you're black and these lads will kick lumps out of you. And three, you're too skinny and you're not going to be strong enough to play in the Navy team. Come back in six months if you're still interested.'

In six months, my trial would be over, and I'd be bigger and stronger, but I'd probably still be black.

My response to this setback was to turn up at every training session anyway. Initially, nothing changed – the coach kept saying no to my requests to play. Then, one day, I was running round the track while the team were warming up for a practice game and the coach called me over. 'Look,' he said, 'we're two players short. You play on one side, and I'll play on the other. Just stay out on the wing, and you'll be fine.'

I'd played men's football from the age of fourteen, so I already knew how to look after myself on the pitch. My gangly legs were like elastic bands, resistant to any battering they could take, and anyway I was able to avoid the heavy lunges from anyone trying to take me out. I scored two goals and got drafted into the team straight away. Suddenly, the six-month trial regulation had been forgotten.

I was selected to play against Portsmouth FC reserves at HMS *Vernon*. I honestly believe life is all about fate. The only other game I'd played until then had been against the Army. I wasn't nervous, although maybe I should have been. I was a kid, a young cadet meant to be performing lowly naval duties, and now here I was on the way to play against a professional team.

As it turned out, I bagged another two goals and ran the game. Pompey's reserve-team manager Ray Crawford and chief scout Tony Barton were there to see it. They asked the Navy coaching staff if I'd be interested in signing for Portsmouth. When the conversation was relayed to me, I thought I was dreaming. Would I be interested?!? This kind of life-changing leap only happened in films, and I knew I wasn't on the set of a Hollywood movie.

I of course said yes, but there was a snag – I still had two months of my trial period to go. Tony Barton asked if there was any way to get me released now and was informed that the only way for me to swap my sailor's duffel bag for a footballer's kit bag was to pay a £200 release fee. Portsmouth duly handed over the cash – it still goes down as the worst deal in the club's history! I was floating on a cloud, totally made up. This was real – I was off to be a pro footballer!

Of course, there was one other obstacle I'd overlooked – Dad. The Navy might have ruled the waves, but they didn't rule him. He was far from happy when I rang home to tell him I was going to meet the new Pompey boss, the ex-Liverpool forward Ian St John. He insisted the Navy send him a letter saying I'd be allowed to continue as a mariner if things didn't work out. As he had blocked my ambition to play for Middlesbrough, I was so glad he let me give it a go with Portsmouth. Perhaps now he could see how much it meant to me. And the Navy's reassurance of a swift return should the idea backfire had softened his opposition to the idea. In my mind, however, one thing was absolutely certain – whatever happened, no way was I going back to the high dock and sweeping the decks. And thankfully, the closest I'd ever get to a life at sea would be waterlogged pitch.

And so, on 8 November 1974, aged sixteen, I became the first signing of Ian St John. My wage in the Navy had been £16 per week. Having now signed apprenticeship forms at Pompey, I'd swapped that for the princely sum of £10 a week for the first year and £12 for the second. I didn't care about the cash – I wanted to grasp the opportunity and give it a good go.

I had a lot to learn. I still laugh at youth team manager Ray Crawford's early impressions of me, as reported in the

Kammy

Portsmouth News – 'His knowledge of the game is scanty. He is weak in the air, his marking is wayward, and he hasn't got much positional sense.' But apart from that, everything was good, although a career as a motivational speaker probably wasn't on the cards for Ray. At least there was plenty to work on – and I worked bloody hard. Even so, being a footballer was much easier than being a Navy recruit. I stayed in Southsea at digs with Keith and Hazel Penney, a lovely couple who really looked after me and treated me just as well as their sons David and Jeremy. I was up at eight, fed by Hazel, and would then walk into Fratton Park for nine. All in all, HMS Keith and Hazel was a lot nicer than HMS *Raleigh*. I couldn't have asked for better care and their home offered me more comfort than I'd ever experienced. I especially loved having my own bedroom after months of sleeping alongside twenty other young cadets – all sharing one toilet! Living beside the coast was also heaven for me – I could run and exercise and kick around on the beach to my heart's content. I loved the place.

At the club, along with the other apprentices, I'd clean and polish the pros' boots, sweep the terraces and scrub the dressing rooms on a daily basis. Some of the lads found it hard work but, to get a bit Uncle Albert from *Only Fools and Horses*, it was nothing compared to life in the Navy. Young pros don't have to do such tasks any more – and I understand the reasons why – but it wasn't sweeping chimneys and didn't do us any harm as young professional footballers. Whenever I swept the terraces, cleaned the bath, or polished the boots of the senior players, I'd dream of the day it would be me the fans were cheering, me in that bath celebrating a win, and some other young lad with big ambitions polishing my boots.

On the pitch, I scored regularly from midfield for the youth team and played a few games for the reserves in the South-East Counties League. We went on to win the FA Youth Cup, but it wasn't always plain sailing – if you'll pardon the pun. I hit a dry spell with the youth team and started to worry about earning a new contract towards the end of my first season. Ray, though, really looked after me. He took me aside before we played Fulham's youth team one day and told me to keep listening and learning – I had the talent to go a long way in the game. I've remembered that advice ever since, because you never stop learning in football, full stop. If sometimes it felt like Ray spent half the training sessions having a go at me, I knew he was doing it for my benefit. And it worked.

Looking back now, Ian St John, known to us all as the Saint – as he would be to millions when he and Jimmy Greaves had their own *Saint and Greavsie* TV show in the eighties and nineties – didn't have a chance at Portsmouth. He was a fabulous coach, coming to Portsmouth off the back of a successful spell at Motherwell, and recommended by none other than his former boss Bill Shankly, who'd turned down the Fratton Park job himself. But the Saint found his hands tied by the fact the owners, husband and wife John and Dolly Deacon, didn't have the funds to back him – at two hundred quid I was considered a big-money signing. That meant that while we had a few old pros, Saint was forced to blood youngsters like me and my apprentice pal Steve Foster. It was Saint who converted Fossie from centre-forward to centre-back, from where Steve went on to win three caps for England after becoming a headband-wearing colossus in Brighton's back four.

My leap to the Portsmouth first team came when Saint picked

me for a pre-season game at Brighton. I was still scoring goals for the youth and reserve teams from midfield, but Saint put me in that day as a striker. I did OK, but it was a surprise nonetheless when, with winger Micky Mellows injured, I was named in the team for the league visit of Luton Town to Fratton Park. I was ecstatic. Six months before, I'd been destined to be riding the waves with the Navy, and now my lifelong dream of having a career as a professional footballer was really about to begin.

I went straight back to my digs in Southsea and called the Newmarket pub in Middlesbrough – the only way to get in touch with my mum and dad, who were usually in there. I also managed to track down Alan Ingledew. I think Alan was more excited than anyone. In fact, he made the 320-mile journey to see me make my professional debut, bringing my parents with him. They were there, sat in the main stand with the other families.

My strike partner against Luton was George Graham, who, as a suave, good-looking fella, was known as 'Gorgeous George' back then. He was coming towards the end of his career and had a huge impact on the young lads in the squad, both on and off the field, although there was no sign of the strict disciplinarian who would go on to become a legendary manager at Arsenal. Winger Peter Marinello, meanwhile, was seen as the Scottish George Best and was nicknamed 'The Cat' because he could sleep anywhere. They were both brilliant players to have around me on my debut, and George in particular talked me through the game and gave me plenty of advice.

We lost 2–0, but I was awarded the sponsors' man of the match, and Saint was pleased with my debut. He kept me in the side for a few games, and I played against legends like Bobby

Moore at Fulham and Bob Moncur at Sunderland as I became a first-team regular. Alan also brought my parents to see me score my first goal against Bolton, who included in their number Peter Reid and Sam Allardyce, both of whom would go on to become good pals and regulars alongside me on the *Goals on Sunday* sofa. Big Sam gave me a good battering that day – on the pitch, not the sofa. One of his first challenges nearly sent me into the English Channel. We went up for a header together, and he came through the back of me, heading my head – and the ball I was heading – and sent me flying. I got my revenge when I sneaked past Big Sam to bury Bobby McGuinness's cross past Bolton keeper Barry Siddall for my first professional goal. After it hit the net, I just ran. And ran. And ran. I hadn't thought about goal celebrations – and if you've seen me dance, you'll understand why – but the fans and the manager loved it. And so did my mum and dad, jumping up and down in the stand.

Saint liked my hardworking attitude and willingness to learn. He was less impressed when I earned my first red card – one of six in my career and another incident my parents were on the south coast to witness. It was my own fault: I'd kicked out at Plymouth's Micky Horswill after he'd chopped me in half earlier in the game with the type of challenge that's now long been outlawed and was actually very close to the mark in the midseventies. The wily midfielder poleaxed me to get a reaction – he got one with bells on, and stood there smirking as I headed for the first early bath of my career. We have since laughed about it together.

There was the compensation that we managed to beat Plymouth 2–0, but Saint was furious and refused to look at me as I headed down the tunnel. Ray wasn't too chuffed either, because it meant I missed an FA Youth Cup semi-final against Villa a few days later. I was called into the manager's office on Monday morning and escaped with a telling-off, a warning and no additional fine. Saint could see I was distraught and just told me to learn from the dismissal, which I did – apart from the five other times I was shown a red card. I said I would learn, not *when* I'd learn.

We were relegated from the old Second Division that season. The Saint was sacked, succeeded by Jimmy Dickinson, a Pompey legend who played 845 games for the club. Surgery was needed on the Portsmouth squad. Jimmy was told to sell players, and my name was on the list.

It might have been the end for me and Portsmouth but eventually I'd return to Fratton Park for arguably the most famous (for all the wrong reasons!) point of my entire career.

6

Secrets

WHILE I MIGHT HAVE NOW KNOWN THAT APRAXIA WAS behind my issues, no way was I going to compromise my working life by making my situation publicly known.

On reflection, that was a bad decision. More than anything it meant my anxiety levels went through the roof. *Soccer Saturday* in particular had become a huge problem. I was dreading every game, praying for a quiet game, no goals, controversies or red cards. That way the director would come to me less frequently, I could get away with short words and uncomplicated sentences, and, because it was a quick over and out, no one would have time to notice the way I was speaking or judge me. I was probably the only football fan in Britain on a Saturday afternoon hoping for a 0–0 result.

Desperate for help of any kind, I went to see a hypnotherapist, Daniel McDermid. I told him if he could get me through the season, I'd then jack it all in. I'd watched hypnotherapists in Las Vegas putting people in trances and getting them to do stupid things and, although I knew a lot of that was play-acting, I couldn't see why such a technique, done properly, couldn't get my voice going again. The stupid things I didn't need any help with – I could manage them all on my own.

Daniel was brilliant and while those sessions might not have been the cure I'd hoped, they did manage to ease my anxiety so that I at least felt calmer on air.

Daniel thought it would benefit me immensely if I went public and shed the burden of keeping my condition a secret. For me, that simply wasn't an option. No way would my pride allow it. Truth is, I was ashamed of my apraxia. Last thing I was going to do was shout it from the rooftops – 'Look at me everybody! It's Kammy. I can't talk properly.'

I was an idiot – and not for the first time.

Of course, my plan to sneak under the radar on *Soccer Saturday* was never going to work. Maybe you can fool casual work colleagues, but these were people I'd operated alongside for years. Jeff clearly thought something was amiss with my health and after one shocking day at Scunthorpe he rang me – 'What's going on?'

As usual I brushed him off. 'Oh, nothing to worry about, Jeff. Nothing a few decent nights' sleep won't fix.'

To be honest, there was still a part of me that thought I'd be able to overcome my problems. I was pulling the wool over my own eyes as well as everyone else's.

Matters came to a head when I slurred my way through a run-of-the-mill match at Rotherham. I was so bad that night, barely able to string a few words together, that I will never,

ever, be able to bring myself to watch it back. It really was that embarrassing.

Twitter didn't make great reading during the game.

'Is Chris Kamara unwell?? Very slurred speech on Sky Sports.'

'Kammy are you OK mate?'

'Noticing you're not at your best today. And I don't mean that in an offensive way. If you're struggling mate, please get some help or talk to someone.'

On my way home from the match, I called Daniel, who once again urged me to go public with my condition. He said it was clear that people had realized something was wrong, and by not opening up I was only going to invite more conjecture, more stress and strain.

Finally, I saw the wider picture. He was right. I was battling a serious problem. Why make it worse by keeping it to myself? There was no need to live apraxia alone. It wasn't something to be ashamed of. It was something that could happen to anyone. How would I have felt if a friend told me they had apraxia? I wouldn't judge. I wouldn't mock. I'd do as much as I possibly could to understand and, if possible, to help. I've always been the first to give people the 'it's good to talk' speech. It was time to do it myself.

I pulled over, took my phone in my hand and called up the Twitter app. What I did next felt a million times bigger than anything I'd ever done in TV or football. Slowly, I typed out my message. 'Just wanted to let a few of you know who tweeted me today that I am ok-ish. Alongside my thyroid problem I have developed Apraxia of Speech & have been working to get my speech back to normal. Some days it can be a little slow and some days it's normal. Hopefully I can beat this!'

I looked at it for a minute or two, finger hovering over the 'post' button. I felt a mixture of fear and nervousness. Should I? Shouldn't I? I jabbed my finger at the screen. Done. Gone.

I put the car into gear and headed home.

7

On the Move

WITH MY PORTSMOUTH ADVENTURE OVER, I HAD TO HOPE
that someone would see me in the shop window before I gathered
too much dust and disappeared, never to be seen again. Luckily
I'd done myself a favour by grabbing a couple of goals on the last
day of the season. That upped the interest and Third Division
Swindon came in with a £14,000 offer that cash-strapped Portsmouth couldn't refuse. I was flattered that another club wanted
me but still wasn't sure about the move, so I met the Saint and
George Graham for a few beers at a Hampshire county cricket
match. There's nothing like a game of cricket when you want
to talk football. George and Saint both told me to go for it. I
had no agent back then – very few players did – and so I also
sought George's advice on what kind of money I should ask for.
George said £50 per week, £20 appearance money and a £1,000
signing-on fee. Swindon said they'd give me £30 per week, £15
appearance money, and a £500 signing-on fee. The manager,

Danny Williams, handed me a pen and a contract – 'Sign it, lad,' he said. So I did. In so doing I became Swindon Town's first black player.

Swindon would add another two grand for moving expenses, not that mine were significant. I didn't need a removals van. I carried all my worldly goods from Southsea to Swindon in a carrier bag. My Swindon digs were run by Phyllis and Jack Smart, who had been looking after young footballers for years. Again, I was being fussed over by a willing landlady, but this time her husband was an ex-policeman. I made a mental note not to overstep the mark.

It so often happens that the minute you move clubs, you find yourself playing against your previous team. Portsmouth was only our second home game of the season, and a section of the Pompey fanbase seized on the opportunity to try to undermine and threaten me.

Sadly, but reflective of the times, Portsmouth, like a few clubs at that time, had a small National Front element among their following. Mad as it sounds, it hadn't been uncommon for them to boo me even though I was doing my level best for their club. Imagine that – being booed by some of your own supporters because of the colour of your skin. I was used enough to idiots by then – remember I'd grown up with this sort of stuff – and so ignored their nonsense. To be honest, most of the time as a footballer you're so in the moment that you barely hear the crowd anyway.

Luckily, everybody else at the club supported me, and we all got along great.

The fact I was playing against Pompey so soon after leaving

was like the proverbial red rag to a bull. I was always going to get stick during the game but things took a sinister turn when death threats, traced back to the National Front by the police, were sent to Swindon in the post. I wasn't worried about it so much as surprised they could write. I also thought it was probably the work of a couple of lone nut-jobs – and it turned out I was right – but the threats were taken very seriously by the club. Secretary Bob Jeffries consulted the police, and they took the same attitude, arranging an escort in an unmarked cop car to get me from my digs to the stadium. After eating breakfast with two plain-clothes officers – they fitted in nicely by polishing off two full Englishes – I was whisked to the dressing-room entrance. I could see there was a big police presence – news of the death threats had been all over the newspapers – and when I got inside I was blown away when Danny Williams named me as captain, which was a wonderful gesture. I was pumping with adrenalin as I led the team down the tunnel to an electric atmosphere, which turned to thunder and lightning eight minutes later when I scored.

These days players often refuse to celebrate against their former clubs. Forget that. As soon as the ball hit the net, I took off and ran the length of the pitch to the Swindon faithful in the Town end and went ballistic. They went crazy too, while scuffles broke out in the away end. The cops made a few arrests as we coasted to a 3–1 win, at which point I was rushed off before any troublemakers could get near me. A police officer even kept an eye on me as I had a drink with my old teammates in the players' bar, before escorting me back to my digs. You can probably blame my carefree attitude that day on my being young and naive. Looking back now I do wonder what might have happened if they hadn't put those precautions in place to ensure my safety that day.

Barely had the furore died down when – again, as always happens – the League Cup draw threw the two clubs back together again. The first leg was at Fratton Park. No police escort this time, but we were hurried off the bus through a police cordon to the front entrance. We got a draw, meaning yet another chapter in the 1977–8 Swindon/Portsmouth saga back at the County Ground. This time I spared the police the bother of having to escort me from the pitch. I got myself sent off in the last few minutes. I made a late tackle on Keith Viney, one of the lads I'd grown up with in the Pompey youth team, and Clive Thomas, arguably the UK's best and most well-known referee at the time, couldn't wait to point me in the direction of the dressing room (there were no red cards back then). Thankfully, the job was done at that point – I'd scored again in a 4–3 win.

The final instalment in the battle was the return league fixture at Fratton Park. With Jimmy Dickinson's side hovering above the relegation zone, I hardly helped their cause when I scored the winner and celebrated in front of the delirious Swindon travelling support. Jimmy's verdict? 'He did rub salt into the wound, didn't he?' Sorry, Jimmy.

Initially, I found it hard to settle in Swindon. While Portsmouth was a port and naval city, a busy mix of all sorts of people, Swindon, a much smaller place, felt a little cut off.

Games coming thick and fast had been a welcome distraction at Swindon. Truth is, at first I struggled off the pitch. Portsmouth had felt like a real home. I'd made connections there, to the extent that I'd often head back there at the weekend after games. I just didn't feel able to lay down any roots in Swindon. That all changed when I met a certain someone called Anne.

It wasn't the standard way of meeting the love of your life. The first time I laid eyes on her she was stood next to a broken-down car at the side of the road. We were on the team coach coming back from a League Cup tie at Portsmouth, of all places, when Kenny Stroud, one of our defenders, spotted his girlfriend Linda at the side of the A34. He'd lent her his car to drive to the match. Stroudy shouted to the coach driver to pull over so he could jump out and investigate. After a few minutes, he returned, saying roadside help was on its way. Obviously, being a coach full of chivalrous young men, we left them to it and got back to our card game. Indeed, I went as far as to seize the opportunity to inform Kenny that the breakdown service would be far from quick and as a result he would now have time for a quick beer back in Swindon. As we enjoyed a deserved pint – we'd held out for a 0–0 draw in the first leg – I quizzed Kenny about the girls with Linda, particularly an attractive girl who turned out to be – you guessed it – Anne. I hadn't scored in the match, but maybe I was about to net the goal of my life.

In the weeks after, I'd occasionally see Anne out and about, but it would take a few months to pluck up courage to call her and ask if she fancied going out at the weekend. When she told me she was tied up because it was her birthday, mistake number one popped out of my mouth. 'Many happy returns. How old will you be?' I asked. I know – never ask a lady her age and all that.

Somewhat reluctantly, she told me. 'Get away with you,' I blundered on. 'You're older than that.'

Look out for the *Chris Kamara Book of Chat-Up Lines* coming soon. It's amazing this chapter isn't called 'Why I Live on My Own'.

The birthday faux pas put me back six months in the pursuit of my future wife. But the Kammy charm, such as it is, finally wore her down. She often reminds me of our disastrous first dance.

In my defence, I'd asked her to dance to Barry White's 'Just the Way You Are', old smoothy that I am, but by the time she finally agreed and I led her (well, pulled her) onto the dance floor, the DJ had upped the tempo, and I found myself hopping around like my feet were ablaze to Boney M's 'Rasputin'. Anne stood there looking dumbfounded. I wasn't revealing myself as Russia's greatest love machine, or even Swindon's, and Anne made a quick exit when 'The Smurf Song' started to ring out. I couldn't believe she'd leave me before I'd had the chance to impress with my Papa Smurf dance.

I called her the next day to see if she'd enjoyed the evening(!) and had got home OK, but for some reason the line went dead and I never got her on that number again. So, fair to say it wasn't love at first sight – at least not from her point of view. I'm always up for a challenge, though, and if something feels right to me I'll 100 per cent pursue it. Clearly, she came round to my way of thinking in the end. At least she can never say she didn't know what she was getting into. The warning signs were there from the start.

8

Out

AFTER SENDING THE 'COMING OUT' TWEET, PUTTING MY truth out there for all to see, I still had a few miles to go before home. Down by the gearstick, my phone had begun to dance. There was clearly a reaction. It's just I had no idea if it was good or bad.

When I got home, I told Anne what I'd done and finally picked up my phone to have a look. I couldn't believe what I was seeing. I was being overwhelmed with messages of support, not only on Twitter but from countless friends and acquaintances from down the years. The relief was unbelievable. Straight away I felt a huge difference. The boot that I'd been under for so long had been lifted. I felt I could breathe again. I felt like I could walk.

9

Growing Up

SCORING GOALS IS A GREAT WAY TO GET SUPPORTERS ON side, and I'll admit that a bit of early on-field success, plus the fact I was spending a lot of time in bookies' and pubs to escape the isolation of my digs, did make me a bit blasé about my situation. When Bobby Smith took over from Danny Williams as manager, he delivered some home truths. After I'd had a miserable game at Sheffield United he accused me of dereliction of duty and of taking my eye off the ball. He had a point.

Again Anne proved a great remedy. Meeting her made me take my football more seriously and I got the rewards. I knuckled down and did extra sessions when training was over for the day and the following season Bobby made me club captain at the age of twenty-one.

While Swindon wasn't the biggest of clubs, it was there I began to get a real taste of what it is to play in proper big games. In 1979–80, we reached the League Cup quarter-finals, where our reward was a tie against Arsenal at Highbury. The Gunners were a great team, reigning FA Cup holders, with the likes of Alan Sunderland, Liam Brady, Frank Stapleton and Pat Jennings in the side. It was the biggest night of my career to that point, and we were all inspired by playing in front of a 38,000-strong crowd, including 7,000 of our own fans roaring us on, in such a magnificent stadium. We scraped a 1–1 draw to take the Gunners back to the County Ground, where those who managed to get tickets, including my mum and dad and uncle Derek, were treated to one of Swindon's most pulsating cup ties ever. I managed one of the goals with a header, and we sneaked through 4–3 thanks to Andy Rowland's late winner.

Our luck ran out against eventual winners Wolves in a two-legged semi-final that ended 4–3. The supporters had been given a rare glimpse of higher league football and they, along with us players, were devastated to miss out on Wembley. I was so proud to be named the supporters' Player of the Year, amid so many other outstanding candidates.

Despite happy times at Swindon, in the summer of 1981 I was on the move again – back to Portsmouth. Frank Burrows, my Swindon first-team coach under Danny Williams, was now manager at Pompey, and asked me to return to Fratton Park. My only reservation was that the small minority of Pompey fans I'd had a run-in with before had got wind of the proposed move back and were not happy.

'Once you put on that blue jersey and run out at Fratton Park they'll all be with you, no matter what colour you happen to be,' he promised. He was right. In light of what had gone on when I'd left for Swindon, there was barely a murmur – how crazy is that? – and the fans were great to me. Just as importantly, Anne and I, by now living together, were happy in the rented house we had in Waterlooville, a lovely spot on the outskirts of Portsmouth. Life by the seaside was good, and it really felt like I had returned home.

Not for long! After only eleven games of the season, I got a call out of the blue from Pompey chairman John Deacon informing me he'd accepted a bid from Brentford manager Fred Callaghan for my services. To say I was disappointed to be leaving so soon, after rebuilding such a rapport with the Portsmouth crowd, would be an understatement.

Anne and I had envisaged opening our doors to friends and family who wanted to spend a few days at the coast. Having popped off to Argos for a spare blow-up mattress to accommodate them we felt a bit cheated that it never got used!

But of course London has its appeal too. A non-stop flow of visitors meant a tour operation every weekend – arrive Friday evening, match or shopping on Saturday, London sightseeing all day Sunday, wave off Sunday evening/Monday morning. It was exhausting but fun, and we definitely made the most of being in the capital.

Fred too was like a best mate. He welcomed me to Brentford, again in the Third Division, and made me feel so special, as he did with all his players. Again, though, I was different from the other players – I was the first black person to play for Brentford in the Football League. And no issues here – the crowd took to me from day one. Meanwhile, Fred's cockney rhyming slang made us laugh on a daily basis – it was like learning a new language for me.

A mix of lively characters and football legends awaited me at Griffin Park, on and off the pitch. It was here I first met all-round entertainer Bradley Walsh, at that time a promising young striker who had played a few reserve-team games for the Bees. His football career was cruelly ended by a nasty ankle fracture the year I joined, but he's not done too badly since and is still passionate about the game. Then there was Terry Hurlock, the long-haired, intimidating cockney hard-man who Fred Callaghan paired me with in midfield. He was the toughest player I ever played with (yes, sorry, that includes you, Vinnie). Stan Bowles was the biggest character of them all. He loved to have a football at his feet, and he loved to play the card game kaluki, a variation on rummy. He was brilliant at both. He also loved to bet. And he was rubbish at it. Over the time I knew him, I became known as the 'Bank of Kamara'. I often had to sub him and pay the bookies when his losses ran out of control – maybe not the best behaviour for a bank, but definitely not the worst. Club secretary Christine Matthews, who has been a good friend and confidant to me and many players over the years, used to look after him and make sure his wages were paid at the right time to keep him out of trouble.

Speaking of staying out of trouble, Anne and I got married in 1982 while I was a Brentford player.

We did so back in Swindon, where we still had roots. Family and friends from Middlesbrough helped us celebrate our special day, along with Anne's family, and players and staff from Swindon and Brentford. I think most of them came to check that Anne really was making an honest man of me. Initially, we'd intended to live in Swindon, adding another income stream by buying an off-licence a stone's throw from the County Ground. If there's one thing being a footballer in the 1970s taught you about, it was alcohol! But while on the surface it seemed a good idea, the reality was that while I was travelling the seventy-five miles to London and back most days for training, Anne was stuck working long hours running the 'offie'. The accompanying accommodation required total modernization, so her limited downtime was spent surrounded by dust and debris. She couldn't even turn to drink because that meant going back to work! I could pick and choose when I wanted a bit of social time behind the counter, but it was full on for Anne. We decided that running an off-licence with shelves lined with booze wasn't really the place for an 'athlete' – I'll leave you to be the judge of whether that's the right word – and so we sold up and made London our home.

On the pitch, things were going great. I took over from Terry Hurlock to become captain and was voted Player of the Year at the end of the 1982–3 season. Getting this award from the supporters meant so much to me, like it had at Swindon. In those days, the supporters were the ones who paid the wages simply by walking through the turnstiles very different to how things are now.

Sadly, even after Fred Callaghan had brought in ex-Chelsea legends Ron 'Chopper' Harris, Mickey Droy and Bill Garner, we were never serious contenders for promotion. We struggled in 1983–4, and Fred left the club. He was replaced by Frank McLintock, who would become a good friend and colleague at Sky. When I joined Sky's Saturday afternoon team, Frank was on the studio panel with Rodney Marsh and George Best, and I was in awe of him and the other two because of their legendary status in the game. I was just the kid from Middlesbrough, remember, and had achieved nothing by comparison.

As a manager, Frank was exactly what we needed, in many

ways ahead of his time. At the end of the season, he gave us individual exercises and running programmes to do over the summer, and because of his achievements with Arsenal the players enjoyed playing and respected him. Even so, I felt uncertain about my future, to the extent that we yo-yoed back to Swindon to live for a while. I didn't want Anne to be left alone in London if I moved clubs again, especially as we'd had the very best of news – we were expecting our first child. Ben, naturally, decided to make his entrance into the world six weeks early – on the first day of the new season. Did this mean he was starting the way he meant to go on? Did Anne have another 'me' to contend with – i.e., unpredictable?

In the event, my fears of being moved on from Griffin Park had been unfounded, and on the day in question, after weeks of tough pre-season training, we were revved up and ready for the opening match, at home to Leyton Orient. I dropped Anne at the hospital in Swindon, where the midwife confirmed that the birth would be that day but probably not for a few hours. I wouldn't get away with it these days, but Anne agreed I could go off and play that much-anticipated opening game. And so off I headed off with Anne's brother Mike, although not until after my first fatherly talk to my son – 'Don't you dare arrive until I get back otherwise your mum will never forgive me!' Anne gave me strict instructions to get club secretary Christine Matthews to keep in contact with the hospital and relay any news from the touchline during the game.

At the end of the match, I swerved the communal bath, grabbed a towel for a wipe-down and told Mike to hit the M4 to Swindon as fast as he could. Luckily for me, Ben did as he was told and waited until I'd got back to hospital before entering the world. We might have lost that opening game, but this was the result of a lifetime.

The footballing highlight of my Brentford days would have to be reaching the final of the Freight Rover Trophy, the tournament set up to give clubs in the lower two divisions a chance of glory, in 1985. It was Brentford's first Wembley final for forty-three years, and Frank took us for a week of warm-weather training in Corfu to prepare. Things didn't go to plan, though, when, as tends to happen when you send a bunch of footballers on a free holiday to the sun, the lads started to enjoy themselves a little bit too much. If anything, we probably set back our cause rather than helped it.

To play on the hallowed turf of Wembley was another dream come true for me. Anne insisted on coming along to watch with Ben, who was nine months old at the time – his first football match, and at the home of football to boot! My one regret was that earlier that season the captaincy had been taken from me and given back to Terry Hurlock after I'd had a falling-out with Frank's assistant, John Docherty. What an idiot I was – I could have been leading out the team at Wembley.

We might have spent a week in Corfu, but we wilted in the Wembley heat and opponents Wigan won comfortably. The Latics were a good young team, managed by Bryan Hamilton, who was a former teammate of mine at Swindon. My mood was raised slightly by the fact that before the game I was introduced to my hero Elton John for the first time – a fleeting handshake but a hello nevertheless. Elton, whose love of football is legendary, was guest of honour, but it was sad that he was handing the trophy to Wigan captain Colin Methven rather than my mate Terry Hurlock.

The old Wembley, of course, is sadly no more. Griffin Park has gone too, and the Community Stadium that's replaced it, only a mile down the road, couldn't be any further removed from that traditional old home. It's hard to believe the club has squeezed a modern 17,000-seater football stadium between the apartment blocks and offices of west London. I am delighted that Brentford are in the top division at last. Griffin Park was a throwback to the good old days, or bad, depending on how you look at it. Four sides of terracing, with a pub on each corner, whereas the Community Stadium looks like a spaceship that's tried to land on the Chiswick flyover.

Having some security at Brentford, we'd moved homes to Bray, between Maidenhead and Windsor, but at the end of that 1985 season I decided I wanted a new challenge and to leave. The club offered me a £10-a-week increase – just enough to buy a pint in their new stadium! – but my mind was made up.

I was out of contract but still officially a Brentford player under the league rules, and therefore was expected to turn up on the first day of pre-season in July like everyone else. My Brentford teammates, more committed to the cause, had taken Frank's inspirational notes and forward-thinking at-home training regime to heart and looked in good nick, while I hadn't really given much attention to my fitness that summer. I took my eye off the ball to the extent that I couldn't get anywhere near the ball!

I had thought my natural fitness and a few runs during the summer would get me through. I was wrong. On the first cross-country run, I was, as ever, among the front-runners, only to seize up after four miles and limp back to Griffin Park on my own.

Kammy

You sometimes took your life into your own hands in the treatment room. The club doctor was actually a retired brain surgeon – not the most useful qualification when it came to dealing with footballers and their leg injuries. On one occasion I needed stitches to a nasty knee injury and the doc duly did the necessary. It was only when he'd finished and I started to move that we noticed a long thin protrusion in my knee. He'd somehow managed to leave the needle in my leg and promptly had to whip it out before it caused any more damage. To be fair, we've all left things behind at work, but, as I told him, I'd think twice about using him if I needed brain surgery!

Eventually, I'd end up relocating back to Swindon – we'd worn a groove on the M4 – after I re-signed for the Robins in 1985. Our second son, Jack, was born there in 1987, a beautiful brother for Ben. At that point, we thought we were going to stay put in Swindon forever. But forever is a word that rarely applies in football. Forget running an off-licence – we should have started a removals company.

10

Ups and Downs

ONCE I'D REVEALED MY TRUTH, I BEGAN TO SEE HOW concerned people around me had been – and for how long.

Friends and family say they'd had their concerns before the first Covid lockdown in March 2020. Anne recalls us visiting her brother Mike and his partner Nettl the previous Christmas. When I disappeared to the loo, he asked her, 'Is Chris all right? He doesn't seem himself.' Anne said I was fine, just tired and overworking at a busy time of the year, which she truly believed at that point.

My good friend Jeff Stelling spotted that I was struggling at that time too. He couldn't quite put his finger on the issue but felt my reports weren't as sharp and fluent as previous years. But, as we left Christmas behind and went into the lockdown, if my voice was occasionally slowing down, I hadn't noticed.

In fact, in a perverse way, I'd quite enjoyed lockdown. Ben and his family moved in with us just before the lockdown was confirmed – they lived in an apartment in the city so it made sense for them to be with us – and with our other son Jack and his family living next door and sharing our land, we couldn't have been happier in the circumstances. We appreciated that so many others were missing loved ones and I felt very lucky to be able to spend countless hours with our grandkids and the animals on the fields at home.

As the lockdown continued, I joined with celebrity friends in trying to bring a bit of fun into people's lives at a very difficult time. For example, Leigh Francis, better known as Keith Lemon, invited me on to a Zoom version of *Celebrity Juice*, which I've always had a great laugh on over the years – usually at my expense.

We kept the grandkids well away – *Celebrity Juice* isn't on CBeebies for a reason – but during the recording Leigh seemed more interested in whether I knew different foreign words for hello than his more usual risqué banter. As usual, I had no idea what he was talking about. I had a couple of guesses, while Leigh and regular guest Holly Willoughby tittered away on camera. Turned out I was sat in front of a huge orange cushion festooned with the word hello in a dozen languages – we're a friendly house, even the soft furnishings are glad to see you. Although I'll be honest, I didn't even know we had it. That's no surprise to Anne; she often says she could redecorate the whole house and I wouldn't notice.

'Are you sure it's your house, Kammy?' enquired Leigh.

I'm not saying I'm rubbish at quizzes, but questions like 'Is this your house?' are about my level.

Eventually, minus the cushion, we set up a camera in our barn to cope with more TV invitations. I made an appearance on

My first communion. I was given the confirmation name Christopher Columbus Kamara after Saint Columba.

St Pius School, Middlesbrough, class photo – can you spot me?!

Returning to my childhood home at Park End, Middlesbrough.

My world in one picture.

Early Portsmouth days –
I managed riding a bicycle
but never perfected the
bicycle kick.

1988: coming up against a
young Gazza and admiring his
play. He scored two goals and
I hardly got near him.

The open-top-bus parade around Leeds after winning promotion. In my arms, my youngest son, Jack, and his brother, Ben, squashed in front of my teammate Bobby Davison.

What a great squad.

Facing my old Leeds teammate David Batty for Sheffield United against Blackburn.

Bradford City, Wembley winners. Nicky Mohan and me celebrate with a massive hug.

Anne and me in competition for
the best perm of the 1990s.

Getting to chat to my hero Elton John –
one of the best days ever.

Kamara-Cam on a Saturday afternoon up in the gantry.

Jack and me after our Kilimanjaro triumph.

Officially 'Singing 4 England' in the studio.

Baring all for England.

Steph's Packed Lunch this way, as well as being a guest on *The One Show* and contributing to a piece about Black Lives Matter for Jeremy Vine's programme on Channel 5.

I could also host events this way, as I did for an online quiz with Mel Giedroyc in aid of Marie Curie.

When football returned, played behind closed doors, Sky tried to minimize my travel by having me covering games in the north. It was an eerie feeling in the stadiums. Apart from the players and officials, we were the only people there. I felt so sorry for the players, trying to motivate themselves, getting changed in boardrooms and canteens as far away from their opponents as was possible, having very little contact with anyone. While my delivery lacked a bit of oomph, I put it down to my own acclimatization to games and players at the bottom end of the league – I had enough trouble with names when I was fully functioning! As a precaution, I decided to stick to short reports and soundbites, which probably hid any growing problems from myself as well as everyone else.

*

It was only later in lockdown that the alarm bells started to ring when I did an interview with Alison Hammond about racism during Black History Month. I simply couldn't get the words out and started slurring – no surprise, then, that they didn't use the interview when the programme aired. I couldn't understand what had happened, worried further by the fact I was making a guest appearance on the Sky comedy *Code-404* the following day with two of Britain's best actors, Stephen Graham and Daniel Mays. It was daunting working with two performers of their calibre, and I told Daniel as much before we started filming. Fortunately for the BAFTA judges, I only had a few soundbites to master and felt content that I'd done OK. I got an even bigger boost when Daniel came up to me before I left. 'Smashed it, Kammy,' he said. 'I don't know what you were worried about.' Again, with this good day cancelling out the one before, neither did I. This was the constant swing in ability to function I was going through at that time. When I covered that match at Rotherham at about the same time, for example, it was starting to eat away at me that something wasn't right. I thought I was still getting away with it, but I wasn't sure, and I felt a swell of the nervousness and anxiety that would soon come to swamp me whenever I reported on *Soccer Saturday*.

But then I appeared on the *Crackerjack* revival – I love being on shows like this because I know my grandchildren will enjoy seeing their grandad on them – and had a good day and a great laugh with all the kids in the audience. Days like this would make me totally write off the bad ones. 'Did I imagine it?' I'd think. 'Was it as bad as I thought? Probably not. Let's carry on.'

Same when I appeared on Mel Giedroyc's comedy show *Unforgivable*, while regular appearances on *Packed Lunch* were going OK too. Every day still felt like an adventure. Despite the odd dip, my mindset was like a lottery winner's – 'How have I had twenty-two years as a football player, two years as a manager and now twenty-odd years in this industry and yet it's still getting better? What's not to be delighted about?'

Even after the darkest days, like the one at Huddersfield where I feared I was going to fall down the steps from the gantry, I'd find myself getting back to normal. In fact, I returned to the John Smith's Stadium for Sky a few days later. My reports were more fluid, I got up and down the steps fine, and I felt happy.

But then a pilot for an ITV show was a total disaster. Lisa Faulkner and I teamed up on a farm in Hampshire to present a show on the different aspects of running a farm shop. We were to interview the family and the workers, sample the work done around the farm, and tell the story of the people and the business. I struggled to get the words out and my delivery was really slow. Lisa was lovely, but I was sure she could see I was struggling. I hoped I'd got away with it, but the commission for the programme was refused. I convinced myself it was my fault and felt awful for Lisa.

Put me in a studio to record another Christmas album, though, and I was happy as can be – maybe because ballads were the right speed for me. Even reaching the high notes wasn't impossible – although it did require me to be having a good day.

Compare that to the nightmare of the album promo appearance on *The One Show*. I was asked to provide a commentary-style voice-over to say what was coming up on the show, and I read the menu from the autocue without any problems. I'd had a little practice chat before we went live and knocked it out the park, so my confidence was quite high before the show went live, buoyed further by the fact I'd been on before, actually presenting live with Alex Jones when Noel Gallagher and Lee Mack were guests. It had been a great show and a good laugh.

Maybe it was the fact that, before we started talking about my new recording, Michael Ball and Alex Jones wanted my opinion on racism and football. It threw me a little. My brain wasn't ready for the switch. Whatever the reason, the result was a complete horror show.

But then I did promos elsewhere that went like a dream. I breezed through radio appearances with Chris Moyles on

Radio X, with Paul Hawksbee and Andrew Jacobs on their talkSPORT afternoon show, and with Scott Mills and Nick Grimshaw on Radio 1. All these people knew me well and no one seemed concerned, or at least they didn't say anything to me.

I then stayed overnight at Chessington Zoo ahead of a piece for *Steph's Packed Lunch*, where I met a penguin they'd named Kammy – a definite compliment, for me anyway. I felt really well that day, although perhaps it was only because I was having so much fun at the zoo. After filming a pre-recorded piece without any problems, again I came away thinking that I was either imagining my issues or somehow bringing them on.

I was brought crashing back to earth when I recorded an in-studio episode of *Celebrity Juice* with Paloma Faith, Paddy McGuinness, Laura Whitmore and Emily Atack. I sang a duet of *Santa Baby* with Paloma, but just couldn't keep up with the words on the autocue. I put my slowness down to the three bottles of beer I'd had pre-show. This wasn't unusual for *Celebrity Juice* – the juice always flowed. If you didn't have a drink before that show, you'd need one afterwards! Paloma was lovely, laughing at me the whole time because she thought I was merry. I was happy to let her think that rather than confront the real issue.

Again and again, I'd start to convince myself I was getting away with whatever was going on in my head, only to receive the jolt that told me that I really wasn't. We went to visit our old friends Bill and Margaret in Sheffield after I'd stumbled through a difficult game at Hillsborough. Bill tends to say things as he sees them. 'What the hell's up with you?' he asked as I walked in the door. 'That fella I saw today, that's not you.' Deep down,

I knew he was right, even if I wasn't quite ready to admit it to myself.

I also covered a game at Middlesbrough in early December, and after interviewing the then Boro manager Neil Warnock, he asked me if I was feeling OK. I told my long-time friend it had been a bit of a long day. I don't know if he really believed me.

What I did know was that these ups and downs were messing with my brain. Every time I felt I was making progress, I'd be tackled to the ground by my own inadequacies.

★

Now everything was out in the open, the time for lame excuses was gone. When I first told Shep about the implications of the apraxia diagnosis, he was stunned. We laughed about the endless times down the years he'd tried to be the voice of reason and talk me down from doing or saying something ridiculous, and now there I was, barely able to say anything at all. He tried to reassure me it wouldn't change the way people see me at all.

I explained my fears about why some of the pilots we'd recorded had slipped through his fingers. I told him I thought the failure to confirm those commissions was down to me. He did his best to reassure me it was simply a coincidence and that no one had noticed I'd been struggling or slowing down.

But, while I was suitably astounded at how long people had been wondering what was wrong with me, my real focus had to be on the here and now. In my new world of unknowns, there was one absolute certainty. I was finished as a football presenter. With the heaviest of hearts, I spoke to the *Soccer Saturday* producers and told them I was stepping down. I couldn't put myself and the viewers through it any more. It was the end of an era.

After twenty-four years with Sky, I'd hit the wall. If I was going to quit, I'd always wanted it to be on my terms. I couldn't help feeling disappointed and resentful that in the end the condition made the decision for me. The upside was the relief that there'd be no more live broadcasting situations to stress about.

11

Moving On Up

In the summer of 1985, Brentford physio Eddie Lyons spent more time with my knee than he did his own family. No matter what his manipulations, nothing seemed to do the trick.

Frank McLintock made no secret of the fact he thought I was pulling a fast one because I wanted a move, so when Swindon boss Lou Macari ended the impasse with a £12,500 offer, Frank couldn't wait to get me off his hands.

Club medicals were a little basic in my playing days – barely a squeeze and a cough. The first time I joined Swindon, all I did was touch my toes a couple of times in front of the manager Danny Williams and the club doc. And because there were still no intensive medicals or fitness tests at that time, my return to Swindon was equally basic. I was clearly injured, but Lou was convinced he would have me playing in a fortnight. Two days after my return to the club, he told me to run around the pitch, but I pulled up within a few yards near the corner flag. The

MRI scan I should have had when I arrived showed a ruptured hamstring – probably originating back to that first day of pre-season training. On the plus side, it didn't show up anything else the club doctor might have left inside me. I missed the first five months of the season but returned to play twenty-three games and was never on the losing side as we won the Fourth Division title and promotion.

I then missed only four games in the 1986–7 season, one of which was the Third Division play-off final replay against Gillingham (the two legs had ended all-square and these were the days when ties weren't settled on penalty shoot-outs). I'd suffered the indignity of a blood clot on my backside after a nasty collision with the Gillingham striker Tony Cascarino. My right buttock ballooned to four times its normal size. Had she been around, I'd have been a credible Kim Kardashian tribute act. I struggled to sit down for a week, never mind play a part in the all-important play-off final replay. Thankfully, the Swindon lads managed without me and we won 2–0. I gave the boys a standing ovation. I had no choice.

I parted ways with Swindon Town and Lou at the end of the 1987–8 season and was on the road to Stoke. Lou's influence remained with me, though. Swindon was one of the most athletic teams I ever played in because Lou was obsessed with his players being at maximum fitness. In training we would just run and run and run. His way of thinking inspired me to the point that when I signed for Stoke I immediately joined a running club so that I could get some yards in if we didn't have a midweek game.

It was manager Mick Mills, the former England full-back, who convinced me to make the move to join the Potters, but once again I signed for a club when I was injured. There's a bit of a running theme here! Maybe I'm worth more off the pitch than on! But it wasn't deliberate, I promise.

Rumours of a new signing had been circulating for a few days, and a few supporters with nothing better to do had gathered at the Victoria Ground for a nosy when I arrived to meet Mick. They must have wondered what they were getting when I emerged from the car on crutches. I'd had a cartilage operation at the end of the 1988 season, but there'd been complications, thanks to my own stupidity. The day after my operation, I'd driven to see Mum and Dad with Anne and the boys, and my leg had started to play up. By the time I arrived, I couldn't straighten it. Yes, I'd injured myself sitting down.

Barely had we said hello to the folks when Anne made the decision to get us all back inside the car and drive home so I could get medical help. As you can imagine, the boys loved that. Jack was one, Ben was four, and their dad was writhing in agony in the front while they were kicking and screaming in the back. I've said it a few times over the years – poor Anne. If I ever want to see a definition of her, I look up 'long-suffering' in the dictionary.

Thanks to internal bleeding and a nasty infection, my knee had swollen to the size of a grapefruit by the time the surgeon saw me the next morning. He drained my knee, put me in plaster, and sent me for two months of rehab. We still went on holiday, though, Anne having to escort me to and from the bar every night while keeping her eye on two lively toddlers. You could say she had three little kids on her hands.

At Stoke, Mick had dreams of promotion to the top flight and wanted me at the heart of his midfield. I was an experienced cog in the wheel along with George Berry, Gary Hackett and Tony Henry. Peter Beagrie, the skilful winger, was Mick's other signing, but as we arrived, two young guns, Steve Bould and Lee Dixon, departed for Arsenal, leaving a hole in the defence. We had the potential to be a really good team, but after a promising start to the season we somehow won only once in the last fourteen games and finished in mid-table. It was a good time personally, though, and after scoring on my debut in the opening game, I went from strength to strength in the lynchpin role.

Mick liked the way I played too, and I loved producing for him. I can't say he built the team around me, but he made me captain almost immediately. The relationship we had, talking football matters off and on the field, was second to none.

The highlight of my time at Stoke came three games from the end of that first season when we played at Swindon and Ben, now five, was the Stoke mascot. We walked on to the County Ground pitch hand-in-hand in front of all the family – another special moment to treasure.

Mick Mills was sacked in the November of my second season after we were thrashed 6–0 at Swindon, his assistant Alan Ball taking charge. I was upset to see Mick walk out the door for the last time and I went to see him at his home in Stafford to tell him so. He had believed in me, and I told him that I would be forever grateful for that. I was playing some of the best football I had ever played, and I had him to thank.

My good form hadn't gone unnoticed by other clubs, including the two that meant the most to me – Leeds United, my boyhood favourites, and Middlesbrough. Hmm – maybe soon I'd have a decision to make.

12

Feeling the Love

AFTER PUTTING A STOP TO MY WORK WITH SKY, I SHOULD have taken a complete break. But that would have been the sensible thing to do.

Instead, I signed up for ITV's *The Games*, in which ten celebrities compete against each other in Olympic-style events, with presenters Holly Willoughby and Freddie Flintoff. The show would run over five nights. What was I thinking? Consenting to do those shows was crazy, but I wasn't finished there. Scariest of all was my agreement to present twenty episodes of a new reboot of *Cash in the Attic* for Channel 5. Anne had tried to persuade me to pull out of that job for months, but I simply didn't get around to it. I was, as always, hoping all would come good for me. When I met the production team a month after the apraxia diagnosis and offered to stand down, they were insistent they still wanted me to go ahead. Deep down, I was hoping they'd feel the opposite and tear up the contract. No chance. 'Whatever we have to do to make this work,' they promised, 'we'll do it.'

The Games came and went. It was actually good fun and ITV took the precaution of pairing me with broadcaster Simon Brotherton to give me a boost on the commentary, Simon taking the lion's share of the load when my speech wasn't so great.

Predictably, though, the workload for *Cash in the Attic* was more than I could handle, a gruelling few months travelling up and down the country, while trying constantly to get my voice right. I felt shattered most of the time simply because of the travelling and overnight stays. Inevitably, there were times I struggled to talk fluently. While we could do multiple takes, and I was always given time to get it right, it could be embarrassing to find myself floundering in front of members of the public who must have wondered what the hell was going on. As must have the crew. The heads of the production company knew about my condition but told no one on the set.

I was having a particularly bad day when we filmed the first auction near London, to the extent I could barely speak. It was the first time I'd met fellow presenter Jules Hudson and I could tell he was taken aback. I was embarrassed by how bad I was that day, but overall, despite finding the series stressful and tiring, I still loved the experience and being part of a great show. I'm a people person and made sure all the contributors felt comfortable, especially when I was rummaging in their drawers!

As you can see, I found the act of stepping away from the work I loved to be difficult in the extreme. *Ninja Warrior* was a case in point. Based on the Japanese game show *Sasuke*, the *Ninja Warrior* competitors had to complete a nine-obstacle course in forty-five seconds. When me and Shep had been offered the chance to host the show, my immediate reaction was 'Bring it on!' I had visions of me and Ben going head-to-head on the course ourselves – he might be twenty years younger than me and a gym fanatic to boot, but I prided myself on my fitness levels and competitive streak. It was that prospect which convinced me to give the show a go. Shep didn't need any convincing – he was a big fan of the US *Ninja Warrior* and was excited beyond belief. Shep would present while I was there to provide a bit of atmosphere and, between the laughter, try to tell the viewers what was going on. Rochelle Humes would be the court-side interviewer.

We filmed the first series in Manchester in 2015, and it was a real eye-opener walking into a bona fide showbiz environment. I'd never been treated like this before – my own dressing room, cuppa whenever I wanted it, someone ironing my shirt, make-up people, hairstylists, even someone to make sure my moustache was on point.

'Welcome to how it should be done,' Ben said.

It didn't take long to get used to that lifestyle, but sometimes I did feel a bit uncomfortable having people run around after me, although I'm sure Anne would find that hard to believe.

I treated the competition like it was the Champions League and did my research, wanting to know as much about each competitor as I could, writing detailed notes and prepared words and phrases I could call upon when the moment was right. I could then add that stuff into the spontaneity that was my hallmark. If you want to be successful when working in TV, you have to be authentic.

Recurring back problems (mine) meant that Ben and I never

did get the chance to go up against each other on the course. But Ben did manage to go solo, while I positioned myself in the commentary gantry just metres from the vast wall he'd have to scale as the finale. I felt sure he'd have no chance of getting close to me. I was wrong. Doing a very good impression of an orang-utan, Shep made light work of the course and was soon at the foot of the wall. 'Come on, mate, you've got this,' I bellowed above the noise of the whistling and applauding crew, before starting the iconic chant all audiences adopted at this point of the course – 'Beat the wall! Beat the wall!'

I was so excited for him but at the same time knew I wouldn't hear the last of it if he reached the top of that mighty obstacle. Putting my envy aside, I gave him one last encouraging shout, offering advice gleaned from observing the contestants: 'Lean back, Shep – and go!' He took a step back and, face fixed with determination, strode forward, timing each step to perfection, before running up the wall like it was flat to the ground. From my position above, I saw his fingers curl over the top of the obstacle before he hauled himself up and banged his palm on the completion buzzer. Shep was ecstatic. As he tried to regain his breath and composure, I stuck a mic in his face – 'Brilliant, mate, but what took you so long?' Good job he had little strength left at that point or else I might not have made Series 2!

Ben was up for trying the more advanced courses reserved for the semi-finalists but was told he was uninsured and if he was injured he couldn't present the show. 'Kammy would have to do it alone,' said the producer. Everyone agreed that wasn't a good idea and that was it – matter closed. Talk about a vote of confidence.

We filmed five series of *Ninja*. The show then disappeared

before a comeback after a three-year break. Naturally, the producers, Michael Kelpie and Martin Scott, were delighted it had been recommissioned and the old gang would be returning. I should have been singing and dancing along with them but instead when they told me all I could say was, 'Oh no!'

'Don't you mean "Oh yes, we're back?"'

I quickly recovered the situation – 'You know me, chaps, confused as ever. Of course, I am happy – it's fantastic news.'

In reality, I was thinking more of my condition. *Ninja* still being prepared to use me for the new series was a massive boost. We'd had great times filming previous series, and I wanted to do it again, but part of me didn't think I was capable. Would I be able to contribute? Would I even be able to speak? I didn't have the heart to tell Shep, Rochelle and the team that I wanted out.

In the end, I had a long conversation with Shep about my future and apraxia. That was when he said I needed to tell everybody. I told him I had already tweeted about it. 'No,' he said, 'you need to tell *EVERYBODY*.' He suggested an interview with him on *Good Morning Britain*.

I was really concerned about people feeling sorry for me, that I was going to be looked upon as a victim, but Ben said it was important people understood what I was dealing with.

'This new challenge doesn't mean you can't do the job,' he told me. 'You're an essential part of the *Ninja Warrior* team. It's important and integral that you're still there.'

We had many long conversations before he finally booked me to go live with him and Charlotte Hawkins on *GMB*. I remained anxious and Shep talked to me the night before to reassure me.

'Trust me,' he said. 'You'll be surprised how people respond, and it will be a weight lifted once you've shared it.'

The following morning, after Shep and Charlotte had relaxed me with a few laughs, she asked the question about my apraxia. The floodgates opened as I unloaded what I was going through and how hard it had been.

Charlotte was so lovely. 'At the end of the day, this is your career, isn't it? And it's a big deal when something like this happens to you. We've had so much love coming in for you.'

I was nearly in tears.

'You might be only firing on six cylinders not eight,' added Shep, 'but Kammy on one cylinder is better than the average person on ten cylinders.' Shep loves cylinders! 'It might have slowed you down, but you haven't lost the glint in your eye and the infectious laugh and joy in your face when you smile. That is still there, and that is why people still love you.'

The response from viewers, who sent messages of support in their thousands, took my breath away. The feedback, not only from the public, but from current and ex-colleagues, was overwhelming. I had so much support it was difficult to digest it all. Lots of advice and help offered, too. Unfortunately, I was not able to acknowledge all of it, but it was gratefully received.

Daniel, my hypnotherapist, had been so correct in his prediction that I would feel so much better having everything in the open. 'The day you accept your condition,' he said, 'is the day you start to recover from it.'

I couldn't have made that move without Shep. I get a lot of support from him, and Shep knows I'm there for him, too. That trust and friendship has been an important part of the past thirteen years of working together.

Kammy

All three of my closest TV pals – Shep, Jeff and Steph McGovern – had noticed something wasn't right before I told everyone about my condition. I'd failed to deceive them. That's because they know me better than I know myself. Thank you to you all.

13

Leeds United

THE MOVE TO LEEDS FROM STOKE WAS A MESSY AFFAIR, TO say the least. Like every manager, Alan Ball, rightly revered as a World Cup winner, wanted to build his own team.

While I got on well with Bally – a bundle of energy who wanted to improve and get the best out of each and every player he worked with, although not so strong on the tactical side of things – I wasn't at all surprised when he said he was open to offers for me.

Leeds, Sheffield United and Middlesbrough showed the most interest. I finally settled on joining the Whites, although it was a tough decision and one which could have cost me my lifetime friendship with Middlesbrough director – and now chairman – Steve Gibson. Bally accepted a £150,000 bid from Middlesbrough and arranged a phone call with their manager, Bruce Rioch. Bruce didn't have to sell me the club, of course, but told me how he wanted my experience to take his exciting young team to the next level. After that very positive chat, Bally told me to get up to Teesside that evening, meet Bruce and Steve, watch the Tees–Tyne derby against Newcastle with them, and then sign. He handed me the papers to complete the transfer, including all the details of how the transfer would be structured.

However, Leeds were also keen, and I was invited to call in at Elland Road on the way up to Teesside. After a quick discussion with Anne, I decided to do exactly that. No harm would be done – would it? – and it was only polite to chat with them since they were showing interest in me. Leeds manager Howard Wilkinson and managing director Bill Fotherby were waiting, and they informed me that they'd contacted Stoke chairman Peter Coates, who'd confirmed he was happy for me to speak with them. Unfortunately, no one told Bally. Thankfully, he fell out with the Stoke board over this and not me, as he felt they'd gone behind his back.

I was in a dream situation that day. When I was a kid, kicking a ball around with my mates, I was Boro or Leeds, Eric McMordie or Johnny Giles. It was my ambition to play for Boro and my dream to play for Leeds. And now I had both clubs wanting to sign me – and it was my choice. I was seriously torn, but Leeds made a little bit more sense. They were top of the Second Division and going places, with a great squad of players and Howard in charge. I loved Boro too – it was a real dilemma.

Not that I told Bill Fotherby and Howard any of this. I listened as Howard told me how desperate he was to add me to his squad, because I covered every blade of grass on the pitch. He'd just signed Lee Chapman from Nottingham Forest, and he said the two of us were to be the final pieces of the jigsaw.

Leeds were going to get promotion and win the First Division title within two years, he said, and he wanted me to be a part of it. He wasn't the only one. *I* wanted me to be part of it.

With my future decided, I felt there was no need to continue on the road to Middlesbrough after all, so I headed home to Anne and the kids. We should have been having the best of celebrations that night. I'd signed the deal of a lifetime, trebling my wages, but there was a cloud hanging over the evening. I kept telling Anne that I was worried what impact choosing Leeds would have on my friendship with Steve Gibson.

I rang Middlesbrough FC as soon as their game was over, hoping to catch Bruce Rioch before he heard the news. When I told him, he was not a happy man. 'No one does this to me or Middlesbrough Football Club,' he raged. 'You'll be a very sorry young man. You'll regret this for the rest of your life.' Then he put the phone down on me.

Well, that hadn't gone well, and I still had my mate Steve to contend with. He rang shortly after. 'I've just spoken with Bruce,' he said. 'How much have they offered you?' I told him about the deal. 'We couldn't have matched that. Remember when we were kids? We were either Boro or Leeds players. You go off to Leeds – and have a great time.'

What a bloke! My oldest pal – we go back forever – and he'd given me his blessing even though it was at the expense of his club. It meant the world to me, and Anne and I were able to crack open the champagne at last.

On signing for Leeds, we bought a family home in nearby Wakefield, where Anne and the boys settled in quickly. We hoped this part of Yorkshire would be a permanent home. For footballers, and more importantly their families, it can become unsettling to put down roots in one place, only to tear them back up and move on. While inevitably I would move clubs again, we did indeed stay put. Ben and Jack grew up there. It's home to them, and so, thirty-plus years later, it remains home to us.

Being football-mad themselves, the boys always followed my career, supporting whichever team I happened to be playing for – promptly throwing their old footie kits in the charity bag as soon as I changed clubs so they could parade around in their latest strips! They had the privilege of meeting many football icons after the final whistle when they waited for me to come out of the dressing room. They were the envy of their school pals on a Monday when they could boast that they'd had their photo taken with Gazza, Ian Wright, Alan Shearer or whoever. These days Jack is a die-hard Huddersfield Town fan, while Ben is in his dad's corner and looks for Boro and Leeds results first.

While West Yorkshire had become our happy home, Mum and Dad didn't have it quite so easy. They were on the thick end of some ugly abuse when I turned down Middlesbrough for Leeds. The worst of it was at their house, with offensive graffiti daubed on the walls. Dad was having none of that. After the property was attacked one night, he basically set up guard at the front door. If he spotted anyone hanging around he'd interrogate them. The message soon got out that he'd handle any trouble his way and it subsided, but it was a tough few months for them. It was terrible that they should pay such a high price for my moving between football clubs.

I made my debut for Leeds against Hull City in February 1990. It was typical of so many of our games: a thrilling 4–3 win that put the supporters well and truly through the wringer. Two weeks later, I scored my first goal – a thumping header from a Gordon Strachan corner – against West Brom. In fact, it would turn out to be my only goal for Leeds. For the first time in my career, I was not the first-choice central midfielder. I was competing with Strach, youngsters David Batty and Gary Speed, and Vinnie Jones to be in Wilko's midfield four, and if I wasn't filling in for the two young lads when the manager felt they needed a rest, I was playing at right-back to cover for an injured Mel Sterland. I didn't care – I was simply happy to be playing for Leeds wherever Howard needed me as we powered our way towards promotion.

After winning our penultimate game at home to Leicester, thanks to an iconic winner from Strach, our top scorer that season, it all came down to the final day and a trip to Bournemouth. It's probably the game I'm best remembered for by the Leeds faithful thanks to my assist for Chappy's winner which clinched the Second Division title and Leeds' return to the big time. It was a huge occasion. With Bournemouth's Dean Court ground holding just 10,000 and Leeds allocated only 2,200 tickets for potentially their biggest game in years, plus it being a Bank Holiday Monday fixture, there was trouble inside and outside the ground before, during, and after the match as thousands of Leeds fans made the long journey to the south coast for the promotion party. When we arrived at the ground, the tension was obvious. It's a game that's remembered for all the right and wrong reasons.

Howard pulled off a masterstroke with his team selection for the game. Our striker Bobby Davison was not fully fit and Wilko knew it. He also knew Carl Shutt, Bobby's obvious replacement, struggled with the pressure of big games at that stage of his career. Carl was a lovely lad, with bags of ability, and he'd scored plenty of goals for Sheffield Wednesday and Bristol City before Howard had snapped him up. But standing in for Bobby, he had only scored a couple of goals. The night before the game, Howard called me, Strach and Bobby into a meeting. He'd decided the unfit Bobby was going to start, and when he inevitably pulled up after a few minutes, he would turn to Carl on the bench and bring him on, leaving him with little or no time to worry about it or get nervous. The three of us were sworn to secrecy and, sure enough, five minutes into one of the biggest games of our lives, Bobby broke down and Carl came on to lead the line with Chappy.

Bournemouth, managed by Harry Redknapp, who was to become a good friend, needed to win the game to avoid relegation. It was goalless at the break, with Bournemouth showing little sign of folding, or scoring at the other end for that matter. I kept bombing down the right wing, trying to find the opening. But Howard was going ballistic. 'Sit in midfield and hold your ground,' he shouted. I ignored him and kept on making the runs. 'Sit in midfield and hold your ground,' he bellowed again – there was a reason he was nicknamed Sergeant Wilko. 'If you don't, I'm bringing you off.' He pointed at me. 'Hold your ground.' But still I carried on ignoring him. He told Batts to warm up. 'If you make one more run, that's it, I'm bringing you off!' he shouted. A few seconds later, Chris Fairclough spotted another of my runs down the right wing and found me with a pinpoint pass. I looked up and saw Chappy, launched a cross to the far post, and he rose to power his header past Cherries' keeper Gerry Peyton. The place went berserk. The Leeds fans went berserk. The whole team went berserk. Even Howard looked quite happy. 'Now I'll sit, gaffer,' I bellowed.

The other good news was that Middlesbrough stayed up that day too thanks to a shock 4–1 win over Newcastle at St James's Park and our victory over now-relegated Bournemouth. That outcome gave me the opportunity to have my say, and I did an interview with the Middlesbrough evening paper, saying how delighted I was that my assist had helped not only Leeds, but also Boro who I'd been praying would win. Thanks to that turn of events, I was confident I could now go out in Boro with my pals without fear of a backlash.

That promotion, and subsequent success, was thanks not just to a great collection of players, but to a style of management that was innovative in the extreme. Joining Leeds was like going back to school – except this time I actually learned something. Pre-Elland Road, I thought *I* knew what being a professional footballer was all about. Leeds United under Sergeant Wilko was a whole new world. Training under Wilko meant stretches and exercises before and after every session, while our diet was assessed for strength and nutrition. Gordon Strachan had precisely the same mindset. Strach always emphasized that diet, exercise and mental strength were vitally important to reach maximum performance.

People talk about Arsène Wenger changing the culture in English football and revolutionizing training methods and diets when he joined Arsenal in 1996, but Wilko and Strach were doing it before the Premier League was even thought of.

Howard spent big that post-promotion summer, bringing goalkeeper John Lukic back from Arsenal and signing defender Chris Whyte from West Brom. But it was the addition of talented young Scottish midfielder Gary McAllister from Leicester

City that was to have the biggest impact on my place in the team.

We'd played Leicester the previous season and Gary had scored a wonder goal against us from twenty-five yards, no doubt planting the seed in Howard's mind that he'd like to bring him to Leeds. The boss had a real go at me at half-time, blaming me for the goal, even though it had been Vinnie's fault. As ever, the big man had kept quiet, laughing to himself and letting me take the blame. There's a reason he plays the villain in films.

In between watching the Italia '90 World Cup and England's heart-breaking journey to the semis, I spent all that summer preparing as best I could for my first season in the top flight. I was already one of the fittest players in the squad, but I was determined to be in peak condition to be part of Leeds' long-awaited return to the First Division.

For the first few months I was in and out of the side before suffering a devastating injury at Coventry. I can still picture it now. I was playing left-back at Highfield Road and went up for a header. As I came down on my tiptoes, my ankle bent in the wrong direction. When I hobbled into the dressing room at half-time, Howard looked at me and said, 'You off and Snods [Glynn Snodin] on. Let's not take any chances.'

I insisted I was fine and not coming off. 'Just strap me up,' I said. 'I'm OK.' Physio Alan Sutton strapped up my ankle, but ten minutes into the second half my body went one way but my ankle didn't follow – my studs stuck in the ground and the weakened ankle ligaments crumpled. The only bright moment in a miserable day was the ovation I got from the Leeds fans as the stretcher passed before them – although Strach slaughtered me afterwards for managing to sit up and applaud and wave before I headed back to the dressing room.

Months later, Howard admitted I should have been taken to hospital in Coventry for an X-ray after the match. Instead I was patched up and helped onto the bus. I even drove myself home to Wakefield from Elland Road. I spent all day Sunday hobbling round the house in agony, unable to put my foot down properly, no doubt causing even more damage to my ankle. It was two days before I found out the extent of my injury – I'd snapped my Achilles. It would be eight months before I was anywhere near a football pitch again – and by then my Leeds days were numbered.

The last thing any footballer wants is to be injured for long periods. Crocked players are no use to a manager, and the physio's room and gym can be very lonely places. Being out of action hits your pocket too. Appearance money was important to players in those days, and I knew I wouldn't be earning any for the rest of that season.

I was miserable. I'd never suffered a serious injury before; spending the rest of that season on the sidelines was the longest and toughest period of my career. I gave it everything to get fit again, but in truth I don't think I ever fully recovered, although I went on to play for a few more seasons.

I became a peripheral figure around Elland Road, missing out on dressing-room banter, and towards the end of the season I stopped going to games because I simply couldn't handle being on the outside of everything.

When I was still nowhere near fitness when we returned for pre-season, I fell out with Howard. He made no secret of the fact he thought I was going through the motions and had slipped into some sort of comfort zone. Of course, nothing could have been further from the truth, and I was more than ready to let him know my feelings when I headed for his office.

I was about to knock the door off its hinges when Howard's secretary Maureen politely stopped me and told me to wait. She went into his office, emerging with the message that Howard would see me when he was ready, which was forty-five very long minutes later. When I walked in, I still hadn't calmed down. I was about to say my piece when his phone rang. He answered it, keeping me waiting for another ten minutes. Storming into someone's office takes longer than you think! When he finally gave me permission to speak, I let fly, barely pausing for five minutes as I poured my heart out and let him know how I really felt. Howard just sat staring at me. 'It's my life!' I shouted. 'I'm doing everything I can to fix it, but all the gym work, all the cycling, all the physio treatments aren't making a difference.'

He nodded but didn't say a word. He then took a pen from his desk and started scribbling. He handed me a piece of paper with a name, address and phone number on it. 'Go and see him,' he said and promptly started shifting some sheets of paper around before picking up his phone and making a call. The meeting was over.

Paddy Armour was a sports injury specialist from Wakefield. He'd worked with Howard at Sheffield Wednesday, and on the day of my appointment Geoffrey Boycott's Rolls-Royce was in the car park. The Yorkshire and England cricketing legend was a regular customer, and Sir Geoffrey apparently attributed much of the longevity of his career to Paddy. He was elderly, stocky and wily, and he diagnosed my issues very quickly: 'You've got an Achilles tendon problem, arthritis in your ankle and plantar fasciitis.'

Up until then, I didn't know what plantar fasciitis was. I thought it might be something you'd find at your local garden centre. Better known as triple jumper's heel, he explained why it meant I was still finding it so difficult to put my foot down. He was right about that – I'd started to run on my tiptoes. I left Paddy's little room with a proper diagnosis and a rehabilitation programme that would have me fit and ready to play within six weeks. And Howard was delighted. Because he'd decided to sell me!

After a couple of reserve-team games, I was finally back on the bench, getting my chance to impress when I came on for the last twenty minutes at Notts County when Gary Mac was injured. A few days later, I started in the League Cup against Tranmere Rovers and managed ninety minutes in a 3–1 win at Elland Road to help us to reach the fourth round. I didn't know it at the time, but it was my last start for Leeds.

While I thought I'd done quite well in what was, after all, my first full game for eight months – an indication that my Leeds career could be getting back on track – Howard called me into his office the next day and told me he'd agreed a fee with Luton manager David Pleat. I was free to nip down the M1 to talk to him. If I could stick around for the game against Oldham that weekend, he said, that would be a help, because Gary was a major doubt.

I was absolutely devastated. I didn't want to leave Leeds, but I knew I didn't have any choice. Because I was 'injury prone' in Howard's mind, he was going to offload me.

Gary passed his fitness test on the Friday morning but I came on from the bench and Oldham's Brian Kilcline scored an own goal from my cross to give Leeds the win to go top of the First Division for the first time in thirty years. I turned to the Leeds fans to celebrate. News of my pending move was out but they knew I didn't want to leave. 'There's only one Chris Kamara,' they chanted, a wonderful moment and one I'll never forget – one of the best and worst times of my career.

★

Two days later, I was a Luton player. David Pleat made me a very good offer, and instead of playing at the top of the table I rolled my sleeves up for a relegation scrap. I got two telegrams on the day of my Luton debut. The first was from Howard, which read, 'Good luck from everybody at Elland Road. And remember, "Stay on your feet."' – something Howard had told me when I'd first signed. He meant it as well. If I slid in for a tackle and got booked, he'd fine me, starting at £50 and doubling each time thereafter. A sending-off was a week's wages. Being a mid-field hard-man was an expensive business at Leeds! No wonder Vinnie disappeared to make his money in films.

The second message was from my former teammates: 'Good luck today and for the rest of your career. See you soon. Gordon and the boys.'

I did see them soon too. Leeds went on to win the last First Division title before the Premier League kicked off the year after. I'd only played three games, so not enough to warrant a medal – nowadays the kitman, the physio, and the press officer would get one! – but I was invited to the end-of-season celebrations and made sure I enjoyed every single minute of them with some of the best teammates, and one of the greatest managers, I encountered in my career.

As for the Leeds fans, they got Eric Cantona as my replacement. I'd say it was a fair swap. Whether anyone else would, I don't know. Eric could play a bit . . . just a bit . . . and helped the club to their first English title for eighteen years, before he was sold to rivals Manchester United. He even managed to score his first Leeds goal when I returned to Elland Road with Luton in February 1992, the home side winning 2–0. I received a wonderful heart-warming welcome from the Leeds fans, who sang my name in the warm-up and before kick-off, and then jokingly booed my first few touches of the ball – brilliant. To make the day even more special, Ben and Jack were the mascots.

Sadly, ultimately our fight was futile and Luton's ten years in the top division came to an end. We had to win on the last day to survive, up against Notts County who had already been relegated. We went a goal ahead after twenty minutes and then the nerves and occasion got the better of us. I had to watch the horror unfold from the bench because a knee injury had forced me off at the break. The defeat was one of the lowest points of my career. We walked around the Meadow Lane pitch in a daze. Having been a top-flight team under Pleaty for ten years, it was a devastating blow for him, the fans and the club. Luton's slide from the top table wouldn't stop until they hit the depths of the National League. And then, incredibly, and brilliantly, in 2023 they made it all the way back again. What a fantastic achievement, great to see them in the Premier League.

My anguish was only heightened by the fact that, at the same time as we were on the floor, my former Leeds teammates and their supporters were up the road celebrating that First Division title – just as Howard had promised me when I'd signed a couple of years earlier.

I didn't have much chance to help Luton return to the top flight. A couple of months into the 1992–3 season, I was on my way again when Dave 'Harry' Bassett took me on loan at Sheffield United.

In some ways it was a relief. The family had stayed in Yorkshire when I'd signed for the Hatters, mainly because the kids were settled in school. I'd rented a house in Luton and they'd join me at weekends and school holidays. After a while, though, driving up and down the M1 took its toll and we were ready to be together again properly as a family.

Three months after the Premier League was launched, I made my debut for the Blades in a 1–1 draw with Coventry City at Bramall Lane. I got a whole minute of action in what is now the world's best league, as a late replacement for John Gannon, and played another seven games before finding myself back at Luton.

Then, in February 1993, I finally achieved my ambition to play for Middlesbrough, albeit briefly. Manager Lennie Lawrence offered me a temporary place back home, and I played five games on loan before that deal ended too. Boro had the makings of a good side, with Bernie Slaven, Colin Cooper and my former Leeds teammate John Hendrie in their ranks. It was a shame we couldn't make the deal permanent, but the club had no money. It was too short, but still lovely to play for my hometown team before the time came to hang up my boots. I was delighted finally to be reunited with my old mate Steve Gibson and it was special to play a couple of games at Ayresome Park with my mum and dad and the rest of the family in attendance.

Kammy

At the end of the season, I signed on a free transfer for Sheffield United. By now I was thirty-five, the oldest Blades player to play in the Premier League at the time, and I was in and out of the side as Dave Bassett chopped and changed his team in an attempt to avoid the drop. I'd made only sixteen appearances when we went to Stamford Bridge on the last day of the season, needing a win to survive. It summed up my season that I didn't even make the bench for the midday kick-off. We started the afternoon in sixteenth place, and by the end of the game, with results elsewhere going against us, we were relegated. For a while there'd been hope. We led Chelsea twice in a tense match, but Mark Stein sealed our fate with two goals, including a gut-wrenching last-minute winner. The biggest blow to our fate was at Goodison Park, where Everton came from two goals down to beat Dave's old team Wimbledon and secure their safety.

It was an awful time, made worse the following day when we had to assemble at Heathrow Airport for a three-week, end-of-season tour to Australia, which some genius in the Bramall Lane marketing department had dreamed up. I don't know what the slogan was – 'We're going down . . . under'? Even though my good pal and former Leeds teammate Bobby Davison and I had been surplus to Dave's requirements for most of the season and were out of contract, we had to make the trip too.

Dave was still raw from relegation and when we arrived at our first luxury hotel, in Perth, he tried his best to impose curfews and fines on the players to keep us in check. Bobby and I had other ideas. Out of contract, out on the town. Results hadn't gone our way, but here was a chance to do something we could excel at. We were fined two nights on the trot for arriving back late from the casino. On the third night, Dave abandoned sentry duties and joined the players. We spent the rest of the trip enjoying late-night drinking sessions around some of the best cities in Oz. We were more like the Barmy Army on a cricket tour than a professional football team, and after attempting to play games in Perth, Sydney, Newcastle, Brisbane, Melbourne and Adelaide, we headed home. The lads went via Bali for a week to finish the trip, while I returned to Blighty to find, hopefully, a new club.

14

Enter the Dragon

SOMETIME AFTER THE *GOOD MORNING BRITAIN* INTERVIEW, and after many refusals, I finally agreed to do *The Diary of a CEO* podcast with entrepreneur and *Dragons' Den* star Steven Bartlett. My agent had been trying to persuade me for months to go on Steven's podcast but I kept saying no because, as ever, I was worried about my voice. Anne laughed when finally I relented – 'I thought you were going to start saying no to these things!'

'I know,' I admitted, 'but I'm hoping they'll be able to edit it and make it appear halfway decent.'

I hadn't met Steven before, but from the second he walked into the room, he charmed me and disarmed me, and I dropped my guard. He said he'd followed my career for years; that I'd been an inspiration to him and his generation growing up, a real trailblazer.

'Do you realize that, and do you feel it?' he asked. I said I didn't. I don't think I'll ever totally believe comments like that. How can I be held in such high esteem by so many? But he totally relaxed me, and before I knew it, I was opening up and spilling the beans.

Steven and I talked about all aspects of my life, including the difficulties I'd been facing with my illness and trying to beat it on my own. I told him how I felt a fraud because I couldn't bring to the table what I used to.

Steven couldn't have been more generous in his reply. 'In my life, growing up, you made me love the game more, made me understand it more. You have been hilarious. You are loved more than anyone I have seen, and you have earned that – it is a skill. I couldn't do a sliver of what you do. I suspect your fear, that you are a fraud, is not as logical as you think it is. And I mean that. I couldn't do 10 per cent of what you do.' I only wish I had an idea for a business – he'd have to invest after all that!

As with the *GMB* interview, the reaction to the podcast really surprised me. It was one of the most popular episodes of *The Diary of a CEO* series and gained more than eight million listeners. It would also lead to a reaction from football fans in my hometown of Middlesbrough that I never could have expected.

15

Boro

HAVING ONLY PLAYED FOR MY HOMETOWN CLUB AS A LOAN player, I was unsure how the faithful Boro fans felt about me. Their feelings were no better illustrated than by their reaction to the revelation of my apraxia.

A few days after my interview on *The Diary of a CEO* podcast with Steven Bartlett, incredibly they unfurled banners of support at the Riverside. I'd watched that Middlesbrough v. Rotherham match at home, but if Sky showed the two banners during the broadcast I must have been looking the other way. Not like me to miss something important happening in a football ground! Luckily, the club quickly put a photo on their social media accounts.

It turned out that the Red Faction, a group of fans in the South Stand committed to bringing colour and atmosphere to the Riverside, had unveiled two banners. 'You're not a fraud. You're unbelievable Kammy,' they read. When I saw the banners and the reaction on Twitter, I couldn't believe the trouble to which Boro fans had gone to show their support for me. It was a truly lovely touch and gave me a huge lift after a tiring week.

It felt as if every person I know in football texted to ask if I'd seen the banners. Shep said he was nearly in tears. Even big Arsenal fan Piers Morgan had something nice to say about Middlesbrough's supporters – 'Love this', he told his followers.

It was so humbling, and I certainly meant it when I tweeted my thanks again the following morning – 'I wasn't dreaming, last night did happen. Thanks so much to all the Boro fans who made it happen.'

I got an email address for the Red Faction from Boro's head of communications, Paul Dews, and sent a message thanking them for taking the time to produce the banners and for their support. I contacted Dewsy again a few weeks later to ask for permission to come to the Riverside Stadium and thank all the fans in person for their support and kind messages. While I wasn't keen to speak in public, I felt I owed it to them to show how much their gesture had meant to me.

I arranged to go to the home game against Bristol City, and Steve Gibson and wife Polly invited Anne and me to stay at their house in North Yorkshire for a couple of nights. We went for a walk together on Saturday morning, along with the former Boro boss Tony Pulis and his wife Debbie, who had also been invited to stay. Having a fresh pair of ears to assault, namely Tony's, Gibbo and I reminisced about our school days, and about playing football non-stop round Park End.

'What would our dads make of us now?' I asked Steve.

Judging by our surroundings, and his success in business and as Middlesbrough chairman, I thought Mr Gibson senior would be a very proud man indeed. I imagined my own dad Albert would have been walking tall too, happy that everything had turned out OK.

Truth is, had Steve not come to its rescue in the mid-1980s, there might not even be a Middlesbrough FC as we now know it. After the club went into liquidation and the gates to Ayresome Park were locked – the club was forced to play the opening game of the 1986 season at Hartlepool United – he helped put together the consortium that secured its future.

Later he instigated the move to the Riverside, brought in world-class stars like Juninho, Fabrizio Ravanelli, Gazza, Alen Boksic and Christian Karembeu – the list goes on and on – and oversaw the end of the club's long wait for silverware, winning the League Cup in 2004. Boro also reached FA and UEFA Cup finals and competed regularly in the Premier League. The team has since spent far too long in the Championship, and Steve's ambition now is to bring top-flight football back to Teesside.

Me and Steve have had many discussions about football and Middlesbrough over the years, and he's often called me for advice or an opinion on a certain player or manager. He doesn't always take it – Steve makes his own decisions – but I see it as my way of giving something back to him, because he's given so much to me over the years. Everybody should have a guardian angel, and Steve is mine. I can't imagine life without him. I know I could ask him for anything and he'd try to sort it for me. I wish I could do the same in return.

I hadn't told Steve about my pending engagement on the pitch. I didn't even know if he knew anything about the fans' banner and their message, or if he'd been at the Rotherham game. On the journey to the ground, though, Steve casually mentioned that he'd arranged for some of the Red Faction fans to come into the boardroom after the match to meet me. That was my cue to tell him I was going on the pitch at half-time, but of course, Steve is Mr Middlesbrough – he already knew.

I was surprised I wasn't more emotional when the moment came. I'd been a bit worried about it on the way to the ground, thinking I might struggle to get the words out because of the emotion of the occasion, not just the apraxia. Thankfully, it was a good day for my voice and I felt confident as I waited in the tunnel. I went through the few words I was going to say and rehearsed them under my breath. When I was introduced and walked onto the pitch, the reception was wonderful, and when the crowd started singing 'Chris Kamara – he's one of our own', I could feel myself welling up. Only by distracting myself waving my arms and conducting them, did I keep my emotions under control. When the fans quietened down, I managed to say a few words – 'Thank you so much, everybody. Thank you from the bottom of my heart. Once a Boro lad always a Boro lad. I'm on the mend thanks to all your best wishes. I really appreciate everything, thank you.'

As I walked off the pitch to the sound of cheers and applause, and waved again to the crowd, it felt like another pinch-me moment. The loving embrace of the Middlesbrough people really is something magical.

16

Lost at Leeds

Going on the pitch to acknowledge the fans' support was becoming a regular thing. In early 2023, Leeds' commercial manager Stuart Dodsley invited me and the family to the Premier League fixture against another of my former clubs, Brentford. It took some persuasion on his part to get me out in front of the Elland Road faithful. To my mind, there were so many former players who deserved to get an ovation more than me, and I didn't want to do it, even though I'd done a similar thing at Middlesbrough a few weeks earlier.

It then occurred to me that it would be a big treat for my grandson Sol, already a big Leeds fan at the age of five. Ben had recently taken him to his first game, at Fulham, but this would be his first ever match at Elland Road. What a way to start – to go on the pitch and have a kickabout with the players. It was already a memorable day for the family. Anne, Ben, Jack and me have seen a few England games over the years, but because

I was either playing or working for Sky every weekend, we very rarely got to watch Leeds together – or any of my other clubs, for that matter. With friends and family we filled a hospitality box in the Jack Charlton Stand before Ben, Sol and I were escorted down to the pitch. One of the Brentford players kicked a ball towards Sol, who tapped it between his feet and passed it back. Looking back, I wish we'd gone over to the Leeds players at the other end of the pitch and let Sol have a kickabout with them too. Maybe one day he'll play for Leeds at Elland Road, although for now he's much more interested in perfecting his Michael Jackson dance moves. He even wore his Jacko hat and Leeds United kit together for the occasion!

After a brief introduction, Stuart handed me the mic. The old Kammy would have loved this. He'd have got the crowd going, recalling great days and teammates and reliving that goal against Bournemouth. I've even sung to an Elland Road crowd in the past, before introducing the Kaiser Chiefs – and no, my singing didn't inspire their hit 'I Predict a Riot'. Instead, now I felt exposed. I'd known all morning I wouldn't be able to get the words out. I'd been dreading this moment – my voice was having a bad day – and knew I had to keep it short and sweet. I basically thanked the home supporters for the memories, then turned to the travelling Brentford fans and thanked them too.

Had I been more fluent, I'd have said what a great day it was for me to bring my grandson, a Leeds fan, and introduce him to the crowd, but there was nothing in my head. I had prepared something, and thought that if it was a good day it would just flow from me. But it was a bad day. And if it's a bad day, I can't remember words – even trying to recite something is nearly impossible. I was so frustrated. All I could aim for was damage limitation.

I took Sol by the hand and he, Ben and I turned to all four sides of the ground to all too briefly acknowledge them, me with my hands above my head applauding and Sol waving. At this stage, he has no idea what his grandad playing for Leeds really means. When he looks back at the footage, though, and starts to understand football even more, I'm sure it will mean more to him.

When I got back to our box, my ex-teammates Mel Sterland, Noel Whelan, Jon Newsome and Bobby Davison, who all work in the Elland Road matchday hospitality machine, popped in to see me. The banter was flowing straight away, but I felt unable to join in. I'm sure the lads could see I was struggling. Then Paul Reaney, a legend from the Don Revie era who made more than 550 appearances for Leeds, came to see me too. I stood up to greet him but knew the younger lads in the room wouldn't have a clue who he was. And so I introduced him as a member of my all-time favourite Leeds United team – 'Sprake, Reaney, Hunter, Charlton, Cooper, Lorimer, Giles, Bremner, Gray, Jones, Clarke.' I was amazed I was able to recite the full team, albeit in a slow and deliberate manner, but I was determined to get it right in front of a true Leeds hero. And I was very pleased with myself when I did. The little victories are important.

Paul burst out laughing. 'How can you remember that, Kammy?' he said before giving me a hug.

'Because, in my opinion, that was the best Leeds starting XI.' Don't ask me my times tables or capitals of Europe, but I'll always remember that team.

17
Gary

One player sadly missing that day was Gary Speed. He was just establishing himself as a first-team player when I joined the club in 1990; as soon as I saw him it was obvious he had the world at his feet. He stood out a mile, not only for his talent, but for his smile, the fun he clearly found in football. I loved him straight away.

Gary had broken into the first team from the Leeds youth ranks alongside his good mate David Batty, and it was clear they both had very bright futures. While I was thirty-one and about to enter one of the most enjoyable and educational parts of my twenty-two-year playing career, Speedo was in his first full season, about to embark on a journey that would see him become the first player to make 500 Premier League appearances and more than 800 in all.

Speedo and Batts were great to be around. They had respect for the senior players but also loved to wind us up and got away with plenty. They were both made for a football dressing room and wanted to learn. Speedo in particular had a maturity about him – there's no doubt about that. When you're in among all those senior players, as he was, it's a sink-or-swim situation. It's hard for a youngster to gel with players who have seen it and done it – you've got to be comfortable in that environment or you won't survive. Speedo, same as he was as a footballer, was years ahead of his time in the way he slotted straight into the first-team environment.

One game that always makes me think of Gary was against our derby rivals Sheffield United in a top-of-the-table clash at Elland Road on a Bank Holiday Monday. The nerves were really kicking as the biggest home crowd of the season packed into Elland Road. Howard played me in centre midfield alongside Vinnie, with Speedo on the left and Strach in his familiar role on the right side. We romped home 4–0, totally unstoppable, and I won the man of the match award – a framed print of a collection of Joshua Tetley pubs. It's not the most exciting picture and looks a bit out of place among the signed shirts and photos from my playing days, but it always brings back memories of that day, in particular Radio Leeds' John Boyd's commentary – 'Go on, Gary Speed, get one yourself, son . . . and what a great goal!' I released Speedo, a lovely pass with the outside of the right boot, and he went on to score one of his most iconic goals, sprinting half the length of the field to drill a hard, low finish into the bottom corner.

When you think of the intense pressure the team was under to win promotion, and the way, despite his age and inexperience – or perhaps because of his age and inexperience – Speedo handled it, he was a player of truly incredible character, never fazed by any of it.

I was sitting on the *Goals on Sunday* sofa when I heard Gary had died. My former Leeds teammate Vinnie Jones was with me. I got a text from Sam Allardyce while the show was on. It was quite common for managers and players to text me while we were on air, because a lot of them watched and they'd often send a message referring to something they'd seen on the show. This text did not sound good, though. In fact, it made my blood run cold – 'Have you heard the news about Speedo?'

I saw it through to the ad break and then texted him back immediately – 'What news?'

When I saw his reply, my first thought was that it couldn't possibly be true. I showed it to Vinnie. He agreed there was no way it could be right. It had to be some kind of terrible rumour.

Shep read it too. 'You don't send texts like that about someone as a joke,' he said. It simply didn't make sense. Not Speedo. We were shocked and dismayed.

We still had about forty minutes of the show to go. Vinnie and I somehow put the news to the back of our minds and got through it. With the report unconfirmed, all I could think was, 'Please God, don't let it be true.'

Within ten minutes of the programme ending, the official news of Gary's death broke. I just couldn't believe it. I still can't. Having known Gary for more than twenty years, and becoming such good friends, discovering he'd taken his own life sent my head into a whirl. I was in total denial at first, not wanting to believe it. Naturally, Vinnie was devastated as well. We went to Grasshoppers Rugby Club next door to Sky HQ for a drink and talked about our time together at Leeds when the camaraderie was so incredible and Speedo such a special presence.

Gary had actually appeared on *Goals on Sunday* a few times, in that group of ex-players we could always turn to if a guest dropped out at late notice. We had a list of reliable regulars who were good on the show – Speedo, Peter Reid, Ray Wilkins, Sam Allardyce, Ray Parlour, Shay Given and David Moyes, to name but a few. I would usually try to meet the guests on the Saturday night and have a couple of drinks if they were staying at a nearby hotel. With Speedo, I would always ring to find out what time he was arriving so we could enjoy a couple of beers together – one of the few times I allowed myself to go to bed at ten o'clock rather than nine. We did that the night before his last *Goals on Sunday*, a month before his death.

On that last show together, I would honestly say that he appeared happier and more content than I'd ever seen him – so good-looking with that wonderful, unforgettable smile. Professionally, he'd massively changed the face of the Wales national side since taking over as manager and looked set to take them to a major tournament for the first time in decades.

To this day, it's hard to get my brain around what happened. I've spoken about Speedo to Alan Shearer and Shay Given, who were both really close to him, and I'm not the only one still shaking my head. I thought I really knew Speedo. I thought I knew what he was like, what he was about. I know he worshipped his wife Louise and his two boys, Thomas and Edward, and on the many times we met up, he always talked about them and what they were up to.

If he was going through mental health issues and inner turmoil, he hid it so well. I saw him three or four times in the two months before he died, and not once did he show any sign that anything was wrong. He always looked like he didn't have a care in the world. I suppose that's the thing about mental health – we often don't know what people are really going through.

★

It's so important to talk. I myself have felt personal torment and a feeling of worthlessness because I didn't think I could do my job any more. But I look at my grandkids and know they don't care how I speak. I've also learned there's a way to tackle my issues. With the support of my family and friends I'm able to work through them. Right there is my escape hatch.

I know also that not seeking help for my problems was wrong. If I had talked, I might have saved my thyroid. Maybe I wouldn't have apraxia. I can't worry about the past, but I can look forward to the future. And I can talk to someone if I have something on my mind.

It's one of the reasons I support the Inside Out campaign run by the mental health charity If U Care Share. Part of World Suicide Prevention Day, the message is simple 'Get what's on the inside, out'. It's something I believe in deeply after my own experience in the past couple of years. If U Care Share gives mental health workshops throughout the Premier League and EFL, and works with players of all ages in their academies and training grounds, which can only benefit the game.

Football is also playing its part to help players – very different to my day, when it would have been seen as a sign of weakness to admit you were having a tough time mentally. Today, if you're struggling, you're encouraged to talk. Back then, you kept that sort of stuff to yourself, bottled it up, which can never be healthy.

Again ahead of the curve, this time in addressing the mental element of sport, was Gordon Strachan. Today, sportspeople use therapists all the time. Back in the eighties, however, it was almost unheard of, but Strach had a therapist when I arrived at Leeds and encouraged all of us to use him.

Strach tried to make sure all the lads were in the right frame of mind, that they were settled at home and their families OK. It mattered to him from a personal point of view, but he also knew players perform better if everything else in their life is on an even keel. I often wonder what would have happened if I'd met Strach earlier in my career. Before moving to Leeds, I always thought I could only offer my wisdom to other players if I was playing well myself. Otherwise people would just tell me to look after my own game and shut up. Working with Strach, I came of age in terms of looking at the bigger picture. He was ahead of his time as a captain and a thinker.

Hopefully, even more so in the wake of Gary's death, the stigma surrounding mental health is long gone, and easily accessible help is there for all players nowadays.

It makes me so sad to think that Gary wasn't able to get the help he needed. A lovely, lovely man. He will always be very much missed.

18

Kammy the Gaffer

AFTER THE DEBACLE OF SHEFFIELD UNITED'S SUMMER tour Down Under, I used the rest of that summer to coach at a girls' summer camp in Dallas. The 1994 World Cup was being held in the USA at the same time and there was a fair amount of interest in the game Stateside at the time.

I wasn't expecting a rush of interest from clubs back home, so when Bradford manager Lennie Lawrence, who had taken me on loan at Middlesbrough, offered me a contract at Valley Parade I jumped at the chance. Bantams chairman Geoffrey Richmond, a larger-than-life character and successful businessman who had big ambitions for the club, then took an age to finalize the deal after I returned home because he didn't want to pay me during the close season. It was the start of what was to be a productive – but turbulent – relationship with the enigmatic Mr Richmond.

Lennie was great to work with, a good man-manager, very

knowledgeable and always so relaxed, calm and methodical. I really enjoyed playing for him and he could see further potential in me, inviting me aboard his coaching staff. I was ready for it. Playing for Howard Wilkinson, and seeing his innovative methods, had inspired me to start working towards my coaching badges. Watching David Pleat in action had also been massively informative. He had a knack for spotting a player's strengths and weaknesses the first time he saw them play and would then work on those aspects in training. At Sheffield United, Dave Bassett had actually let me take coaching sessions. It was something I enjoyed more and more as the clock ticked down on my playing days.

While Lennie also wanted me to keep playing, I had in fact played the last of my 641 games, a 1–0 defeat at Blackpool, managed by my old pal Sam Allardyce. I was ready to retire. I'd been quite lucky with injuries, up until Leeds, and had played for longer and in more games than most footballers, but the years of being at the heart of battle had taken their toll. I knew I hadn't really recovered properly from the Achilles injury. I was an old warhorse looking for new pastures – not a one-way trip to the knacker's yard.

In time, Lennie began to clash with Geoffrey Richmond, a man used to having the final say and who loved the attention he got from the local paper, the *Telegraph and Argus*. He wanted to know everything that was going on and would often call Lennie into his office for meetings that could go on for hours. Lennie wanted to get on with the job, but his cause wasn't helped by us struggling at the wrong end of the Second Division. We survived and towards the end of that season, Lennie appointed me his assistant. We went into the 1995–6 season aiming for promotion, and thought we had the squad to do it, but still the results wouldn't come; Lennie was sacked in December. I think he was relieved in the end – Geoffrey had that effect on you.

Within minutes of letting Lennie go, the chairman called me into his office and offered me the job of caretaker manager. I had until the end of the season to prove myself by making sure we didn't get relegated. I took a punt on saying we could win promotion. He loved that. And that was how I decided to play Geoffrey – tell him what he wanted to hear.

I was desperate to succeed and gave it everything I had. I knew I could be good at management and had the personality to get on with players, the press and other bosses. I knew also that the job needed hard work and commitment. I still had an awful lot to learn, though.

With thirteen games to go, I told *Argus* football reporter David Markham we'd reach the play-offs and win promotion. I suppose, as predictions go, it was confident. At least the paper put it in the sports pages, not with the horoscopes! I knew we could give it a go and the fans liked the positivity and got behind us.

One of the first things I introduced into our routine was small-sided possession games of the kind I'd seen Ajax play in pre-match warm-ups. I'm not sure if that was the difference, but we only lost three games in the run-in, leaving us needing to win at relegated Hull on the last day and hope other results went our way to make the play-offs. Unexpectedly, there was a mini riot outside Boothferry Park, with Hull supporters upset that their traditional home end had been surrendered to accommodate the Bradford supporters. Hull needed the cash and knew the home end would be a sell-out for the first time in years. The fifteen-minute delay caused by the demonstration worked in our favour.

We were drawing 2–2 when the results from elsewhere came in and worked out we needed one more goal to take the last play-off place. We threw everything at a resilient Hull defence until my old Leeds colleague Carl Shutt popped up with a late winner.

We faced Big Sam's Blackpool in the play-off semi, and I was convinced we were out after we lost the first leg 2–0 at Valley Parade. I was also pretty sure at that time that my short management career had come to an abrupt end. It was my first meeting as a manager with Sam, and he got the better of me tactically that afternoon, putting a player in front of the back four and cutting out the service to one of our danger men, the lanky Ian Ormondroyd – or 'Sticks' as everyone knows him – who was handy in the air, to say the least. We were left with a task as high as Blackpool Tower for the second leg.

I was furious with myself after the defeat and stewed on it for hours and hours. It was so much worse being a manager than a player – every loss felt like another step towards me being out of football for good. I was no company when I got home, and Anne, recognizing how low this was taking me, and trying her best to lift my rock-bottom spirits, suggested to my chief scout Andy Smith and our good pal John Allott that they take me out for a drink. Over those couple of pints in O'Donohue's in Wakefield, I pondered how I could get one over on Sam in the return game. Then came a lightbulb moment – not quite the Blackpool illuminations, but it'd do. I decided to drop Sticks and not rely on deep crosses. Instead, I'd get the players to cross the ball from midway inside the Blackpool half. We worked on it for the two days of training in the build-up to the second leg and the players responded brilliantly. They had felt the pain of that awful first leg too.

I couldn't believe my luck on the night of the game – the Blackpool programme writer had inadvertently done my work for me and more or less printed my motivational pre-match team talk. They had jumped the gun, to say the least, by printing double-page adverts for trips to the final at Wembley. I left a few programmes with the offending pages open scattered around our dressing room and pinned a few more on the wall.

'This lot think they've reached Wembley already!' I told the lads as we got ready.

'Don't forget! Their coaches are booked!' I reminded them as they headed out.

We blew Blackpool away. Shutty scored, then Des Hamilton, before Mark Stallard banged home the aggregate winner. What a night for Bradford City. At the final whistle I leaped up and ran on to the pitch, sprinting towards the players and Bradford fans to celebrate. We were off to Wembley. I felt for Sam, who told me later that he made his players sit in silence listening to us celebrate through the paper-thin dressing-room walls. They could probably hear me singing – lucky them.

All the talk in Bradford was about the final. While the supporters were securing tickets and booking coaches to the Twin Towers, Geoffrey was doing his bit to prepare us for the big day – by falling out with the players. The lads wanted appearance money, a promotion bonus and a cut from merchandise sales. While I agreed they had a point, I said the players had to go through the chairman not me. Eddie Youds, Paul Jewell and Wayne Jacobs made their case in a meeting, with me as mediator. Geoffrey listened, and as the group read their demands, he slowly changed colour from his usual affable red to fuming, bursting-at-the-temples, purple. He stood up. 'Forget it. I'll play the youth team at Wembley,' he shouted, and stormed out of the room, stopping at the door to triumphantly pull his arm from behind his back and stick two fingers up at everyone. The players sat there open-mouthed. I just wet myself. 'He'll calm down,' I assured them.

He was in the corridor, seething of course, and mortally offended anyone should be asking for money, but I talked him around. The players got some of their bonuses, and Geoffrey made a few quid from the Wembley merchandise. And there was plenty. The roads from West Yorkshire to Wembley were covered in claret and amber – we took over the place.

The planning was meticulous and, to this day, I take great pleasure that I insisted on getting the lads kitted out in new suits for their Wembley appearance. Geoffrey agreed with the idea, and every member of staff wore the blue suit with the club badge and tie. We stayed at a top hotel for three days, went to the cinema, an Italian restaurant – I even told the lads they could have a beer if it helped them relax and settle their nerves.

On the day of the final, Anne pulled up outside the team hotel to collect the buttonholes for our boys. Brilliantly, they were to be the Bradford mascots for the game, leading the team out alongside me – an incredible moment which we still all cherish. The photos take pride of place in our 'Footie Gallery'. As I came out of the hotel to meet them, M People's 'Search for the Hero' was playing on the radio, an inspirational song for me at the time. Maybe it was an omen.

Before the police escorted the team bus to Wembley, with Anne and the boys instructed to follow close behind, I asked the lead officer to find a way of delaying our arrival so Notts County got there before us. That would mean they would go on to the pitch first in front of their 12,000 supporters, before we arrived with a bang and soaked up the volume from our 30,000 fans. That little psychological trick could have worked against us – it might have given the Notts County squad more determination to put us down. But, as we emerged onto the pitch, our players and staff looking resplendent and ten feet tall in our club suits, waving to the sea of City fans, I looked at the Notts County lads in their own mish-mash of suits, each with a black-and-white carnation. I honestly knew from that moment that we were going to win. They simply never stood a chance. We made Wembley ours. Des Hamilton and Mark Stallard got the goals, and I lost it at the final whistle. So much emotion. So much effort and commitment. Hours and hours away from Anne and the kids. And it was all worth it. We stayed on the pitch for ages. My dad had tears running down his cheeks in the royal box, and I eventually got to see him in the bar – I'd had to dry off after making the most of the celebrations in the famous Wembley baths.

It was without doubt one of the best days of my career. There was one sour moment, though – which may well have been the beginning of the end of my relationship with Geoffrey. We were handed a trophy for winning the play-off final, but I had never been comfortable with the idea. Let's face it: we'd finished sixth in the division. It seemed mad that we should be rewarded with a cup – a medal was more than enough. After all, Oxford United had finished second and hadn't got anything.

I didn't put my medal on. I put it in my pocket and didn't take a hold of the trophy during the lap of honour. Geoffrey, though, insisted I pose for a photo with him holding the cup aloft. I told him I didn't want to do it, and why, but he put his arm around me, held up my arm and the cup, and said, 'Just enjoy it.' It's another photo on the wall, and the only one where I'm smiling through gritted teeth!

I was still caretaker manager at this point, but after the obligatory civic reception, Geoffrey gave me the job full-time and we started planning for a crack at the First Division, the second tier of English football, now termed the Championship. It involved a lot of wheeling and dealing, and Geoffrey backed me in the transfer market as we signed Darren Moore, Peter Beagrie, Jamie Lawrence and Robbie Blake, who would all go on to play in the Premier League. One of our best deals was the goalkeeper Mark Schwarzer, who was only at the club for three months and made us a £1.1 million profit. We signed the big Aussie from Kaiserslautern for £150,000 and after a handful of appearances Middlesbrough came in with a £1.25 million offer we couldn't refuse. We got Gary Walsh in return.

Geoffrey loved a bargain buy, and he loved the new Bosman ruling, meaning that when players' contracts were up they could leave for free – previously clubs had held their registrations back and demanded fees for players they didn't even want to keep. Our chairman quickly latched on to the idea of signing players for nothing and was forever sending me to games in Sweden, Holland, Portugal, all over, to sniff out any talent recommended by the agents who were continually ringing him and me. We did some good deals and some bloody terrible ones. It was exhausting, and I was never at home, but I knew the hand Geoffrey was dealing me and continued to give everything to improve the squad and our chances of success.

One amazing, if slightly unlikely, signing was Chris Waddle.

I'd have him in my team any day – even if I wouldn't play 'Diamond Lights' on my stereo. I sent Andy Smith up to Scotland to watch Chris, who was playing for Falkirk after being released by Sheffield Wednesday. Chris was only thirty-five and I knew he still had plenty to offer – I just needed to know if he was fit enough for the demands of the English First Division. 'Decent, Kammy,' was Andy's verdict after Chris had run the game against Clydebank and scored the winner. 'He can still play.'

We signed Chris on a six-month contract, and he was a joy to work with. Some people thought he was after my job, but he wanted to play football and enjoy himself, which he did, picking passes, shimmying past defenders and scoring wonder goals.

His standout game for Bradford came in a plum FA Cup fourth-round tie at Everton. When he saw me in the tunnel before kick-off, the Toffees' legendary keeper Neville Southall asked me if Chris, an injury doubt in the run-up to the game, was fit to play. 'He is indeed,' I told him.

If the big man was worried about Chris, then that concern was entirely justified. We'd done our homework. Nev was increasingly playing as a sweeper-keeper, hovering near the edge of his area. Chris and I had discussed this during the week. When he came out to warm up, I reinforced the message – 'If the ball falls to your feet anywhere around the halfway line,' I told him, 'just whack it.'

Chris was immense, not only did he provide two perfect passes so John Dreyer and Robert Steiner couldn't miss, he scored one of the best goals I've ever seen. When Andrei Kanchelskis lost the ball forty-five yards out, Chris didn't even look – he scooped his left foot round the ball and watched as it flew over Nev, who was only on the six-yard line, and landed in the back of the net. He ran to the Bradford fans, bouncing in front of them with both arms in the air. Not knowing how to celebrate myself, for some reason I chose to do a somersault on the touchline – well, more of a forward roll, I suppose! As I pulled myself back up from my amateur gymnastics, I saw the disapproval, maybe even disgust, on the face of Everton boss Joe Royle. What did I care? Life's for living – and when the final whistle went Bradford had won 3–2 and enjoyed one of the biggest days in their history.

Chris played about twenty games for us, and he was brilliant to have in the side, but his form inevitably caught the attention of teams in the Premier League. It wasn't long before Sunderland manager Peter Reid offered him the chance to play for his dad's boyhood team. I'd promised Chris that in the unlikely event of a Premier League club coming in for him I'd let him go the same way as he'd come – on a free transfer. I'd reckoned without Geoffrey – the chairman was having none of it.

'He's one of our best players and you want him to go on a free?' he seethed. 'How will we explain that to our supporters?'

I'd given my word to Chris; if Geoffrey felt differently he'd have to deal with it. Somehow he managed to squeeze £100,000 out of Sunderland and Chris was on his way.

★

For more than two years of my life I lived and breathed Bradford City. It absolutely consumed me and fair to say I wasn't exactly – as the forward roll at Everton would indicate – a calming influence in the dugout. In fact, at times, I was a raving lunatic. From that touchline I kicked every ball, won every header and made every tackle. I might have been a young and naive manager, but I still had the energy and enthusiasm of a pro.

I needed every ounce of that energy because competing in, and staying in, the First Division was tough. On the final day of my first season, to ensure safety we had to match Grimsby Town's result. Nigel Pepper, a feisty young lad and late-season signing from York City, scored twice with a couple of crackers, and Tommy Wright scored the third to ensure another year in the second tier.

There was a big celebration at my house and I invited Geoffrey and his wife Elizabeth, other club staff, family and friends, and press lads like Ian Dennis – now BBC Radio 5 Live's lead commentator – who was working for Radio Leeds at the time. There was booze, loads of good food, more booze, and a jazz band playing in the garden.

It was here, in the most unlikely of ways, that I irrevocably soured my relationship with Geoffrey.

As the drinks flowed, inevitably I took to the mic for an impromptu sing-song with the band. Keeping me off the stage at a party is like keeping me in the dugout on a Saturday. It's a three-man job, and there was no one there to stop me.

For some reason I took this opportunity to perform my own tribute to Geoffrey. To the tune of George Gershwin's 'Summertime', it went something like this – 'Summertime, working for Geoffrey ain't easy . . . he wants to pick the team and sign the players as well . . . all I can say is, Geoffrey, please don't pry . . .'

I'm told I could hardly get the words out for giggling, finishing with a flourish – 'So hush now, Geoffrey, but don't you cryyyyyyy.'

Given how Geoffrey had made his fortune, you'd have thought the crowd might have held up lighters. But no. There was a short smattering of applause, before, according to Ian Dennis, who stills remembers it well, the most agonizing of silences as everyone looked towards Geoffrey for his reaction. He was sat there with a steely grin fixed to his face and shortly afterwards left with Elizabeth in tow. It was less summertime, more P45 time. I might as well have handed in my notice there and then. And, boy, did I get it in the neck from Anne the next morning. No more garden parties for us.

After my balladeering, the relationship became increasingly strained. Signings and transfers became more difficult as Geoffrey tested my patience and continually tried to save money. We made a great start to the new season, going top as we headed into September, and I thought I deserved to be trusted in the transfer market. Instead he was always testing me.

The *Daily Mail* linked us with signing my old Leeds pal John Hendrie from Barnsley, which was news to me. I angrily confronted the author of the article, Yorkshire football reporting stalwart Alan Biggs, after a night match at Valley Parade. Instead I was made to look a fool when, during the blazing row with Biggsy in the main stand, he revealed the source of this information. Yes, you guessed it – Geoffrey.

Resigning on the spot is normally a pretty dumb move. But, after Geoffrey tried to make me apologize to Biggsy, I did just that. The pair of us calmed down the next day, and, despite growing reservations, I carried on. It was only putting off the inevitable.

After we lost 3–0 to Manchester City in the FA Cup third round, Geoffrey rang me on the team bus and told me I had to sack one of my coaching staff because 'our season was over'. Geoffrey's mood seemed to change with the wind direction.

Only a week earlier, he'd taken me and Anne out to celebrate the second anniversary of my appointment, sending a limo to the house and playing TV footage of the Wembley play-off win on the screens in the back. And now he wanted me to get rid of one of my coaches and close confidants. No way was I losing either of my valued assistants Paul Jewell or Martin Hunter, so I dug my heels in. Geoffrey's reaction was typically uncompromising. 'If you won't get rid of one of your staff, we're going to get rid of you instead.'

'OK, Geoffrey,' I said. 'You win. Do the necessary. Tell the press, pay me up, and I'll be out of your hair.'

While naturally he tried to backtrack and persuade me to change my mind, I'd had enough. And, in hindsight, severing the cord with Geoffrey was one of the best decisions I ever made. Although that cord did take a fair bit of severing. When it comes to messy break-ups, Geoffrey could teach Hollywood a thing or two. He decided he didn't want to pay me a penny in compensation, as he thought I'd soon find another job. I was determined he couldn't have everything his own way. I eventually got only about a third of the money I was entitled to, but I was just glad to be out of Geoffrey's clutches and put his antics behind me.

Before I disappeared, I did recommend Paul Jewell for the job, and I was pleased to see the great things he achieved with that squad – with or without Geoffrey's interventions – taking the club to the dreamland of the Premier League. I visited the old place a few times with Paul in charge. In fact, on one occasion, with a *Soccer Saturday* cameraman in tow, I burst into Geoffrey's office and pulled out a cigarette lighter in the shape of a pistol. 'Now here's something I should have done years ago,' I said as I pulled the 'weapon' on my former boss. Maybe it was a bit extreme, but Geoffrey saw the funny side, especially when he saw it was a Ronson lighter – one of the successful businesses that had helped him shape Bradford City in the first place.

*

Even if I had wanted to sit and mope over leaving Valley Parade, I didn't have time. A couple of weeks later a dream job came along – to manage Stoke City. I'd had such an enjoyable time during my playing career there, made captain in my first season, voted Player of the Year, and I had such a special affinity with the crowd in the Boothen End, that going back as boss was a no-brainer.

The club had by then relocated to the spanking new Britannia Stadium, and, smarting from my Bradford exit and still desperate to prove myself, I relished the challenge ahead. What an opportunity.

Three months later it was over. I'd dropped straight into the heart of a club in turmoil. The week before I joined, the team had lost 7–0 at home to Birmingham City, prompting angry scenes among the fans and the inevitable sacking of manager Chic Bates, who'd endured a run of one win in twelve games. The club insisted Chic stay on as my assistant, while his right-hand man, the Stoke legend Alan Durban, also remained as part of the backroom staff. Agreeing to that arrangement was a big mistake – and one which led to my downfall. I'd expected Chic to be given a pay-off and go. Who wants to stay at a club that's just sacked you as the number one?

It was sad to see how a club which had been such a friendly place when I was a player had now descended into one riddled with rumour and infighting.

At the same time, on Teesside, my dad was dying. I'd spend hours on the motorway heading to and fro to see him in those last few days. Looking back now I wish I'd realized earlier that the job at Stoke was hopeless and spent more of those last weeks of his life with Dad. At the time, though, I believed I could turn things round and make a difference.

In reality, of course, I didn't have a chance. Chic was unhappy he'd been sacked and understandably didn't like the fact I'd taken over his job. I'd have felt the same if the boot had been on the other foot. Keeping Alan Durban on didn't help much either. Maybe I should have tried harder to work with the pair of them, or insisted that Peter Coates and vice-chairman Keith Humphreys dispense with their services. This middle-way worked for nobody.

Another hammer blow was the sale of Andy Griffin, our best player, to Newcastle in a £1.25 million deal. The young full-back made up his mind very early on that he wanted to join Kenny Dalglish on Tyneside and refused any attempts from Stoke to get a better deal from Leicester, who'd pulled out all the stops to get him – an offshoot of which was a strained relationship with Foxes boss Martin O'Neill for a while.

My only cash signing was striker Kyle Lightbourne from Coventry City, billed as the club's record acquisition but whose actual fee was £150,000 less than the £500,000 reported. Kyle picked up a virus soon after signing, struggled to make an impact and didn't score a single goal in my time at the helm.

In the end I gave eleven players their debut in fourteen games in charge, winning only once and drawing five. After a terrible 3–0 drubbing at Tranmere in early April 1998, I was finally, thankfully, relieved of my services. In a bizarre reversal of roles,

Alan Durban was appointed caretaker manager, Chic Bates installed as his assistant, and Stoke were relegated.

I'll be forever saddened that I was not able to produce the goods for the faithful Stoke followers who had supported my return to the city. Maybe it was a case of right club, wrong time, and I was delighted with the success Stoke went on to enjoy under Tony Pulis when they became an established Premier League club.

19

Lost for Words

A LOT OF TV PEOPLE APPROACHED ME REGARDING MAKING a programme about apraxia. Initially I was nervous at the prospect and not interested in doing any of them.

I could think only of how bad my public appearances had been. Towards the end of the 2021–2 season, for instance, Brentford had invited me and Bradley Walsh to their Premier League clash against Southampton. The invitation came from Peter Gilham, the club's PA announcer, who is the longest-serving matchday announcer in the country. Peter, along with Mike Sullivan, the club's legends liaison manager, had organized pre- and post-match events at the nearby Novotel in honour of the 1992 Brentford side, the Third Division title winners. Terry Evans, the captain of that team, and manager Phil Holder were there to enjoy the day, along with former striker Marcus Gayle, who is now the club ambassador, plus Graham Benstead, Bob Booker, Paul Buckle, Keith Millen, Graham Pearce, Neil Smilie and Brian Statham. Brad and I had lunch and a few laughs with them at the hotel, then a car picked us up to take us to the ground, and we all had a few photos by the side of the pitch before kick-off.

At half-time, the club asked us to go back up to the directors' box to acknowledge the fans with former chairman Dan Tana, who was also a guest of honour. As we all stood there waving and receiving warm applause, the club put up a lovely message for me on the screens, congratulating me on my twenty-four years with Sky and wishing me all the best. Unbeknown to us, it was aired live to the *Sky Sports News* viewers, with Jeff Stelling adding his own tribute.

We couldn't have been invited to a better game from Brentford's point of view. Any fears that they might struggle on their return to the big time for the first time since 1947 had long since disappeared. The Bees had taken the Premier League by storm under Thomas Frank, and they were already well clear of the dreaded drop when they met Southampton. There was a brilliant atmosphere inside the ground, where the fans are right on top of the action, and they completely outplayed Southampton in a 3–0 win which put them safely in mid-table with a couple of games to go.

When we went back to the hotel, I was starting to tire and really battling with my speech. It had been a long day, and I was glad I hadn't had to do any public speaking or been asked to take a microphone at any stage. I tried to keep the conversations with our hosts and the other guests to a minimum, but Brad knew I was struggling. I'd filled him in on the problems I'd been having over the past few months, particularly while broadcasting, to the point that I'd eventually been forced to give up the job with Sky that I loved so much.

The hotel bar was bouncing, and Brad got up in front of a small audience in one of the rooms to say a few words. And he stormed it, of course, ad-libbing, telling jokes, laughing at himself – and at me – all the while looking dapper in his smart suit, bright yellow tie and handkerchief. He looked so at home. And the whole time all I could think was that I should have been up there with him. The old me would have been taking the mickey, sharing those laughs. I loved watching my old pal doing what he does best, but I had to grin and bear it before he eventually, politely, called me up to join him. And when he handed me the mic, all I can remember managing to get out of my mouth was 'Thank you so much for everything' as slowly and precisely as I could manage. I didn't want to say much more because I knew the words would stumble and sound slurred, and I wasn't ready to do that in public. I was still raw from standing down from Sky yet desperately wanted to be up there on stage with my pal. It was one of those moments when I just wanted the old me back for five minutes. Instead, by the end of the evening, I couldn't wait to get out of there and head home.

When Shep then asked if I would be prepared to do a documentary with his production company, my first reaction was the same as with all the other offers. No.

But Shep made a good argument for me to take a more positive approach. As he pointed out, I was in a unique position to help raise the profile of this little-known condition – a voice for those, young and old, who live with it. I told him about my concerns – mainly that I didn't want people to feel sorry for me. He explained what the documentary would be like and the story we would tell. Under those circumstances, and knowing Shep would oversee the production with my well-being in mind, we embarked on making *Chris Kamara: Lost for Words*.

It was 100 per cent the right thing to have done. Not long after the programme had aired, Shep and I were in Italy to record a podcast with former Arsenal and Chelsea midfielder Cesc Fabregas when we were stopped by a couple who'd watched the documentary and wanted to thank me. A family member of theirs had apraxia and couldn't believe someone on television was going through the same thing.

'I told you,' Shep said to me. 'That's how much it means to people.'

Lost for Words couldn't have been a better title for the documentary. Inevitably, during the making of the programme, my speech was up and down. Recording the voice-over, I couldn't nail the word 'therapist'. Eight, nine times, I tried, and it simply wouldn't come out. The annoying thing is that I can say that word. I'm sitting here saying it now and it comes out just fine. That day, however, it simply wouldn't. And that's hard. Embarrassing and frustrating. All I could do, as ever, was accept it and get on with it. The sound recordist managed to find one version of the word that was close enough and put that into the final edit. To my mind it was far from ideal.

There are some people who immediately stop you thinking of your own problems, and Mikey Akers is exactly that. Twenty-two-year-old Mikey was diagnosed with apraxia at the age of two and a half. He has been campaigning since he was thirteen to help improve treatment and education, increase awareness among teachers, doctors and nurses, and raise funds for more speech therapists. As Mikey pointed out in the documentary, many kids receive only scant speech and language therapy sessions – and then they stop.

Children with apraxia need speech therapy to help them learn how to talk – but for too long that funding has not been there. Why should Mikey and many others have to battle for support? There are kids out there who deserve the best chance they can get in life, like football-crazy lad Zach Wilson, who I also met up with at his home and we had a kickabout in his garden.

If by raising awareness, I can secure more help for people who in many cases are literally voiceless, it will mean more to me than anything I've achieved in life. It's one of the main reasons why I wanted to write this book. People can't support something they know nothing about.

Mikey once said to me, 'You can't stop working, Kammy, because the more you do, the better it will be for you – but it will also have a HUGE impact for all of us and our cause.'

That's a big responsibility, and I never want to let anybody down, so I'll do exactly as he says. There has to be investment in apraxia. There has to be change.

20

Sky Calling

MY TWENTY-FOUR YEARS AS PLAYER AND MANAGER MIGHT have come to an end at Stoke City, but I was always going to work in football in some capacity.

I got lucky when, after winning a Manager of the Month award with Bradford, Sky called me and asked if I'd join the pundits for the first live broadcast of a Football League game on the channel – Sheffield United v. Sunderland at Bramall Lane.

I said yes – Sheffield is just down the road from my home – only to be told they wanted me in the Sky studios in west London. I still agreed and joined presenter Marcus Buckland for what would turn out to be a six-hour stint of live TV when fellow pundit Gerry Francis was unable to make it in for the second game of a double-header. Sky must have liked what I did as from then on I'd work on occasional matches while still Bradford boss. When I got the sack from Valley Parade, Sky offered me a contract. Believing my future was in management, I turned it down, but quickly changed my mind when I was fired by Stoke a few months later.

Initially, I thought the media work would help me maintain a high profile with a view to another crack at management. But the more media work I took on, the more I enjoyed it. It wasn't only Sky – 5 Live were also good to me and I became a regular co-commentator on Premier League and Championship matches for them, alongside John Murray, Alan Green and Mike Ingham.

When Sky launched *Soccer Saturday*, Rob McCaffrey, a reporter I'd got to know during my time at Bradford, convinced producer Ian Condron to give me a go. *Soccer Saturday* was a groundbreaking live TV innovation, and the idea took a bit of getting used to for some. Patsy Kensit once said that in those early days she couldn't believe how her then husband Liam Gallagher had become addicted to a Saturday afternoon programme where basically you watch blokes watching football matches. I'm sure she wasn't alone in being mystified.

When I started on the programme in 1999 I routinely found myself alongside legends of the game such as Rodney Marsh, Frank McLintock and George Best, the latter being one of my heroes and among the very best players the game has ever seen. I'd had a half-decent playing career, but I couldn't help feeling a little bit daunted.

Besty and Marshy were great to work with, perfect on screen together, and always kept host Jeff Stelling on his toes. I also became a regular on the midweek shows, which Jeff hosted at that time too, keeping us in order with a combination of quick humour, superb knowledge and perfect timing.

I only met Jeff the day before we were first on air together.

We'd both been on Teesside in the early 1990s when I was on loan at Middlesbrough and Jeff was cutting his teeth at BBC Radio Tees, but our paths had never crossed. Ian Condron introduced us in the canteen at the Sky studios in Isleworth and we hit it off immediately.

Under the regulations, broadcasters weren't allowed to show any live action on a Saturday afternoon. Condo, however, wanted to add an extra live feel to the programme. So after six months he decided he had a different role for me – he wanted me to go on the road and deliver reports live from the grounds with the crowd in the background.

And so Kamara-Cam was born.

I was far from convinced it would work, and I wasn't the only one. Jeff thought it was an unnecessary intervention and interruption in his fast-flowing results service. He couldn't see the benefit of watching a reporter talking with the crowd behind them if the viewer couldn't see the match.

To his credit, Condo stuck with the idea and sent me off for my first attempt, at Cambridge United. The piece wouldn't be live but filmed by the touchline as a report to be broadcast the following week. Seemed simple enough, but the post-match interview with Cambridge manager Roy McFarland was a disaster. He kept laughing because I was having trouble with the microphone – 'You don't know what's going on, do you, Kammy?' The report was never aired. I was devastated but Condo assured me it was an issue on the day of the broadcast, not the quality of the report, and we decided to go live the following week at Oxford United versus Walsall.

We arrived three hours before kick-off to set up. I wanted everything to be right, especially the angle of the shot from the gantry. It would be the way I prepared for every game for the next twenty-plus years.

My very first link-up with Jeff was set for 1.50 p.m. Condo had asked me to give the viewers a flavour of what was going on outside as well as inside the stadium. I was ready and prepared, feeling confident – until, two minutes before we were on air, an irate cameraman turned up, demanding that we move because we were 'in his spot'. I was still trying to reason with him when I heard Condo through my headphones – 'Going live in thirty seconds.'

The cameraman was having none of it. 'I've been filming Oxford United for nineteen years and this is my spot. You're going to have to get out.'

'OK, but we're going live now – we'll move in a minute.'

'No. You'll move now.'

Jeff was now coming across to me for the first ever airing of Kamara-Cam. 'Here's our man at the Manor Ground today. Afternoon to you, Chris.'

'Afternoon, Jeff,' I said, and with that our angry cameraman walked across the shot in front of me to the other side of the gantry.

'Sorry about the cameraman walking across there,' I said through smiles and laughter. He then tried to walk back across the shot. This time I was having none of it. As I struggled to keep him at bay with my left arm, I tried to continue the broadcast through gritted teeth, somehow managing to keep him out of shot. When the studio cut the feed, the pair of us went toe-to-toe until my cameraman Colin McDonald pulled us apart.

I came away from the game convinced that would be the first and last time we would see Kamara-Cam in action. They only came to me once more during the whole game, and Condo wasn't exactly enthusiastic when I called him afterwards. I didn't expect to be out on the road again the following week – or any time soon for that matter – but at least we'd tried.

Rescue came in the unlikely form of *Soccer AM*. Tim Lovejoy and Helen Chamberlain, who presented Sky's Saturday morning comedy football show, had seen my altercation with the cameraman in Oxford, and featured it the following weekend, wetting themselves as I wrestled with the interloper. It did look funny, and those who hadn't seen it live loved it. And so we survived.

At the same time I received a very important piece of advice from Rob McCaffrey. He felt I'd looked uncharacteristically nervous and stilted. 'That wasn't the Kammy I know,' he said. 'You're coming across like a TV news reporter on location. Like Kate Adie on the front line.'

He told me to be myself; to combine having a laugh – and especially laughing at myself – with being knowledgeable and informative. I got what he was saying. Kamara-Cam would only work if the audience wanted to watch me. I increasingly made the most of my brief moments on screen. The 'Kammy' character started to emerge.

I was a very small part of a huge show in those early days, but I always wanted everything to be perfect. Under strict rules that meant no players were in view, the best background was always the crowd. If a camera operator hadn't worked with me before they soon learned I was a stickler for making sure we had the best possible camera position. I always hated girders or anything that made it look like I was in a broom cupboard. My attitude was 'I'm at a football match, so show I'm at a football match.'

No one's entirely sure when I first said, 'Unbelievable, Jeff!' I didn't decide one day that I needed a catchphrase. It was simply natural excitement that made me say it. Now, of course, I hear it everywhere I go. I don't think there's been a day in recent times when someone hasn't said it to me, even when I've been abroad, and I really don't mind it at all. In fact, it would feel very strange if it suddenly stopped now. Just because I'm no longer on *Soccer Saturday* doesn't mean people can't shout 'Unbelievable, Jeff!' at me!

The most unexpected place I've been recognized is downtown Las Vegas on a family holiday. We were walking down the street one night when suddenly we all heard, 'Here comes Chris Kamara. Unbelievable, Jeff! Give us a wave, Kammy.' I looked round and saw a ventriloquist entertaining passers-by. The greeting had come from the puppet on his right arm. Anne was convinced I'd set the whole thing up – I couldn't possibly have been recognized so far from home – but actually the ventriloquist had spent time in the UK, and told us he had played the *Soccer Saturday* drinking game on a few occasions. Not that there's a definitive *Soccer Saturday* drinking game – all over the country people are slugging beer, shots or who knows what, every time a pundit shouts 'Gooaalll' or a reporter messes up a scorer's name.

When people aren't shouting 'Unbelievable, Jeff!' at me, they're sending me photos of themselves pretending to be me, inside a cardboard telly and holding a microphone, at fancy-dress parties. I love it that people are prepared to go to those lengths. If it lightens their day, bring it on.

I'm not sure Jeff always feels the same. He's also subjected to the saying everywhere he goes, and I'm sure there are times my mate curses the Saturday afternoons I kept on saying it.

Kammy

Mind you, there was also the time when I was witness to one of the most dramatic equalizers in the Premier League and somehow managed to forget to say it.

It was at Bournemouth in 2015, soon after Ross Barkley had put Everton 3–2 in front at the Vitality Stadium, and with the game about to go into the eighth minute of added time, Jeff came over to me. 'They are still having a go, Jeff. They've got another chance, Jeff. It comes across the box. It's a goal! Stanislav makes it 3–3.' And then I just stared at the camera, breathing heavily.

'For the first time he could have said, "Unbelievable, Jeff," and he didn't,' cried Jeff, holding his arms open. 'It WAS unbelievable.' It wasn't the first or last time that he was one step ahead of me.

21

I Don't Know, Jeff

ASIDE FROM THE ODD 'UNBELIEVABLE JEFF!', THE OTHER thing people often remind me of is the time on *Soccer Saturday* when I appeared to have no idea what was going on behind me.

The game in question, at Portsmouth, came at a time when Pompey had restricted access to the broadcast gantry for health and safety reasons. Instead, for their game with Blackburn, I positioned myself in the corner of the Fratton End and North Stand, by the home supporters. With the camera in place, I went closer to the pitch to keep an eye on the action. That's when Sky's production coordinator Carly Bassett, daughter of my former boss Dave at Sheffield United, and the cog who has kept the show running for so many years, mentioned in my ear that I was next on air.

As I moved back to the camera, and got ready to speak to Jeff, a series of goals went in at the games being watched by the studio pundits. Carly kept saying, 'Don't worry, we'll come to you next,' only for there to be another delay. I was stuck between looking over my shoulder and looking back to the camera, ready to go live. And that's when I heard Jeff – 'We're off to Fratton Park, where there's been a red card. But for who, Chris Kamara?'

I had no idea what he was talking about. 'I don't know, Jeff! Has there? I must've missed that – is it a red card?' I could hear the lads back in the studio laughing.

'Chris!' Jeff spluttered, 'have you not been watching?'

I kept looking back to the pitch to work out what had happened. 'I don't know, Jeff! The rain must've got in my eyes!'

The laughter in the studio increased, and Jeff seized on my confusion in typically quick fashion. 'Chris! Chris! Let me tell you, according to our sources, Anthony Vanden Borre has been sent off for a second bookable offence. Get your fingers out and count up the number of Portsmouth players that are on the field.'

I'd seen Vanden Borre trudge off, but I hadn't seen ref Steve Bennett brandish a red card. 'No, you're right, I saw him go off, but I thought they were bringing a sub on, Jeff.'

As they went back to the studio, to more laughter, I managed to shout, 'Still 0–0!' Professional 'til the end.

'Cutting-edge reporting on *Gillette Soccer Saturday*,' noted Jeff.

The laughing continued in the studio, and Jeff made the most of the incident for the rest of the afternoon, but I got an immediate dressing-down from *Soccer Saturday* director Karen Wilmington. 'Watch the game, will you? I know they're laughing in the studio, but you're there to watch the game.'

Turned out I wasn't the only one who'd missed Vanden Borre's dismissal. I asked a few of the press pack about it later and apparently the Dutch defender had received a second yellow for deliberate handball and headed straight for the dressing room. That's my excuse anyway.

On the way home, I rang Anne and said that I might be in trouble. I then called Condo to apologize. 'You can just about get away with it because it's you,' he reassured me.

I tried to talk Ben Shephard out of showing the gaffe on *Goals on Sunday* the next morning. I was afraid I'd be in more trouble and wanted to forget it. He insisted, saying it was hilarious and should be shared. Later that afternoon, Fox News rang and asked if I could go to a local studio to talk about it because the clip had gone viral in the USA. Then a radio station in the Netherlands also interviewed me, and so did a TV show in China. It was relentless for days – and I've been asked about it constantly ever since.

One of the funniest upshots was recording a version of the mess-up for a Sky Super 6 advert in which Jeff painted on a pencil-thin moustache and we swapped places and mimed the conversation. But the original will never be surpassed. Thirteen years on and it's still viewed thousands of times a day. The most successful failure I've ever had. Although there have been a few competitors, like the time I was at West Ham for their clash with Southampton and was oblivious to being called to action.

'Second half is just about under way at Upton Park. Who's started the better, Chris?'

For some reason, my earpiece wasn't working. When Jeff came to me I was facing away from the camera, watching the game over the top of the gantry. Again, the lads in the studio were killing themselves. Sensing a comedy open goal, Jeff came back to me immediately. And there I was, in the same position and still with absolutely no idea I was on live TV. By now the amusement had spread to the entire crew in the studio. Jeff and the producers decided to have one more attempt.

'Second half is well under way at Upton Park now,' said Jeff with a glint in his eye. 'Southampton back on level terms against West Ham. Who's started the better, Chris?' The screen switched for the final time to me staring out on to the Upton Park pitch. I don't think I'd moved a muscle. The director cut back to Jeff – 'He does not have a Scooby-Doo.'

I did manage to get my own back a couple of years later after West Ham had moved out of Upton Park to take up residence at the London Stadium. 'Let's go and find out what's happening at Upton Park,' Jeff said. 'West Ham 0, Sunderland 0. Does this look like it's going to be a deadlock to you, Chris Kamara?'

'Ha, ha,' was my response. 'The London Stadium, you mean, Jeff. Upton Park is long gone. Get it right, come on.'

Jeff was crestfallen. 'That's the lowest point in my career. Chris Kamara telling me to get it right! Unbelievable, Kammy!'

Another time, he came to me at the Tyne–Wear derby between Newcastle and Sunderland with the words, 'Alan Pardew called this fixture mad, Gus Poyet called it mental. There was only one man we could send – Chris Kamara!'

I did my best to live up to the billing. 'It's pretty even here,' I told him. 'Well, not pretty even because Sunderland are slightly on top.'

Jeff laughed – 'Pretty even, but Sunderland are on top. We've certainly sent the right person.'

When he came back to me for a penalty to Sunderland, I must admit it wasn't the strongest live commentary of my career. 'Anita has given away the penalty, and I'll have a quick look over my shoulder, Jeff, to see who's taking it . . . And it's . . . Santon who's taking that penalty. He's been on most of the free kicks and he's going to take it . . . No, sorry, it's not Santon, sorry. My apologies – Santon plays for Newcastle . . . errr . . . it's errr . . . one of the Sunderland players. And he's scored, Jeff! Borini with his right foot, Jeff. Into the top corner. It's 1–0 to Sunderland.'

Jeff's response: 'Mad. Mental. And that's just Kammy!' I don't know what he means . . .

Often, the laughter came because it was so unexpected, like when Newcastle keeper Rob Elliot's wife made an appearance in my chatter.

'If it was not for Rob Elliot, or for the misses, then South-ampton would be well in front,' I told Jeff. 'Not Rob Elliot's missus – the missed chances is what I meant to say.'

Once again Jeff struggled to contain his laughter before saying, 'And Mrs Elliot's first ever mention in a match report.'

It wasn't the only unusual reference that would grab Jeff's attention. In a north London derby, Spurs had gone ahead and the Gunners were pushing for an equalizer.

'Spurs are fighting like beavers,' I told Jeff, 'defending for their lives.'

'Did I hear that correctly?' asked Jeff. 'Fighting like beavers? Not tigers or lions, but beavers? Those ferocious little devils.'

Another time, Carly Bassett inadvertently gained fame one afternoon when I asked, 'Do you still need me at the end of the game, Carly?', having no idea I was live on air.

'I've told you before, Kammy, stop calling me Carly in public, for goodness' sake,' Jeff replied. Later, when he signed off, he added, 'Next week, I've only got two requests. One is a win for Hartlepool and, please, nobody call me Carly.'

The great camaraderie between everyone on *Soccer Saturday*

arose because we genuinely enjoyed each other's company. Fun was never far away, like when we did the *Soccer Saturday Christmas Specials*. One year we had a *Superstars* challenge in honour of the old TV show where sportspeople from various fields competed across different disciplines. I turned up for the swimming event in a gown with 'UNBELIEVABLE JEFF!' scrawled in marker pen. I pretended I couldn't swim and then stormed it to win the heat. Meanwhile, poor Jeff nearly drowned.

★

Me and Jeff were lucky to spend a good deal of time together away from the usual *Soccer Saturday* routine. For instance, one of the first times we realized we were part of a cult show was when we travelled to the 2002 World Cup in Japan. Everywhere we went, fans shouted, 'Unbelievable, Jeff!' at us from across the street and asked for photos and autographs.

Karaoke bars are a major feature of Japanese culture, so I was in heaven. One night we went to the Church, a converted nightclub in Tokyo, where we were joined by former referee Dermot Gallagher and a few hundred Ireland fans. I kept trying to get Jeff up to do a song, but all he could manage, tone-deaf with a voice like a bullfrog, was 'Come On You Boys in Green'. How it didn't crack glasses on the bar I don't know.

Together we went to the England and Ireland matches, and a few in between, on what was a trip of a lifetime. That said, I've lost count of how many times I've told Anne I'm off on a trip of a lifetime. I've had enough for several incarnations.

Me and Jeff saw more evidence of fans' love of *Soccer Saturday* when we travelled together for a week to record *Jeff and Kammy's Journey to Croker* in 2017. We went round Ireland, learning about Gaelic football, finishing off by commentating on the All-Ireland Football Final live from Croke Park. Who could refuse a 'once in a lifetime' opportunity like that?

We went all over the country to learn everything about the sport, and everywhere we went the crowds followed. In the first town we encountered we went into a pub and within an hour there were queues out into the street. By the end of the night, Jeff and I were behind the bar, serving pints. No one would let us put our hands in our pockets – it was like that everywhere we went.

On the day of the final, I had a slight issue. Throw-in was in Dublin at 4 p.m., but I had *Goals on Sunday* to do in London. I had three hours to get from one to the other. As soon as I finished in the Sky studio, I was on the back of a motorbike to an airfield forty-five minutes away, where I got a private jet to Dublin, all laid on by the bank that was sponsoring our *Journey to Croker* show. This was a definite first for me – the only passenger on board, and any food or drink I requested. It was just a shame it was only a hop and a skip to Dublin!

On landing, I was whisked through security to another motorbike which was ready to take me to Croke Park. It was great fun but as we approached the stadium, weaving our way in and out of the traffic in our quest to get there on time, a police bike came up beside us and flagged us down. I lifted my visor and smiled. 'Oh, crikey!' shrieked the officer and, blue light flashing, promptly took up the challenge to help us navigate the last leg. I got into my seat beside Jeff with fifteen minutes to spare – it was lucky I could still shift in those days.

After the game we walked round the pitch, meeting the players, and even getting a slurp of champagne from the winners' trophy, the Sam Maguire Cup, a dream of many an Irishman. It was a fitting end to our brilliant trip to the Emerald Isle and another highlight of the good times me and Jeff spent together. I feel very lucky that I worked so closely with him for so many years.

22

Soccer AM

AFTER THE FUN AND GAMES AT OXFORD ON ITS DEBUT outing, Kamara-Cam was always on the radar of Tim Lovejoy and Helen Chamberlain. The more they saw of my escapades on *Soccer Saturday*, the more they wanted me to present live reports on their show, this time from the inner sanctums of Premier League clubs. My segment was called 'The Home of Football' – basically a fun, slightly mad, made-up-on-the-spot, behind-the-scenes report from a club on a Saturday morning before the serious matchday preparations started. Players, managers and clubs were happy to buy into it.

The access I had to stadiums was incredible. I could go pretty much anywhere I liked, bursting in on managers, raiding dressing rooms and having a great laugh along the way. I was usually at a Premier League ground for *Soccer Saturday* anyway, and always liked to set up early, so it made perfect sense for me to have a laugh with Helen and Tim.

Very early on we surprised manager Harry Redknapp and his assistant Jim Smith when they were in charge at Portsmouth. Harry had given me access all areas, apart from his office, before Pompey's lunchtime game. Despite Harry's ban, I headed straight for his den. I appeared on screen stood before a blue door with a big sign in huge red letters – 'KEEP OUT. KNOCK & WAIT. BOOTS OFF!'

I didn't knock. I waltzed straight in with the cameraman in tow behind me. Harry and Jim were sat opposite each other at Harry's desk with a tray of sandwiches and some reading matter. If I'd expected them to be studying the team sheets, I was wrong – 'They're reading the *Racing Post!*' Jim looked up, somehow restraining himself from telling me and the cameraman exactly where to go.

We went from there to the home dressing room, where Paul Merson, their playmaker at the time, was about to get changed for the game. 'Here's John Travolta,' I said as the camera focused on the dapper gent on the bench wearing a cream suit that wouldn't have looked out of place in *Saturday Night Fever*.

Kitmen were especially good sports. Birmingham City's kitman once let me loose on the shirts in the away dressing room at Leicester. I turned over the first shirt and it belonged to Clinton Morrison. 'Oh dear,' I laughed. 'I must be at the rubber dubs' (subs) end.'

Before the game, Clinton spotted me by the side of the pitch. 'Somebody rang me,' he told me, 'and said you took the mickey out of me this morning. Well, I'm not on the bench, I'm playing and I'm going to score.'

He did, as well, and agreed to an interview with me after the game for *Soccer Saturday*. He was laughing his head off.

'You said I'd be with the rubber dubs this morning, but I proved Morrison is the man.'

Props were a great addition to a ground visit, and when Chris Coleman let me roam free at Craven Cottage, I placed a gold bar (from a joke shop, not real!) in each bright blue boot of new signing Andy Cole and announced that they'd been gifted by Fulham and Harrods owner Mohamed Al-Fayed.

When David Moyes gave me the green light to go into the Goodison Park dressing rooms, little did I know what gems I'd uncover as I trawled round Everton's famous old home. As kitman Jimmy Martin walked me round the home dressing room, we came to the shirt of Alan Stubbs. I told the viewers how much Stubbsy was missing Wayne Rooney, who'd just been sold to Manchester United. I then rooted under Stubbsy's bench and pulled out a picture of Rooney I'd planted there earlier. 'Poor old Stubbsy,' I said. I finished that report with a swig of Chang beer from one of the bottles in the fridge in the dressing room, supplied by the Thai brewers who were Everton's shirt sponsors at that time.

I'd earlier asked Moyesy if I could pop in to see him in his office at the end of my report. He'd happily agreed. When I knocked on his door, though, I found he'd stitched me up. He'd locked it from the other side and had no intention of letting me in. I banged a few times as I stood there laughing, but he refused to open it.

I liked to finish these reports by having a shot at goal, so I bolted towards the pitch – no ball to be found! Everton had popped my bubble big time.

I didn't always mess about. When I was granted access to the Old Trafford home dressing room, thanks to José Mourinho, for *Friday Night Football*, I was on my best behaviour because I didn't want to overstep the mark and ruin my relationship with the 'Special One'. Don't get me wrong. I still had a rummage around – finding Paul Pogba's luminous green boots – but I wasn't about to start running around topless in the showers.

I did occasionally get in trouble with my Sky bosses – and Anne – for some of the stunts I pulled. One time we were filming in one of the hotel rooms that overlooked the pitch at Upton Park before the ground was demolished. When the camera panned round to the bathroom, a young blonde lady emerged, wearing nothing but her underwear. 'Chris, are you coming back in?' she asked.

'April,' I said. 'I've never seen you before in my life.'

Helen was in hysterics in the studio: 'How do you know her name if you've never seen her before in your life?'

Suddenly, the phone in the room rang. This was not part of the routine. The Upton Park stadium manager was watching the show and had called just to see if I'd answer during my live report. Goaded by Helen, I picked it up. 'Hello?' I said, deciding to style it out. 'It's my boss, Vic Wakeling from Sky.' I left a pause and looked at the camera. 'What do you mean, I'm sacked?'

Vic was watching at home and thankfully loved every minute of it – he sent a note to *Soccer AM* saying, 'A bit near the knuckle but absolute quality.'

I used to love winding Helen up and leaving her speechless, like the day Steve Bruce gave me the green light to go into the home dressing room at Sunderland's Stadium of Light. I picked up striker Kenwyne Jones's boots, which were size 12 or 13.

'Look at these, Helen,' I said, showing them to the camera. 'You know what they say about a man with big feet . . .'

Helen sat open-mouthed for a second. 'No Kammy!' she said. 'You can't say that!'

'What? I mean he's got big toes!' I clarified.

I paid a painful price for messing around that day. When I got to the players' tunnel, I pointed out the pictures on the walls of successful Sunderland teams: 'Some of them show the glory days from when they were promoted. There's Mick McCarthy, and there's an old friend of the show, Liam Richardson, celebrating.'

'Liam Richardson' was, in fact, Liam Lawrence, who had since joined Stoke City. He sent me a message straight away. 'You pillock, Kammy. You got my bloody name wrong.'

Fans of the programme might remember 'Taking One for the Team' – a punishment for making a mistake on air which involved the victim sitting with their backside through a hole in the middle of a twenty-foot-high target while players took pot-shots at it. I went down to Stoke's training ground with this contraption – much to the amusement of Peter Reid, who was now on the club's coaching staff. There Liam and his teammates tried their very best to maim me. Thankfully, only Matthew Etherington managed to hit me, with an absolute zinger.

Soccer AM were never afraid to ask me to do daft stuff – mainly because they knew I'd seldom say no. One rare occasion I did refuse – and one of my biggest regrets – was when I didn't take the Red Arrows up on their offer to join them in the skies. They invited me to their training base at RAF Waddington in Lincolnshire with the opportunity to go up on a practice run. I was up for most things but on this occasion I bottled it. Mad really, especially when you think of some of the challenges I did accept, like sparring in the ring with boxing champions Ricky Hatton, Amir Khan and Anthony Joshua, or trying to match the skills of Olympic gymnast Louis Smith while dressed in a fetching red leotard, white headband, and matching sweatbands and leggings.

I loved those crazy reports for *Soccer AM*, some great memories, and was sad when the show came to an end in 2023. The good news is that, thanks to the internet, so many great and ridiculous moments will be preserved forever.

23

Goals on Sunday

SUNDAY MORNING WAS A LITTLE MORE SERIOUS ON SKY. Still relaxed, but a time for contemplation of what had happened across the football landscape the day before. Sky Sports' bosses felt a Sunday-morning analysis programme was in order – and that me and Rob McCaffrey were the perfect pairing to host it. Thus, *Goals on Sunday* was born, complete with the Commodores' 'Easy Like Sunday Morning' as the theme tune to give it an appropriate feel. Vic Wakeling was very keen for me to use my contacts book to get the best guests, and throughout my more than twenty years presenting the programme I continued to entice top names onto the sofa.

Rob was the first co-presenter I worked with, and a great character. Even though we got on famously and worked well together on screen, we would often have huge rows about what each of us wanted to do with that day's show, minutes before we went on air. We were both very passionate about getting it right. We'd both be seething, but the brilliant thing was that no one watching could ever tell, although I'm sure our battles must have amused many a guest.

When Rob left to work in the Far East, Sky tried me alongside a number of alternatives – Paul Boardman, Clare Tomlinson, Rob Wotton, Ian Payne, Vicky Gomersall, even Jeff sat beside me for a brief spell. And then I was introduced to Shep, who'd joined Sky to present Premier League and Champions League coverage. As a starting point, they offered him *Goals on Sunday*, and he jumped at the chance. Shep was like a breath of fresh air – the chemistry between us was there from the start.

Being able to justify any job I was given at Sky was important to me. When I'd first joined *Soccer Saturday* and had started recording features, I'd made sure I knew how to edit the material. That was hard on Anne as I'd be in the editing suite for six or seven hours on a Friday just to produce a five-minute piece, but it was important for me that no one could ever say I didn't deserve my chance. I wanted to show that I was always willing to learn, to make myself as good as I possibly could. When eventually I'd proved myself, Condo told me I didn't need to edit any more, enabling me to spend more time concentrating on content.

When the opportunity to present *Goals on Sunday* came along, I adopted exactly the same attitude – learn my trade and do the job properly – and was proud that, better than any other programme, *Goals on Sunday* became renowned for the depth of its analysis and scrutiny. Sounds daft for someone who'd played as long as I had, but one of my first jobs was to make sure I knew the laws of the game, particularly when they were changed or tinkered with during the close seasons. As a player, the laws aren't a priority. On a basic level, they're simply there. As a presenter on *Goals on Sunday*, however, I had to be 100 per cent certain in my view if I was going to criticize referees for errors. I'd look stupid if I was wrong on a point of law. A lot of refs watched our programme and I wasn't always the most popular bloke in those circles, but I never said anything that wasn't an honestly held opinion. And I always highlighted good calls too, such as a ref playing a great advantage which led to a goal.

I get that an official sat at home on a Sunday morning, watching me rip them to bits, might not like either me or what I had to say very much. But it was never personal. I didn't want referees to make mistakes – I just highlighted them when they did. Having had thirty-plus years as a player and as a manager, I knew how important those decisions are – they change seasons, cost managers jobs and have real consequences.

Sky bosses did occasionally ask me to rein it in a bit if I got carried away, but for me it says a lot that during my time on the show, I actually got on very well with Keith Hackett, who ran the referees' representative body, the Professional Game Match Officials Board. Even if he didn't always agree with my analysis, he knew I was just doing my job.

Making sure I was as well informed as possible for *Goals on Sunday* meant an early night on the Saturday. I'd have a couple of beers at our regular hotel in London, head for bed at about nine, and made sure to give *Match of the Day* a wide berth. I was usually fast asleep by the time the famous theme tune started and Gary Lineker introduced the Beeb's highlights package, and that's how I liked it – it was important to me that I wasn't swayed by someone else's opinion. Next morning, I'd head into the deserted Sky studios at 4.30 a.m. and go through the goals, saves and major incidents from the previous day, which the producers had compiled for me to watch. I'd sit for hours poring over the footage to provide the best analysis, with the best angles for the goals or incidents, and then help the team put together the highlights packages. That sounds extreme, but it's hard work to put together a three-hour show.

I always said to Shep that the most important part of analysis or co-commentary wasn't to talk about the obvious stuff but to tell people about the things they might have missed. He'd come in at eight and we'd have breakfast and the first editorial meeting together. I'd explain the edits and analysis I was looking for. Before the guests arrived at 10.30, Shep and I would go through questions and work out where we'd fit in the highlights packages of their careers. We both took it really seriously.

Goals on Sunday helped me to establish good relationships with managers and players because of the strong analysis I provided, all based on thorough preparation. Credibility was vital because managers wouldn't come on the show if I was talking crap every week. They could see I was still, deep down, one of them, and was simply speaking the truth.

Over time our opinions became so well respected that a lot of scouts and coaches would record our set-play analysis and use it to highlight an opposing team's training-ground routines. The show was a must for coaches. Half the time we were doing their work for them!

I was always careful with the language I used when it came to talking about a player who'd made a mistake or a manager going through a bad patch. If I could deliver those words with a smile or a laugh, then that wouldn't do any harm either. That came from my experience as a manager. It's easy to say a player isn't trying – as a boss you know they always are. It's just that sometimes it's not physically possible to perform as well as those other days when you're flying. Having that understanding was another key factor in making the show more authentic for football people.

That doesn't mean I couldn't be a bit of a maverick, and Shep was always on alert in case I went a bit off piste. Unsurprisingly, there were many times when he had no idea what I was talking about – and neither really did I.

Fabrice Muamba's appearance is a case in point. Naturally, much of the conversation centred around Fabrice's collapse on the pitch at White Hart Lane when effectively he 'died' for seventy-eight minutes. He talked about the events leading up to the cardiac arrest, the medics who performed miracles to keep him alive, and how he was coping after being forced to retire from the game. It was incredible stuff.

In an attempt to lift the mood, I asked whether he'd seen our red setter Sasha, my favourite dog, who'd died about ten years earlier, while he was hovering in that strange world between life and death. Shep was completely floored by the question, as was Fabrice, who laughed as he reported that, funnily enough, no he hadn't seen Sasha that fateful day. I haven't asked about contacting a daft dog in the afterlife since.

Shep was an expert at helping me weave my way out of self-inflicted craziness. While I'd laugh and say, 'What? There's nothing wrong with that!', he'd make sure to put right anything he thought viewers might be slightly offended by. It made him the perfect foil. Off camera, meanwhile, he'd tell me off if I'd said something he felt was inappropriate. 'It's fine,' I'd tell him. 'It's me, I'll get away with it.'

'One of these days you won't!' he'd warn me.

As well as being one of the best live broadcasters around, and a huge sports fan who loves interviewing people, Shep is the nicest man you could meet. He also knows precisely what you can and can't say on live TV. Working alongside him I learned a lot. But he never stopped me being me. We dovetailed from the start and built a brilliant partnership. Shep knew what he was good at and was always prepared to let me add some joy and energy.

When we had quieter guests on, we worked between the two of us to get the best out of them. I'd disarm them with the funnier questions and attempts at humour, while Shep would direct the chat and help them forget they were going out live, which could be daunting for some. He could also steer guests through the more serious sides of their careers, which might have included contentious or controversial moments.

★

Goals on Sunday went from strength to strength, and the list of guests over the years reads like a who's who of football – Eriksson, Venables, Hodgson, Capello, Southgate, Allardyce, Dalglish, Rush, Gullit, Vialli, Zola, Wilkins, Ranieri, Mourinho, Dyche, Moyes, O'Neill (Michael and Martin), Pulis, Warnock, Coleman, Pardew, Strachan, Souness, Bruce, Martinez, Rodgers, McCarthy, Reid, Kenwright, Redknapp (Harry and Jamie), Shearer, Speed, Henry, Drogba, Gerrard, Berbatov, Cole, Ferdinand (Les and Rio), Ginola, Vidić, Lampard, Fowler, Wright, Crouch, Defoe, Campbell, Schmeichel, Sheringham, Schwarzer, Petrov, Pearce, McCoist, Di Canio, McGrath, Seaman, Dyer, Saunders, Wise, Cahill, Sansom, Anderson,

Parlour (apologies to anyone I've left out). And we had guests from other sports too, including two brilliant mornings with champion jockey AP McCoy and golfer Rory McIlroy, getting an insight into their achievements and love of football, same with comedian and Liverpool fan John Bishop and singer Paul Heaton.

Not many top names slipped through our net – Sir Alex and Kevin Keegan spring to mind, and sadly Pep Guardiola and Jürgen Klopp came on the scene a little too late – but nearly everyone I asked came on. Admittedly some took more persuasion than others, like defender John Terry, who took nearly ten years of nagging before he finally made an appearance on the sofa.

But *Goals on Sunday* was never just about the big one-off guests. Our regulars could surprise us too. Graeme Souness, for instance, chose the show to talk for the first time about his time managing Liverpool, and how difficult it had been for him. It was a deeply emotional interview, providing an early glimpse of the passionate pundit Souey would become. For me, Souey's appearance was an unmissable opportunity to tell him how big a hero of mine he'd been back in his playing days at Boro. He confessed he'd loved his time there under the managership of Big Jack Charlton and would have liked the opportunity to manage Boro under 'your mate, Steve Gibson'.

The show was also innovative in partnering up great players, such as Kenny Dalglish and Ian Rush, Sven-Göran Eriksson and assistant Tord Grip, and the late, great Gianluca Vialli with Gianfranco Zola and Dennis Wise.

We were fortunate that Gianluca came on the show a couple of times – such a lovely man, who became a good friend.

Gianluca was a fighter and inspiration and I was devastated when he passed away at such a young age.

Ruud Gullit, meanwhile, came on with Vinnie Jones and his former Wimbledon boss Dave Bassett (brave man, Ruud). Surprisingly, the three of them really hit it off. For a Ballon d'Or winner and legend of the game, Ruud was so down to earth. It was the tradition after the show to take our guests to Grasshoppers Rugby Club next to the studio, but unfortunately Ruud had to shoot off to catch a flight to Amsterdam. What he didn't know was that the clothes in the small suitcase he was carrying had been cut to shreds by Vinnie, unimpressed that Ruud wouldn't be joining us for a post-show pint. Dave, Vinnie, Shep and I were enjoying a drink when Vinnie received a text from Ruud. He'd just opened his hand luggage at airport security – 'I'll get you back,' he vowed.

If the walls of Grasshoppers Rugby Club could talk I'm sure they'd make for interesting listening. It was surreal taking the likes of England managers Fabio Capello and Sven-Göran Eriksson down there, having a couple of pints, and simply chatting about football and life in general.

Not that things always went to plan. Paul McGrath went AWOL for three days after missing a flight to Manchester. Then there was George Best. Not long after his liver transplant operation, George appeared on the show with his old mucker Ron 'Chopper' Harris. Afterwards, George overheard me inviting Ron for a drink. It wasn't long before he was there with a glass of red wine in his hand. Alcohol has been the enemy for more than a few players down the years.

Despite their standing in the game, guests never minded when we had a laugh at their expense and showed some dodgy footage or hairstyles. For example, Peter Reid had a colourful and successful career and so there was plenty of material from his days with Everton, and as Manchester City and Sunderland boss. He was always up for a laugh too, whether he knew it was coming or not. One time he came on the show with a shirt that was slightly dishevelled. Reidy had brought a spare, so when he was getting changed I told one of the crew to film him. Later, we showed him stripping off in slow motion to some slow sexy music. Reidy of course took it in his stride and laughed his head off. He's the type of bloke who'll always run with that type of thing and enjoy it, although he wasn't smiling quite as much when we made him sit through Diego Maradona's 'Goal of the Century' against England at the 1986 World Cup in Mexico – poor Reidy was one of several players left trailing in the Argentinian maestro's wake. We showed Reidy that goal a few times. He always claimed it was Terry Fenwick's fault, not his.

That mix of humour, analysis and outstanding guests was what made *Goals on Sunday* stand out above all the other football shows out there. We all liked putting it together, the guests loved coming on and viewers lapped it up because it was something different – enjoying the analysis while being entertained and seeing another side to our guests. Shep credits me with helping his career because *Goals on Sunday* was the first show he could have a laugh on and be himself rather than being a serious newsreader or presenter. I'm not sure about that – he's a TV natural whatever he does.

When I took a call from Sky during the first month of lockdown to say that *Goals on Sunday* would be suspended, I more or less knew then that was the end of it. Even though it was popular, the viewing figures were good and the programme was still on top form, I got the feeling that people within the organization had other ideas. I've since been told by managers and players alike that *Goals on Sunday* is irreplaceable, and they cannot understand its demise. All good things come to an end, though, and I remain proud of my contribution to a show that everyone who loves the game watched week in, week out, for the best part of twenty years.

★

Probably the moment I'm asked about most of from all that time is an episode of *Goals on Sunday* from February 2015. It was one of the most memorable in its twenty-year history.

The Saturday was like any other day at the office, really. I was in Birmingham for Tim Sherwood's first game in charge of Aston Villa. At the final whistle I jumped in the car to head to my hotel in London ahead of *Goals on Sunday*. As I drove I flicked the radio between 5 Live and talkSPORT to get a handle on any controversial incidents that might have occurred during the day's fixtures and listen to the managers' post-match reactions. It was pretty clear that the story of the day was at Stamford Bridge where Burnley's Ben Mee had scored a late equalizer to earn a shock 1–1 draw. Chelsea's Nemanja Matić, meanwhile, had been sent off for reacting angrily to a challenge from Ashley Barnes and pushing the Burnley striker. The red card meant Matić would miss the Capital One Cup final against Spurs the following weekend. To make matters worse, Chelsea had also had two penalty appeals turned down by referee Martin Atkinson. Already I was looking forward to getting into the nitty-gritty of the incidents and putting together the analysis in the early hours.

Chelsea manager José Mourinho was fuming. He gave one of those brilliant interviews where by saying virtually nothing, he said everything. It was compelling radio.

A couple of minutes later my mobile rang. José Mourinho's name came up on the hands-free. I pretended I'd no idea why he might be calling. 'Hey, José, how are you?'

'I'm angry. Have you heard what went on today? We should have had two penalties. They should have had a player sent off.'

'I've not seen anything yet,' I told him. 'I'll see it when I get to the studio in the morning, José.'

There was a pause. 'I'm coming on your show tomorrow.'

Every time I saw José, I'd ask him when he was coming on the show. I did the same to virtually every coach, but José was the one I really wanted to appear. I was desperate to sit with him and go through his amazing career; to get some real insight into how he managed some of the best teams in the world, and how he'd handled players like Ronaldo, Lampard, Terry and Drogba, to name but a few. Not to mention the rivalries with Ferguson and Wenger. We could fill a whole programme. I was beginning to get excited!

'Are you sure this isn't a knee-jerk reaction and you'll change your mind in the morning?'

'No, I need to nip this in the bud. Referees are not being fair to my team –' that's the polite version of his reply! – 'and if I come on your show, you're going to say, on my behalf, that we should have had two penalties, and Ashley Barnes should have been sent off for his shocking challenge on Matić. Is that OK?'

I thought about it for a moment. 'Yeah. Of course, it is.' I knew full well I could only back him 100 per cent if what he was saying was true, but a little white lie to tide me over until

I saw the evidence with my own eyes was what was needed at that time. There was no way I wouldn't give my own opinion, no matter who the guest was. But I'd tell him that once we had him in the studio.

Before he signed off, I wanted to make sure his promise wouldn't be forgotten. 'José, I need to tell my producer, so you're not going to change your mind in the morning, are you?'

'Kammy, my word is my bond. I will be there.'

I told him we'd book a car to pick him up and he gave me his address in Sloane Square, the posh part of Chelsea, which I suppose it was always bound to be!

I called the producer, Sean Boyle, straight away – 'Are you sitting down?'

'Why?'

'Because José Mourinho's coming on in the morning.'

He laughed.

'No, I mean it. He is.'

Sean was both flabbergasted and over the moon at the same time: 'Are you sure this will come off?'

'Yes,' I said, crossing my fingers.

Sean said the production team were getting ready to leave for the night, but we agreed he should call them back and put together a montage of José's fantastic career, pinpointing all the talking points and his incredible achievements.

I was still an hour away from my hotel at that point, so I called Ben Shephard to tell him the news. 'Awesome, Kammy.' Shep's more cautious than me, so his next words were, 'What about the club press officer, Steve Atkins? Does he know? He might talk him out of it when he gets to hear about it.'

'Oh, yeah, good point,' I said. 'Well, we'll see. Don't forget, though, it was José who rang me, and he says he won't pull out.'

I got to the hotel at 7.45 p.m., had a couple of pints, and was just tucking myself in at about 9 p.m. when my phone rang. I looked at the screen and my heart missed a beat. It was Sean Dyche, the Burnley manager. My first thought was, 'How the hell does Sean Dyche know that José is coming on the show?'

'Dychey! How are you?'

And he was off, that husky voice huskier than usual at the end of a long match day: 'Have you seen what Mourinho's been saying about my team today?'

'No,' I said, lying. 'I was at Villa and not long been back. What's he saying?'

'I need you to do me a favour tomorrow. When you show the tackle by Ashley Barnes on Matić, I need you to highlight it – and I'm not saying it's not a bad tackle by Ashley – but you watch the Chelsea dugout. No one reacts. No one.

'When Mourinho went into the press conference and started having a go at me and my team, saying Barnesy should have been sent off, it's only because he's watched it back on the video. In real time, no one knew it was a bad tackle. Matić got sent off for the retaliation, and that's why José's pissed off. You need to highlight that.'

There was silence. 'Well, that might be a bit difficult . . .' I replied, laughing silently to myself. 'Can I call you in the morning?'

'Yeah, do,' he said and put the phone down.

Everything was going off in my mind. How was I going to deal with all of this tomorrow? I was normally asleep pre-show at 9.30 p.m., but I got to 11.30 p.m. and my mind was still racing, wondering how it would all play out the next day if José turned up.

I got into the studio at 3.45 a.m., desperate to see the incident for the first time. I looked for the Chelsea bench's reaction to Barnes's challenge and Dychey was right – there wasn't one. I didn't need Dychey to tell me – it's the type of thing I'd have noticed without being tipped off. I love looking out for the aftermath of incidents, along with the positioning of the players, managers and officials. But it was a really bad tackle. Matić was lucky, and clever, to ride it, but it could have been nasty – you could understand why he'd retaliated.

Should Chelsea have had two penalties? In my opinion, possibly one. That was no surprise – I'd expected I'd see things differently to José. I knew also that no way could I sit opposite him and agree with every word he said simply because he was José Mourinho and he was on our programme. I was in a tricky situation. Not least because by the time the pre-show meeting started at 9 a.m., we still didn't know if he was going to appear.

I put my mobile on the desk and waited for him to call. Finally, just after 9.30 a.m., my phone burst into life.

'Thank you for arranging the car. I'm on my way.'

'Fantastic,' I replied. 'See you soon.'

'And don't forget our deal.' Oh no! I was hoping he'd have forgotten about 'the deal'.

'OK, no worries,' I replied as I gave the thumbs-up to Shep and the team. We put the final touches to the José package and prepared for his arrival.

I always did a quick stint on *Sky Sports News* right after the 10 a.m. bulletin to announce who'd be our *Goals on Sunday* guests and to talk about the upcoming highlights in the programme and any discussion points from the previous day. When I revealed José was on his way, *Sky Sports News* got very excited. Suddenly it was 'Breaking News: José Mourinho's coming into Sky.' They made a mega deal out of it and even filmed him arriving at the building. I was heading back to the *Goals on Sunday* studio for the last preparations when my mobile rang. It was Dychey.

'I knew it,' he started up. 'I said to my missus last night, "I've just put the phone down with Kammy and he was being really weird."' I started laughing. 'He's using you,' Dychey continued. 'I'm telling you, he's using you. Whatever you do, don't stitch me up.'

'Dychey, you know me better than that,' I replied. 'I would never do that. I would not compromise myself in any situation.'

'Make sure you don't,' he said. And hung up.

I told Shep everything: 'Look, I'm screwed here. On the one hand, I don't totally agree with everything José says, because they should have had one penalty, but not both. And he's right about the Ashley Barnes challenge. I also see things from Dychey's point of view – there was no reaction from the Chelsea bench. I can't mention that in front of José. He might walk off. Meanwhile, Dychey's told me, "Don't stitch me up!" What am I supposed to do?'

Shep calmed me down. He said we'd let José have his say, and I didn't have to agree or disagree. Let him do the talking. It turned out he was right. I didn't have to say a word.

On my way to the dressing room to get ready, my phone rang once again. It was Steve Atkins, and he wasn't happy. He got straight to the point. 'You know if you want José on the show you have to speak to me first, don't you?' I explained to Steve that José had phoned me. 'Ah,' he said. 'Did he?'

'Yeah, I promise you, Steve.'

'Right. OK, have a good show.' And he was gone. Phew, I'd feared the worst, but that was easy!

The buzz around the production staff for *Goals on Sunday* that day was something I'd never experienced in all my time of being involved in the show. It was like God himself had walked through the door.

José came into the studio with a smile on his face – but it was short-lived.

Shep introduced our esteemed guest: 'We're both very excited this morning because we're joined by a man who has won seven league titles in four different countries, as well as, among other things, two European Cups. He's quite simply the "Special One".' That seemed to be a good start, and José appeared to be relaxing.

Whenever we had a guest manager on the show, we'd normally discuss their game halfway through the programme. But with it being José, we thought we'd start off with the controversy.

At the end of the highlights package, Ben said, 'Were you happy or far from happy?'

Not a peep from José. Silence.

I was trying not to look at him, but I could see he was staring at me and trying to get my attention. I sat there sheepishly trying to keep my eyes away from his. I felt awful. I'd reneged on a promise to a man I had so much respect for, someone I held in such high esteem.

This was when Shep came into his own. He knew how to handle José and get the best out of him, and that was to just let him talk. After the show, we were accused by a small number of people of going too soft on him, but why would you interrupt

José Mourinho with repeated questions when he was in full flow? Shep has always been brilliant at knowing what to ask and when to ask it. He knew José would deliver a box-office performance if he let him talk.

'It's not going to go very well if you don't say anything, José,' he said. 'We've got two hours.'

'What can I say that everybody doesn't know?' he finally replied. And once he'd broken his vow of silence, there was no stopping him.

'It's like the lawyer who is consistent because he lost fifteen out of fifteen cases, you don't want that lawyer. It's not because I am in your house that I'm not going to be honest with myself,' he said as he smiled and patted the sofa.

Shep had lit the fuse. Bang. A twenty-seven-minute rant.

The show was stocked up with other highlights from the previous day waiting to be aired, but hardly any of it got used. He went on and on and on, non-stop, producing evidence and blaming referees for this, referees for that. He remembered games long gone in which he felt he'd been wronged and certain referees hadn't given decisions. I sat there astonished – 'How on earth does he remember these things, in chronological order, without pausing for breath, in a language which isn't his first language? How?'

Eventually he stopped, and Shep was able to ask a few questions before cutting to a break. 'I think we need a drink!' he said.

It was a great show and made big headlines. One paper said it was like watching Bert and Ernie from *Sesame Street* interviewing José. I told Shep I didn't mind as long as I was Bert. When we looked back on it after he'd gone, Shep said the only thing wrong with the show was that we weren't able to celebrate him as we did with all the other guests. We had all this fantastic footage of his career, put together brilliantly by the team, and we wanted to hear all about his amazing achievements, but we hardly covered any of it.

It was the best *Goals on Sunday* I was involved in, without actually being involved much at all, and José really delivered. It was also the hardest show I had to do because I had to hold back on what I really thought in case he walked off the set.

In later years, Ben and I spoke to Dychey about that game and its aftermath during our *Proper Football* podcast, and he remembered it well.

'Ah, yeah,' he said. 'When you two pandered to him.'

'We didn't!' I replied. 'I told you I wouldn't stitch you up, and I didn't.'

'To be fair, you didn't, Kammy, and I appreciated that,' he said.

Truth is, I never pandered to any of the guests, but I did try to stay on good terms with everyone, including José, who certainly lived up to being the Special One that day, on a *Goals on Sunday* to remember.

24

Shep and Steph

When I started at Sky, I had no idea it would lead to a career that would last so long and be filled with so many happy memories. Even more of a surprise is the number of amazing TV opportunities that came my way. I was always so grateful to be asked and jumped at every chance, especially if Ben Shephard was involved.

I've been hugely lucky to work alongside Shep on a number of projects, and in 2022 we branched into podcasts with the afore-mentioned *Proper Football* for the BBC. I wasn't very confident of its success when it was pitched to us and was reluctant to get involved due to my apraxia, but the BBC persuaded me to keep working. I kept saying that I wasn't the person I used to be, but they were insistent, mainly because it was another chance for me and Shep to interview great guests. Shep was the ideal part-ner, as I could rely on him to help me through the interviews if I was having a bad speech day.

For me and Shep, *Proper Football* is the perfect replacement for *Goals on Sunday*. I don't have to get up first thing on a Sunday morning – and neither do the guests – while continuing to meet great football people. The real plus is that I still get to work with my mate; it's always a great experience.

As anticipated, Shep looks after me and has really helped me through the interviews. On one episode, we chatted with Peter Schmeichel, ex-Manchester United goalkeeper, and he played us a quick burst of him singing with a Danish band that he regularly gigs with. We also had a revelation when Stuart Pearce told us that during the early days after he'd turned pro, he also continued to play for his Sunday-morning team as goalkeeper, adopting a Russian persona and calling himself Yak Jensen so that he wouldn't be disqualified for being professional. Not sure that anyone checked this out – Yak sounds at least a little bit Russian, but Jensen? The Danes would surely have something to say about that being a Russian surname. And when it came to names, Jimmy Floyd Hasselbaink confessed that he isn't really called Jimmy – a former manager named him Jimmy, it stuck, and he never reverted to his proper name of Jerrel.

Peter Reid, meanwhile, reflected on not swapping shirts with Diego Maradona after the 'Hand of God' goal in 1986 (we do occasionally talk to Reidy about things other than Diego). Reidy told Maradona to stick the shirt where the sun doesn't shine, which led to his teammate Steve Hodge, who had no such pride, swapping shirts with Diego and eventually selling the one he'd acquired for £7 million – oh, the hefty price of pride.

Andy Townsend had some crazy and hair-raising stories on life with Gazza when they were both playing for Middlesbrough, and Olly Murs had us in stitches when he told us tales of the great Soccer Aid matches, particularly the day the team bus, en route to Old Trafford, had to make a stop at the services on the M6 to pick up another passenger: none other than the great Brazilian Ronaldinho. He'd flown into Manchester Airport and needed to get to the team hotel. Standing in the service station car park, he went unrecognized by the public.

As I mentioned, Shep and I also travelled to Lake Como in Italy to interview Cesc Fabregas, and while it was a great trip, I was not having a good day when we met the former Arsenal, Chelsea and Barcelona midfielder. I struggled through the interview, leaving most of the questions to Shep. I just felt slow and awkward, and I told Shep afterwards I wasn't happy. He said I was fine, but he always does, and he knows I am my own biggest critic.

Although I never thought I'd be doing podcasts – certainly not with my health concerns – I really look forward to these informal chats. They're such good fun and have helped to keep me going. I hope they continue – it's been great to get such positive feedback.

★

Working with Steph McGovern has been huge for me too, although I can't confess I'd watched her a great deal on *BBC Breakfast*, as *GMB* with Shep or *Sky Sports News* was always on in our house at that time of the morning. But I'd recognize that Middlesbrough accent anywhere when I did catch a glimpse of her, and I was chuffed when Channel 4 asked me to go on *Steph's Packed Lunch* when it launched during the pandemic. Initially it was a live Zoom call from my house to hers, which didn't really work for me. Much better when it was relaunched from its permanent home at Leeds Dock, at which point I met Steph face to face for the first time, spending the day as her co-presenter, a moment which stands out in my mind for two reasons: one because it was the start of nearly two years working on a new show with some fabulous people; and two because, as I've mentioned, that very first day I realized I was struggling to keep up with the speed of the autocue. The mind was willing. The voice wasn't.

We got talking afterwards and Steph told me she'd been desperate for me to come on. She's a massive Middlesbrough fan and a regular at the Riverside Stadium, so we got on like a house on fire from the start. We share that Boro humour and really take the mickey out of one another, with some great put-downs that only we would get away with. She's very grounded, is our Steph. Turns out she and her family were avid viewers of *Soccer Saturday* and she was genuinely so pleased to finally meet me and tell me how much she'd loved that show growing up. Steph was desperate to get me on the programme regularly, and as it was close to home, I was happy to get involved. As she said, *Packed Lunch* was ideal for me because I could be myself, 'transcend generations' and have some fun.

Steph and the crew even let me take my granddaughter Connie in a couple of times. She was very much at home in front of the camera making sweet treats and was made to feel so welcome by a lovely group of people.

Although some of the on-location pieces were time consuming, I loved doing them, but eventually I only wanted to be in the studio. It somehow felt safer to be surrounded by people who'd pick up and take over if I flagged. Of course, when I did confess all regarding my health, everyone was fantastic.

One show in particular had a huge impact on the audience – and me and Steph. It happened when we were discussing Black History Month in October 2020. Steph asked me about my experiences, and I told her how hard it had been for me and my family growing up in Middlesbrough. I recalled the story of the racist woman in the corner shop. It shocked her.

'And you really think people would stop your progress because of your race?' Steph asked.

I told her how racism was the norm. How when I'd first started playing football, sitcoms such as *Love Thy Neighbour* – based around a white man's constant jibes at the black family next door, and *Till Death Us Do Part*, which featured Alf Garnett's racist diatribes – were top-rated shows on the telly. I recalled how I'd walk into changing rooms and the other players would stop talking. Or if they were talking about a black person, they'd say, 'Oh, you're all right, Kammy. You don't mind.' As I pointed out to Steph, I couldn't mind – because I was the minority.

Steph was moved. 'I think that deserves a round of applause,' she said. 'I get a bit emotional listening to you, Kammy.' She started to well up.

All I could manage was, 'Don't make me start crying,' and with that co-presenter Russell Kane took over and headed for the ad break. When we came back on air, Steph apologized.

'I had a bit of a moment earlier. It's because I'm from Middlesbrough. That's where Kammy's from . . . he was a massive role model to me. And just to hear about things he's experienced . . . I got a bit overwhelmed. And having had a baby recently as well, it's hormones. Anyway, welcome back everyone. Sorry about that!'

I was gutted when I had to step away from *Steph's Packed Lunch*. I was becoming increasingly worried that I'd become a bit of a freak show. Steph keeps telling me the viewers are missing a bit of Kammy and they're desperate for me to return. I know I'm welcome back anytime, but for now I am saying no – although never say never.

I have met up with Steph, though. We did an ad together, and I saw her at a Boro match. I even managed a visit to the *Packed Lunch* Christmas party in 2022 to catch up with everyone and wish them happy Christmas. I arrived quite late, and Steph seemed to be even more excited to see me than usual. I then realized they'd all been partying for hours at that point, and so after downing a quick sparkling water I left them to it – I'm not sure many of them will even remember me being there! But I know her happiness to see me was genuine. We really bonded during our time working together, and, just as with Shep, I couldn't have asked for a more supportive host.

25

Be Yourself

I LAUNCHED MY FOOTBALL CAREER THANKS TO PORTSMOUTH FC when they paid for me to leave the Navy. And you could say the club did the same with my TV career. After the very public, and soon to be infamous, debacle of missing the red card at Fratton Park on *Soccer Saturday*, I was launched into mainstream TV without even trying. It seemed that making a balls-up on live TV was pretty much the best thing you could do to get yourself noticed, and in no time at all the offers started flooding in. As Anne knows only too well, I don't like to say no. Coming from the world of football, where you can never take anything for granted, my attitude was always that I should take advantage of every opportunity that came my way. I just wanted to enjoy each moment. My aim was always to entertain and add some fun. If people saw Kammy was going to be on a show, I wanted them to know there were going to be some laughs.

It's no coincidence that a lot of my good mates from the world of TV are comedians or entertainers. They always gave me a very simple brief when I appeared on their shows – simply be yourself. That meant some amazing laughs.

I struggle to watch myself in my pre-apraxia days – not that I was ever a big fan of watching myself on TV in the first place – so I haven't had a trawl through YouTube, but I have many happy memories to carry me through, such as the six years I appeared on *Saturday Night Takeaway* with the brilliant Ant and Dec. I'd have seen even more of them had I said yes to the regular requests to go on *I'm a Celebrity, Get Me Out of Here!*, but I always turned the jungle down because of my commitment to *Soccer Saturday* and *Goals on Sunday*. My intention was to do it one day, once my Sky contract came to an end, but I'm in no shape to do so now, sadly. Neither my body nor mind could cope. I couldn't face hearing the words, 'Chris Kamara is exempt from this task due to health issues.' No chance. It's a big regret.

I did, though, get to compete on *Strictly Come Dancing* – told I was one of the worst dancers the judges had ever seen when I recorded a celebrity version for Sport Relief. The producers had asked me to participate in the proper show a number of times over the years, but, like *I'm a Celebrity*, it was impossible to fit it into my schedule. Again I put it on the back burner until I stepped back from the Sky work, and again that meant I never managed it. A Sport Relief episode filmed over one evening at Wembley Arena was much more manageable.

I competed against Alex Scott and David Ginola for the Glitterball Trophy. First, though, I had to spend a week rehearsing and practising the moves to my chosen song, New Order's Italia '90 tune 'World in Motion', with professional ballroom dancer

Anya Garnis. For someone so competitive she was remarkably patient, but with me as her partner she really didn't stand a chance. As I struggled to keep up over the first two days, she spent most of the time laughing at me – maybe crying as well!

When it came to the big event, not all the judges were impressed with my efforts. I can't say I blame them – I moved like the Tin Man in *The Wizard of Oz*. In my defence, I couldn't dance at all before Anya got hold of me for those couple of days. I was also a year shy of sixty and my back was in a terrible state. I even secretly drafted in my daughter-in-law's talented sister Rose to give me extra lessons. I'd have hated to see the end result *without* her help!

The highlight of my performance was a special rendition of the famous John Barnes rap from 'World in Motion' – it certainly wasn't the dancing. In Craig Revel Horwood's view I was a 'complete dance disaster'. 'Your feet looked like they were Velcroed to the floor,' he told me. The entire crowd booed and fellow judge Bruno Tonioli brandished a red card at him.

No surprise then that I finished third (sounds better than last). Despite all the swagger and the talk, and the fact he'd appeared on the French version of the show, David finished second, with Alex winning comfortably in the end. Maybe my performance was better suited to Comic Relief than Sport Relief!

Afterwards I was again invited to be a contestant on the main show, but to be honest, aside from the difficulty of committing to a reality show during the football season, I don't think my body would have coped. I'd recently had to stop playing five-a-side football regularly with my boys and their mates, so there was no way I could throw shapes around the dance floor without doing myself an injury.

*

Thankfully, there was no chance of me pulling a hamstring when Jeff Stelling and I were asked to play ourselves on the hit US football comedy *Ted Lasso*. We had no idea what the show was about – or that we'd one day go on to win a major Hollywood award – when we were invited to feature the character Roy Kent as a *Soccer Saturday* guest. We were told the basic premise of the show and that Roy, played by comedian Brett Goldstein, was a recently retired player looking to get into punditry. It didn't take long to work out that he was probably based on Roy Keane. We were also joined by the actor Bill Fellows – who I was to find out is another Middlesbrough lad and Boro fan – who was playing a pundit called George Cartrick, seemingly a combination of Rodney Marsh, George Best and Frank McLintock.

The main difference between the real *Soccer Saturday* and this fictional version was the choice language, particularly from Roy. 'Chelsea were shit today, they were shocking,' he said. 'Have some pride in wearing the f***ing shirt.' I can't see that going down too well on the real thing!

'Again, we apologize for just about every word Roy just said,' says Jeff, trying desperately to save the situation – a phrase he must have been tempted to say every week about my efforts!

My main concern was getting the delivery right and trying to keep up to speed. The script itself was very simple and read like any other Saturday on the panel, plus I had no more than about five lines to learn in each of the three episodes we appeared in.

We only needed one or two takes and we were done. All Jeff and I had to do was change into three different suits and remember the lines.

It was a surprise then to receive an envelope in early 2023 with a United States postmark that contained a letter of congratulations from the Screen Actors' Guild American Federation of Television and Radio Artists and a Screen Actors' Guild award for 'Outstanding Performance by a Cast in a Comedy Series'. Turns out that, by appearing in three or more episodes, we qualified for the accolade. It's a shame we didn't know we'd been nominated! I'd have quite fancied attending the red carpet ceremony in Los Angeles.

It was another guest star slot that took me to the set of *Murder in Successville*. You'll not be surprised to learn that I'd not heard of the programme and had no idea what I'd let myself in for. All I was told when I arrived was it was a murder mystery and I was playing an undercover policeman. There was no script, no pep talk, no hints, no feedback after scenes. I was given a police uniform, sequin dress and blonde wig, told to stick on the uniform, stand on a spot on the set, and get ready to improvise.

The episode was titled 'A Horse Called Alan', and I played PC Chris Kamara, working with Inspector Sleet, played by comedian Tom Davis, investigating the murder of leading racehorse Alan Shearer. In one scene we had to interview one of the main suspects, Cara Delevingne, played by another comic, Ellie White. The three of us tried really hard not to laugh, but ultimately failed. As for the dress and blonde wig, I'll let you find the episode and see for yourself, but I think I was quite fetching as the undercover Kammy Cop, dressed as a lady of the night, not that I've taken up wearing the gear full-time.

★

Almost as ridiculous was my appearance on a Sport Relief version of *The Great British Bake Off* with Ed Balls, Victoria Coren Mitchell and Kimberley Walsh. I didn't get the legendary handshake from Paul Hollywood, but I did eventually win his approval for my showstopper. And, more importantly, Mary Berry liked my baking too.

Before going on the show, Anne had told me I had to curtsy for Mary. Maybe that persuaded her to be kind when assessing my first effort – twenty-four identical banana and sultana muffins – despite their somewhat reduced size. I had practised each recipe in the kitchen for a couple of days, and the measurements had worked at home without any problems. Once inside the *Bake Off* tent, under the watchful eye of Paul and Mary, however, my creations seemed to reduce substantially in size.

'They're like mini muffins,' noted Mary, as she took her first bite.

'They taste like paint,' said Paul, who was keeping his other hand deep in his pocket.

'Paint?' I said, somewhat surprised – that really wasn't the word I was expecting from the master baker. 'I've never tasted paint, to be honest, so that could be a compliment.' It wasn't.

The next challenge was to make savoury pies, and as a man who's enjoyed his fair share of pastry products over the years, I thought I'd be in my element. Once I'd worked out the difference between cling film and baking paper I thought I was doing fine. But as I moulded, stretched, and thumbed the pastry, I just couldn't make it thin and flat, while everybody else seemed to be coping so well. Eventually, with the time ticking by, I caught the attention of fellow baker Kimberley and asked, 'How on earth do you get this pastry flat? I've tried squashing it and poking it and stretching it in all directions, but it's not having it.'

She glanced over the worktop and retorted, 'You're having a laugh, aren't you?'

'Why?' I replied, confused.

With that she marched round to my workstation, opened the drawer and pulled out a contraption. 'A rolling pin would help, Kammy,' she said, eyes rolling, before quickly returning to her own masterpiece. Whoops!

I made the pie bases and fillings, but when it came to putting the lids on found myself a little bit short of the right amount of pastry to cover the meat and veg and complete the job. Even with my newfound gadget I didn't have enough. The tops were full of holes. The show's presenter Jennifer Saunders came over to the bench. 'Oh, Chris,' she said, putting her head in her hands, and laughing. 'What have you done?'

There was better news in the showstopper round – even if the judges burst out laughing when they saw my Strawberry Extreme Body Boarding Cake. The three-tiered sponge was covered in light blue icing complete with a figure supposed to represent me. As Jennifer acknowledged, creating a human body in icing is extremely difficult. When I took my offering up to the judging table, sad to admit that Paul, Jennifer and even Mary burst into laughter. But the proof is in the pudding – or the cake – and Paul absolutely loved my sponge, ignoring the effigy of me with my little legs. 'Chris, that is a fantastic sponge. In fact, it is the best we have had this year.' I've driven my family mad with that quote ever since – 'Did I tell you what Paul Holly-wood said about my sponge?'

I let out a little cheer. 'The only thing that ruins it', he said, 'is you.' Maybe he was right – I actually looked like a dying turtle on the top of there.

I might have come good in the end on *Bake Off*, but I was hopeless on quiz shows and usually fell at the first hurdle. So much so that I believe I might have gone down as one of the worst ever competitors on *Pointless* – mainly because I didn't really understand the rules. This was a celebrity edition of the BBC teatime quiz. I was partnering former rugby league star Martin Offiah, and he was in it to win it. Only he hadn't con-sidered the brain-dead Kammy factor.

The show is simple. Alexander Armstrong asks a question that has been put to one hundred members of the public. Con-testants then have to give a correct answer that they hope is matched by the fewest people. Zero matches is good. A hundred bad. For my question, I had to name a country that had won Eurovision.

'Don't worry,' I told Martin. 'I've got this.'

I was bubbling inside with excitement. 'So, Kammy,' Alexan-der said. 'What are you thinking? The most obscure country that has won Eurovision. Do you follow it all?'

'Not really, no,' I said, cockily – I didn't need to follow Euro-vision to know this one. 'But I would probably say, with Abba being a Swedish band . . .' a slight pause for the drumroll playing in my head, '. . . Sweden.'

Alexander looked a little taken aback. I couldn't under-stand his reaction. I was already mentally humming the tune to 'Waterloo'. 'Nice obscure answer from Kammy there – Sweden,'

Alexander said, professional to the last and no doubt stifling his smirks.

What I didn't know until I watched it back later was that Martin's eyes nearly popped out of his head in sheer horror. Nobody could have been more surprised than me when he told me we were on our way to losing. How could that be? Everybody knew that Abba won Eurovision with 'Waterloo'. And that was exactly the point – everybody knew. I hadn't brushed up on the rules.

Martin showed off his own Eurovision knowledge with our second guess, naming Israel as one of the winners – which I certainly didn't know – but we were finished on the show. 'How do you feel, Chris?' Alexander asked.

'Devastated,' I said, while Martin could not manage a word between gritted teeth. He was fuming and could barely look me in the eye.

'And what are you taking away from your *Pointless* experience?' our host asked.

'Nothing,' I replied, to laughter from Alexander and the audience. Martin's face did not crack, and he had the hump with me for a long time. In fact, I think he has only just forgiven me – and the programme aired in 2012!

Away from TV, I've also been invited to join some amazing performers on their shows and tours, including John Bishop, who once tripped me up live on TV in the bowels of Wembley, the swine. We were there for *Goals on Sunday*, ahead of the 2016 League Cup final, which featured John's beloved Liverpool against Manchester City, and we were replaying a penalty shoot-out competition we'd had with a giant football at Leeds Arena during his stand-up tour. On that occasion I let him win – honest. Here was my chance for revenge. As I started to take my little jog up to the ball, John grabbed my ankle and I fell in a heap. While I lay there in hysterics and tried to catch my breath, Bish walked away and smacked the ball into the back of the net.

'Referee!' I shouted as I got to my feet.

Where's VAR when you need it?

Another stand-up I love is Johnny Vegas, although our friendship nearly cost a runner his job on one production. We were appearing on *Celebrity Storage Hunters*. It was a very warm day, and after a morning of rummaging through junk-filled containers, Johnny and I fancied a bit of light refreshment at a local hostelry rather than the production company's canteen. We asked one of the runners to drive us to a pub Johnny and I had clocked on the way in. He refused at first, saying he'd get sacked. After some gentle persuasion from Johnny, the poor runner reluctantly obliged.

Our one quick pint turned to two, both paid for by Johnny as I'd left my wallet at the shoot location. The runner was visibly nervous and kept looking at his watch. Eventually, the producer rang him, and Johnny took full responsibility for the runner's absence. We returned to complete the filming, and, thanks to our northern charm, Johnny and I managed to smooth over the situation. The runner kept his job, even receiving a well-deserved tip from each of us, although Johnny never fails to remind me that I owe him a pint whenever our paths cross.

★

Jeff and I have also both done our fair share of advertisements over the years. Incredible how much work goes into a thirty-second commercial. Something as simple as standing in a room with the crazy Italian commentator Tiziano Crudeli and saying 'Game on!' can take twenty to thirty takes from all sorts of different angles. With *Ted Lasso*, we were done in an afternoon and home for tea!

26

Hollywood

ALTHOUGH I FEATURED ON PRIMETIME TV FOR MANY YEARS, my Screen Actors' Guild award for *Ted Lasso* was the closest I ever got to Hollywood. However, one former teammate who did rub shoulders with the silver screen's elite on a regular basis was Vinnie Jones. He was one of the biggest characters I ever played with, but I don't think anyone, including Vinnie, could have predicted his glamorous future as a huge star of the big screen.

When Anne and I were in Los Angeles in 2009, we took a sightseeing tour in a twelve-seater open-top jeep. With the famous huge letters spelling out 'HOLLYWOOD' above us, our Peruvian driver Arturo pointed out the homes of the rich and famous. He'd give us clues as we passed the mansions and we'd try to guess the names of the residents. When we came to Mulholland Drive, he got very excited.

'You might not know this actor's name but I like him very much. He starred in *X-Men* and *Gone in 60 Seconds*.' No one had a clue. 'His name is Beenie John-ess.' Anne and I looked at each other blankly – still no idea. Arturo just kept saying, 'Beenie John-ess,' until he pulled up outside a house with a Union Jack flag flying behind huge black gates. Then it clicked.

'I know him,' I said. Anne looked at me as if to say, 'Yeah, right.'

'How do you know Beenie John-ess?' she asked. 'What sort of name is that?'

'It's Vinnie!' I said, laughing. 'Vinnie Jones.'

Arturo started tooting his horn, shouting in his broken English accent 'Beenie! Beenie! Come outside! Come out and give us a wave!' Thankfully, it looked like 'Beenie' was not at home. And a very impressive home it was too.

We continued our tour, the driving encyclopaedia Arturo pointing out mansion after mansion, including those of my hero Elton John, Rod Stewart, Denzel Washington, Brad and Angelina, Oprah, Samuel L. Jackson and Michael Douglas to name but a few. As we were driving round, I sent Vinnie a text – 'U've made it pal. Wd u believe the 1st house we stopped at on the Hollywood tour woz yrs!'

We'd moved on to Venice Beach in Malibu when Vinnie rang. He'd been playing golf with Dave Kemp, another former teammate of mine and his – 'Now that you know where I am, why don't you come over later for a beer?'

When I told Anne, she went as white as a sheet. 'We can't do that!' she said. 'Not looking like this. There's sand everywhere, and we look like a couple of backpackers. How can we go to a Hollywood home like this?' But in the end she agreed it was a once in a lifetime opportunity to hobnob in the Hollywood Hills. Vinnie wouldn't be bothered what we looked like – we had to go.

When we arrived at the gate, I pressed the intercom buzzer. 'Beenie! Beenie! Let us in!' It had been a few years since I'd seen him, but he was still the same old Vinnie. We had a great couple of hours and met his beautiful wife Tania. She got on like a house on fire with Anne, and of course she and Vinnie laughed at our apprehension about visiting.

'Whose house did you go to next?' Vinnie asked.

'I think it was Ron Howard's,' I said.

'Oh, didn't you go next door?'

'No. Why? Who lives there?'

'Quentin Tarantino,' he replied nonchalantly.

We couldn't believe that Arturo had got so excited about taking us to Vinnie's but Tarantino's place hadn't even got a mention. Impressive neighbour to have, Vinnie!

We freshened up and Vinnie and Tania gave us a guided tour of their palatial home. It was obvious Tania had been a calming influence on the Vinnie I knew at Leeds. His heartbreak was there for all to see when she so tragically died of skin cancer in 2019.

The old Vinnie was never less than full on. After Leeds won promotion to the top flight, the team headed to Majorca. We were sat outside the hotel having a beer when a police car bowled up. All the lads were inquisitive and taking guesses at what was happening. Gordon Strachan was sure from the start it would be Vinnie. We all laughed but, sure enough, there was Vinnie, handcuffed, in the back. The two officers took him to the hotel foyer, and because I was his roommate, I went to see if he was all right.

Apparently, he'd been drinking on the beach when a couple of Brits had started on him. 'I need some money, Kammy,' he said.

'These coppers want paying off, and I haven't got any Spanish currency on me. They need 2,000 pesetas.' I went to my room and got the cash, and, as I reminded him every time he came on *Goals on Sunday*, he still hasn't paid me back, even with all those Hollywood millions he's earned.

★

My other brush with Hollywood royalty came about thanks to Alan Carr. I've worked with the funny man on numerous shows, including a pilot for *Play Your Cards Right*, in which I played Alan's Dolly Dealer. Because I'm cack-handed, I couldn't hold the large playing cards correctly. I was supposed to be hiding them from everyone but unfortunately the audience could see which card was coming next and, when Alan asked, 'Higher or lower?' could confidently shout out the correct answer. Alan was in stitches, but the production staff didn't see the funny side and tried to devise a way for me to hold the cards without revealing all. The show was eventually recommissioned but – surprise, surprise – I didn't make the cut as a Dolly Dealer!

I was amazed when I was asked to join Alan for his *Christmas Cracker* show in 2018 as it was being made by the same production company. The comic was to be joined by famous faces including Danny Dyer and daughter Dani, Lily Allen, Olly Murs, Derren Brown, Russell Howard and Alesha Dixon, plus Vicky McClure and Martin Compston of *Line of Duty* fame.

When I arrived at the studios, Olly Murs was already on set recording with Alan, and I was taken up to the green room, passing Alesha Dixon in the corridor as she headed off to be next on stage. I was surprised, to say the least, to learn that I was to be last on with Alan – the final spot is normally reserved for the bigger stars. When I looked around at all the names and faces, I began to panic, knowing full well I wasn't worthy of the honour. The green room was pretty full, and I spotted the Dyers, Lily Allen, plus Vicky McClure and Martin Compston, all sitting around on the sofas.

I said a quick hello to Danny and had a chat with him about football and his beloved West Ham, then I went over to catch up with comedian Russell Howard. We laughed about the piece I'd done for *Soccer AM* where I'd performed a fifteen-minute stand-up routine on *Russell Howard's Good News*.

The Dyers were next up, and Vicky and Martin were told to get ready to go on afterwards. I went to the green room fridge and asked Lily Allen if she wanted a drink. She refused but I definitely needed one to calm the butterflies. I took my beer and turned to a guy sat on his own in the corner, who I didn't know, and asked him if he wanted a drink too. He also declined, and I detected an American accent. As the minutes passed, he wasn't very talkative, and I had no idea whether he was a star or a friend of one of the guests. I didn't really know what to chat to him about, so I left him to it and settled down with my beer to watch the show. As well as watching the recording on screen, we could also see the stage from the seats in the green room.

Eventually, one of the runners came to get this American bloke. 'It's Channing Tatum!' echoed across the studio. I'd never heard of him.

No kidding, the quiet American stranger got a five-minute standing ovation. Alan was bowing and worshipping him, positively drooling while the whole audience – and the other guests – were standing and applauding. This wasn't the first time everyone around me knew something I didn't, but usually people are less obvious about it. I'd have started clapping, but I'd have had no idea who I was clapping for or why.

The music began and Alan started gyrating on the floor, somehow getting Channing Tatum to do the same – which, I was later to learn, is a nod to the film *Magic Mike*, in which Tatum plays a male stripper. Alan doesn't greet all his guests this way, so at least I didn't have to start twerking when it was my turn to appear.

I quickly texted Anne to ask if she'd heard of Channing Tatum.

'Of course I have,' she replied. 'Haven't you? Typical. If it's not on the football channels, you haven't a clue.'

'Who is he?' I asked.

'He's a Hollywood actor. Eve [our daughter-in-law] absolutely loves him. Try to get a picture for her.'

After another ovation, Channing finally sat down on the sofa alongside Vicky and Martin. The runner came up to collect me from the green room, and as I walked down to the stage entrance, there was another standing ovation. The cheering seemed to last an eternity. As I waited for my moment to go on, it occurred to me that, following all the noise and applause, Channing Tatum would be coming off stage.

I decided I needed to know a bit more about Channing if I was to introduce myself, so I quickly googled him while the cheers rumbled on. Channing Tatum 'starred in this film, starred in that film . . . done this, done that . . . *Magic Mike*, *21 Jump Street* . . . a major star and actor . . .' Suddenly, there was Channing. I stood back and shook his hand.

'Oh, well done, well done. That was brilliant. They loved you. What a reaction. Unbelievable,' I said.

'Oh, thank you,' he replied.

'Can I have a selfie? Would you mind, please?'

'No, not at all, it would be a pleasure,' the actor replied.

I got my phone out, and there for all to see, including the superstar before me, was my Google search for Channing Tatum. I was flustered beyond belief, and I let out a little scream.

'Ohhhhnooo. I'm so sorry,' I blurted out in a panic, laughing awkwardly. 'I'll be honest, I didn't know who you were but my wife loves you.'

Looking back at that selfie now, he's definitely showing two fingers to the camera. And I am sure they were for me. I have since been told it is an American salute, but you never know. His face was like thunder, and he didn't crack a smile before heading off.

The mystery of me being the last guest on stage was solved when the show was broadcast. Due to clever editing, I appeared long before the Hollywood superstar, who of course finished the programme as the last guest. My appearance in front of the camera saw me on the sofa with Vicky and Martin, who is a huge football fan and played the game to a decent standard himself, and we got on really well.

I ended up telling a Quentin Tarantino story – or trying to – but managed to forget the legendary film director's name when I got to the punchline. And, of course, Alan absolutely destroyed me. 'Who could it be?' he shouted. And the audience joined in and started shouting out the names of famous people.

'What's his name? *Pulp Fiction*,' I said. With that, they started to go through the cast list: John Travolta, Bruce Willis, Samuel L. Jackson, Tim Roth, Uma Thurman? Eventually someone shouted 'Quentin Tarantino'.

'Yeah, that's him,' I said, and everyone cheered. I think it was relief more than anything – we could've been there all night. That show had some clever editors, but it would take a real genius to make me look like I could remember names.

I got in the car after the show and told Anne what had happened when I'd met Channing and how awkward it had been. 'What are you like?' she said. 'Another embarrassment for the records.' I didn't tell her about forgetting Quentin Tarantino's name. The embarrassment record books were filling up fast enough as it was.

A few months later, I was working at the Champions League final in Spain between Liverpool and Tottenham at Atlético Madrid's fantastic new stadium. Among the guests was Jessie J, who happened to be Channing Tatum's partner at that time. By now I knew all about him. Even who he was going out with. She was delighted to meet me and introduced me to her dad Stephen, who was a Spurs fan and loved to watch me on TV. After we'd chatted for a bit, I said, 'I've got something to tell you.'

'Go on,' she said.

'I did a Christmas show with Channing.'

'Oh yeah, I remember he was on with Alan Carr.'

I proceeded to tell her the story about how I'd had to look him up before asking for a selfie because I was hopeless at recognizing celebs, and she started laughing. Then I told her how I had opened the phone screen and showed him that I'd just googled Channing Tatum. She laughed again and said, 'Ooooh, he would have hated that.'

I could only say, 'Oops. Please pass on my apologies.' Luckily Jessie saw the funny side of it. At least, I think I said all of this to Jessie J. With my track record, it could have been anyone.

27

Crooner

AS A KID, I ALWAYS LOVED MUSIC, AND THE FIRST TIME I saw Gilbert O'Sullivan singing on *Top of the Pops*, I fell in love with both him and the piano. I remember Gilbert wearing a cloth cap, braces and a tie, and singing 'Nothing Rhymed' – I was hooked. The Beatles, the Rolling Stones and Thin Lizzy were all great, but Gilbert was my first love . . . before Elton John came along.

We had a black-and-white pay-as-you-watch telly with a slot meter in the back that the Radio Rentals man would come to empty every week. I'd sit in front of the set every Thursday night at 7.30 p.m. to watch *Top of the Pops*. It makes me smile now to remember the sound coming on while you waited for the set to warm up and the screen to kick into life. *Top of the Pops* was the show millions of us watched, and the idea of becoming the lead singer in a band or a solo artist was something I couldn't bring myself even to contemplate because the stars on the screen seemed as though they were from another planet.

My mum wasn't heavily into music – not unless she'd had a few milk stouts and found her voice – but the one song she would always sing on my birthday was Harry Belafonte's 'Mary's Boy Child'. And she would change the lyrics to suit the Kamara family: 'Irene's Boy Child Christopher was born on Christmas Day!' That was sometimes the best treat on my birthday – which just happened to be Christmas Day. Yes, I'm a Christmas Day baby – not something I'd recommend, although I'm more comfortable with it now. The one birthday gripe I had as a young lad was that my brother and sister also got a present on my birthday, because it was Christmas Day, so it never felt like my special day.

Being a professional footballer from the age of sixteen until I was thirty-eight also made the festive season tough – that's twenty-two years of playing football on Boxing Day. After training on Christmas Day morning, I was never really in the party mood when I got home, because I was either heading off to a hotel before an away match or going to bed at ten to prepare for what was usually a big game. I don't think I had a full Christmas dinner until I was manager of Bradford City, when I didn't have to worry about eating the day before a match.

Now I love Christmas, and it has definitely meant more as I've got older and have two boys and four grandchildren to enjoy it with. Christmas is about family, and I can enjoy every moment with them and make sure they have a fabulous time. And Christmas gives me the chance to indulge my passion for singing – not that I need much of an excuse to break into song. I've always enjoyed belting out a tune, especially over the festive season, so when the opportunity came to record my very own

Christmas album, I could hardly believe it. What a chance to make a lifelong dream come true.

Not many ex-footballers can claim to have recorded a top-ten album. In fact, I can't think of any. Kevin Keegan, Gazza, Chrissy Waddle and Glenn Hoddle had hit singles a few years back. Oh, hang on . . . Julio Iglesias might claim that title, as he played for Real Madrid, although I don't think he had a Christmas album.

My debut album went straight in the UK charts at number eight and even topped the jazz charts for five weeks. Not bad for an old crooner from the Boro! But I have to admit, when it was first suggested that I could record an album, it was in such unexpected circumstances that I couldn't help but think it was a wind-up. At so many points during the whole experience, I was convinced Ant and Dec were going to burst into the room, reveal the hidden cameras, and tell me it was all a *Saturday Night Take-away* prank. Because I had a regular slot on their series for nearly ten years and got to know the Geordie duo well, I was convinced they were going to get one over on me.

But months of planning went into *Here's to Christmas*. I had a voice coach and did my vocal exercises in front of our three horses. Throughout the summer months I was belting out Christmas songs to them in my wellies, with my headphones on, above the din of the M1 traffic in the middle of a field near Wakey. And throughout the whole process, right up until I first sang with a big band in a London studio, it felt as though it was all too good to be true.

The album came about when my agent was approached by the makers of *All Together Now*, a BBC Saturday singing contest with Rob Beckett and Geri Halliwell as hosts. They wanted me for a one-off celebrity edition. The contestants are judged by one hundred cabaret entertainers and singers lined up in booths across the back of the stage. If they like what you're singing, they stand up and might even join in; if they don't, they stay sitting down. The votes are counted after forty-five seconds, and you're judged on the number left standing.

Of course I said yes!

My agent asked what I wanted to sing. I suggested 'Brown Eyed Girl', one of my all-time favourites, as the customers and staff of the Hole in the Wall in Las Americas in Tenerife can testify, because I sing it every time I get up on stage with owner and resident artist Fergal Flaherty. And I knew the judges would stand up and join in with my well-rehearsed version of the Van Morrison classic.

But the producers came back and said they had too many people choosing 'singalong' songs, which seemed a bit odd as it is billed as a singalong show. They wanted me to perform a ballad. I was reluctant at first. While I could see a panel of professional singers standing up, rocking away and getting into the full swing of Van-the-Man Kammy, I couldn't see many joining in with a ballad and giving me as many votes. The agent was a bit taken aback. 'This is not like you,' he said. 'You don't normally go into these things to try to win them.'

And he was right. 'Yeah, it's just a bit of fun,' I said. 'I'll do a ballad – but it has to be Elton John's "Your Song".' To me, it was still a singing contest – not just a TV show – and a chance to raise funds for Marie Curie. I was in it to win it.

When it came to the day of filming, at Media City in Manchester, I didn't want to let my hero Elton down, and I really gave my rendition of 'Your Song' everything. Geri was beaming when the cameras went back to her after I'd finished. 'Would you believe "Your Song" was the song I walked down the aisle to at my wedding?' she said. 'You sang it so well.' Suddenly I wasn't that bothered about winning – a Spice Girl liked my version of 'Your Song'.

Reality-show regular Gemma Collins did a great version of 'Hey Big Spender' to win the contest, and *EastEnders* actress Laurie Brett came second. I was more than happy with third but would have been much closer to winning if they'd let me have a go at 'Brown Eyed Girl'. But Geri liked my version of 'Your Song' and I hang on to that still.

Adam Greenup, from Silva Screen Records, was watching the programme and emailed a couple of days later. He thought it would be a great idea to speak to me about recording in a studio. He'd been convinced since seeing me on *All Together Now* that my voice and personality would be ideal for recording Christmas songs with a twenty-two-piece orchestra and conductor. When shown Adam's email, I simply started laughing. That's when I became convinced that Ant and Dec must be behind it. I think we both were. We googled Silva Screen, and it all seemed legit, as Adam had released albums by composers Hans Zimmer and John Carpenter and had worked with the BBC, bands like Placebo, and many other well-known performers. It was either genuine, or he was the perfect person to be hired by Ant and Dec and their devious team.

It turned out that Adam and I had actually met by chance a few months before the *All Together Now* airing, in a pub in King's Cross when he was with the Silva Screen staff for their Christmas night out. To me, it had seemed like any other night in any other pub. He was sitting with his colleagues when

I walked in, and within minutes I'd been bombarded with requests for selfies, autographs or a chat. Often people will offer to buy me a drink – or just buy me one anyway – which is always a nice touch. What had particularly fascinated Adam was that the majority of requests came from men. I'd never really thought about that before, but wherever I go, blokes, mainly football fans, do like to come over for a chat and are not afraid to ask for a photo. Nowadays, since going on more mainstream television, the balance has gone the other way and more women recognize me and aren't afraid to ask for a selfie.

Watching me interacting with the public that night had planted a seed in Adam's brain. He didn't know I could hold a tune then, but he was convinced my 'personality', profile and the reaction he'd witnessed among the punters in the pub would help album sales. And to make sure, he too asked for a selfie, which he showed me several months later when we met properly for the first time to discuss the possibility of recording an album. I had no recollection of our meeting – or the selfie – even when Adam said he had promised me that night that he'd be in touch to discuss working together on a recording.

An April meeting with Silva Screen was arranged, and we went to their headquarters in London. There were fourteen people in the room, including Adam and the big boss, Reynold D. Silva. They mapped out how they thought the recording would go, and despite my apprehension – and still convinced we were being set up – we agreed to meet again in July. Ahead of that, Adam sent me a couple of sample songs to get an idea of what he had in mind, which was a big-band swing ensemble with me crooning over the top.

Before we could sign the deal, Adam explained that the record company would need to test my vocal range and breathing capabilities, and be completely certain that I, and more importantly my voice, could handle the recording and all that came with it. There were also the promotional demands on my voice to consider, as we'd be going hard and fast into the Christmas season.

We went to the studio round the corner to test my vocals. Adam took me downstairs to the recording booth and asked me to sing the notes he was playing on a keyboard. At the start, I was simply going through the motions. It was only for Ant and Dec, after all. Adam told me off. 'You need to take this seriously, Kammy,' he said. 'This is important. Come on, with a bit more aplomb.'

I started laughing. 'OK, let's go.' Before I knew it, I sounded like the bloke on the Go Compare adverts. Every note . . . nailed. Adam was delighted. He told me to sing 'Let It Snow' to a backing track, and I gave it everything.

'Never in doubt,' Adam beamed. 'Within thirty seconds, I knew you had the energy, enthusiasm and the voice to make this work.' He said that as long as I could sing within the range we'd just practised, everything else would work.

But I still had that nagging doubt. 'Is this a wind-up?' I asked.

'I promise you, Chris,' he said, 'this is not a wind-up. Trust me.' So I did.

Adam and Silva Screen Records weren't messing about. 'We've got a list of all the songs we have in mind,' he said, fishing a piece of A4 paper out of his pocket, 'and we'll get you new songs. We've even got Robbie Williams's songwriter lined up.' One of Richard Scott's creations, 'Here's to Christmas', became the title song of the album.

Adam asked me what I thought. 'My own Christmas album?'

I replied. 'Written especially for me? I'll believe it when I see and hear it . . .'

The record company arranged for me to see Lily Moharrer, a vocal coach with the difficult task of getting me in shape and testing my voice to the limit, as I still had to prove I was 100 per cent good enough to record in a studio. For two days a week I went to her place in Leeds. At first I thought it would be a breeze – I'd turn up and start singing. I soon learned there's a huge difference between getting up on stage in an Irish pub with Fergal Flaherty, saying 'You play it and I'll sing it' with a couple of beers inside me, and delivering in a studio with a big-band sound.

Lily said this was normal for a rookie singer – anyone can sing with a few beers in their belly, but you have to know when to hold your breath, when to breathe, and of course when to sing. She started me off with some breathing exercises and showed me techniques to work the muscles to my mouth – they make a huge difference in controlling your breathing and the pronunciation of the words. It's about control of your diaphragm and relaxing and smiling. You don't sing flat if you smile when you sing. Maybe that is why I love singing so much.

When I wasn't under the watchful eye of the wonderful Lily, I was religiously going through her exercises when I was with the horses in the stable and fields at home. Those poor animals! No matter what the weather – drowning in the rain in waterproofs and wellies; in shorts, T-shirt and baseball cap in the bright sunshine – I'd go through the routines. When Adam sent through the sample songs in June, I'd put the headphones on, get the song sheets out and treat the horses to the sounds of Christmas six months early, whether they liked it or not. And they probably didn't! But it was important to me. I wanted to be word perfect and work without the song sheets when it came to recording.

When July came around, we met the record company in a posh restaurant near King's Cross. The place was packed. As I waited to be shown to our table, I could see a group of people sitting near the window on the other side of the restaurant. I was still utterly convinced I was being set up by Ant and Dec. I even checked to see if the waitress showing me to my table had a camera hidden under the tea towel on her tray, and I was looking out for the hidden lenses as I headed over to the group.

Partly to make an impression, and partly to give the cameras something extra special to record, I burst into song as I walked towards them. 'Oh, the weather outside is frightful,' I sang to the whole restaurant, my arms wide open, big beaming smile across my face. It was the middle of summer, and I am not sure what the rest of the diners thought of my entrance, but Adam absolutely loved it. He stood up, walked across, gave me a high five, hugged me and said, 'Yes, Kammy. That's the voice we're looking for!' It was amazing.

The first recording sessions were arranged at the Steelworks studios in Leeds with Larry Hibbitt, a pop producer who's worked with hundreds of artists. Lily met me before the session. I was all over the place. For once, I was absolutely terrified. On the outside I looked super confident and always had a smile on my face. Inside I was a nervous wreck. Once again, Lily reassured me that this was perfectly understandable for a rookie singer – that's what the exercises and hours and hours of practice and crooning to the horses had been for. I simply needed to calm down, and once I'd spoken to Larry and got the headphones on, with the music piped into my ears at full blast, I was fine. We had a few goes at 'Let It Snow' and 'Frosty the Snowman', eventually working through all of the songs on the list. Although I couldn't quite reach all of the notes on 'Jingle Bells' for some reason, Adam seemed pleased with our progress.

But while he was very happy with my voice, he wasn't happy with the style of the recordings. The songs were swing arrangements, and swing demands that the vocals are delivered in a laid-back tempo slightly behind the main beat of the track. It's an art, a tricky one for a novice like me – just when I thought I had it all figured out, I was back at square one.

Adam introduced me to Graham Stokes, who had managed and worked with Peter Andre, Alvin Stardust and Engelbert Humperdinck and knew how to promote a celebrity record. More importantly, he knew how to produce one. He was certain we needed to get in touch with a recognized producer of swing records and suggested Richard Scott, who was clearly more than a writer of great songs – he could make them sound great too.

The long-awaited meeting and first recording session with Richard was arranged by Adam and Graham at the Chairworks studios in Castleford, renowned as the go-to place for artists such as One Direction, the Kaiser Chiefs, and Paul Heaton and Jacqui Abbott. I was about to lower the tone, if not belt out the wrong tone altogether!

Now we were getting serious. Singing for a laugh and recording an album with someone who's worked with the very best and writes his own songs are very, very different things. I'd experienced working in a recording studio when I sang the official

England football song 'Sing 4 England' for the Euro 2012 finals, but this was on another level. And recording that England song had been tough. I was seriously nervous again.

Lily came with me, as she did for every recording, to go through half an hour of exercises. Richard came in when we'd finished. When we first met, we were fine. Like his big mate Robbie, Richard's a Port Vale fan, and we chatted about the club and the old rivalry with Stoke City. I love talking football with anyone, and Richard knew his stuff.

When I went into the booth, however, it all changed. Suddenly he was really short with me. 'Flipping heck,' I thought, 'this is no way to talk to someone and motivate them.'

Richard wasn't going to take any nonsense. There was no sympathy just because I was Kammy, the well-known football pundit who thinks he can sing. I might have been out of my comfort zone, but his attitude was, So what? As far as Richard was concerned, I was there to record and that was that. There was no ad-libbing, no doing your own thing and laughing and joking your way through it. So we clashed.

We spent eight hours in that first recording with me responding to him through gritted teeth, mindful that if I really lost it – well, it would be TV gold on a hidden camera.

'Oh, the weather outside is frightful . . .'

'That's awful. Do it again.'

So I did it again. 'Oh, the weather outside is frightful . . .'

'That's dreadful. Do it like this.'

Then he'd sing it and tell me to do it like that. And I'd say, 'But I'm not you. This is me.'

'I don't give a monkey's. Don't do it like that, do it like this . . .'

I did my best not to bite but came away that night feeling I'd failed and let Richard – and myself – down. I was really struggling with his motivational techniques.

Next day I started to see his point of view. He was laying down a marker. He was saying, 'You think this is a bit of fun? It's not. Basically, you need to take this seriously.' And he was right. In all those years with Sky Sports, no matter what my role, I liked to have a laugh, but I took my job very seriously. I clashed with some cameramen working on *Soccer Saturday*, but I had high standards because that programme meant so much to me, and I made no secret about it.

The way Richard treated me was perfectly normal to him. And I needed to be told this was not the time to be Kammy – it was time to be a singer. Do it Richard's way and I might just get the rewards.

At the start of day two, Richard took me to one side. He must have been thinking about our first session together too. 'You have two ways to go,' he said. 'There is a door over there. If you want to walk through it, you can. Or you can trust me and hopefully we'll get a result. Hopefully.'

'I'm staying,' I said. 'And I am in your capable hands.'

We get on brilliantly now. Richard's a very clever man. It was a privilege to work with an expert in their field, someone who knows what they're doing and sets such high standards that the final version is perfect. I love that.

In the end, he wrote three songs for me – 'Here's to Christmas' on the first album and 'Happy New Year' and 'Dear Mr Claus' on the follow-up – and I've told him if Robbie sang any of them, they would be instant chart-toppers. They're brilliant.

Over the course of a few weeks, we recorded all twelve songs for the first album about a dozen times, including 'Let It Snow',

'Winter Wonderland', 'Rudolph the Red-Nosed Reindeer', 'Santa Claus Is Coming to Town' and other festive favourites.

Richard was pleased with the final outcome, and Adam liked what he heard too. Next, he wanted to record with the big-band sound and invited me to Angel Studios in Islington to sing with the Chris Kamara Big Band! A big band named after me? I seriously thought he was kidding. Now the nerves really kicked in. We were going to record 'Let It Snow' live and shoot a promotional video at the same time.

The first recording was scheduled for ten o'clock on a late October morning. I got the train from Wakefield at 7 a.m. and was due to arrive at King's Cross at 9 a.m. Then it was on the Tube to Angel and a quick 400-yard walk to the studio. Easy . . .

'Ladies and gentlemen, we regret to inform you . . .' You know that dreaded announcement. We were near Peterborough, and we were told it was at least an hour's delay. I'm a real stickler for time – I hate lateness and always make it a point to arrive on time. Of all the days for this to happen. I was mortified. I thought of the musicians and the conductor, people who had played the Royal Albert Hall and with the Royal Philharmonic Orchestra, absolutely fabulous top-of-the-tree performers, who must have already had some doubts about recording with me, and were now going to be sitting waiting for at least an hour. I couldn't have felt any worse. I rang Adam to explain, but I still felt terrible despite all of his reassurances.

I got to King's Cross at about 10.30 a.m., quickly got on the Tube for one stop and sprinted (well, jogged quickly) from Angel station to the studios. I was nearly fifty minutes late, out of breath, sweating profusely, and all over the place. Richard, Adam and Lily were waiting with the stern-looking conductor Evan

Jolly, who I'd never met before, standing in the background. Talk about first impressions. I kept apologizing and the three of them kept repeating, 'It's fine, it's fine.'

Then the conductor spoke: 'As soon as we can, we need to get you ready and get you in the studio.'

I got changed and went through the routine with Lily. I was a nervous wreck. She did her best to calm me down, but it was a struggle to control my breathing as I headed downstairs to the studio.

For all Adam's promises, and the trust I had in him throughout the whole process, there was still a tiny thought at the back of my mind that this could be the moment of the reveal. If I was being set up by Ant and Dec, this would be an ideal time for them to surprise me. Could they be disguised as musicians in the big band?

It was hard to tell when I walked into the room. It was vast, about the size of half a football pitch, and much bigger than I expected. I shouted a polite 'hello' into the abyss, but it was clear the orchestra was getting ready to start. No one looked up as they went through their warm-up routines on their individual instruments, which echoed through the room: bass player, violinists, the entire brass section, you name it – even the pianist wouldn't catch my eye.

'Forget Ant and Dec,' I thought. 'Everyone is just really p***ed off with me.'

I was under intense pressure to justify all of us being there.

When it came to recording, I was slightly raised on a rostrum, like a priest ready to deliver a sermon to his flock, with the band and the conductor surrounding me. After a few moments in the room, the conductor gave me a nod and said, 'Are you ready?'

'Yeah,' I said nervously, and the band started to play 'Let It Snow'. I was expecting to be given a list of the songs, but I was singing completely blind, although I obviously knew the tunes and the words to every song. The sound coming from those instruments was immense. To be among it was a completely new experience to me. Was I out of my depth?

The conductor was swinging his baton, and I watched him, ready to start singing. Eventually he looked up. It wasn't a good look. I'd obviously missed the cue. He stopped the band. 'When I go like that,' he said, swishing his baton through the air in my direction, 'that's your cue to sing.' I'd never worked with a big band and conductor before, so had no idea when to come in. It was the worst possible start, and I was furious with myself. I looked across to the band, and still no one was looking at me. If the TV crew was going to burst in, it had to be now. Thankfully, they never came.

We went again, and this time when the conductor looked at me and waved his baton, I started singing. 'Oh, the weather out-side is frightful . . .' A few of the musicians actually looked up, and I was pretty sure some of them were quite surprised, even delighted. That was when I knew I had their seal of approval. It was a huge moment and such a relief. I started to relax and smile. All along, Adam, Lily and Richard had emphasized how important it was to enjoy myself and smile because it would enhance my performance.

We got through 'Let It Snow' unscathed. At the end of the song, the conductor gave me a big thumbs-up and a smile. I looked across the room at Lily behind the glass, and she was applauding and had a huge smile on her face, which was all the reassurance I needed. Adam gave me a big thumbs-up too. I knew I'd cracked it.

I then spoke to the assembled band and apologized once more for being so late – but I still didn't get much feedback from them.

'We will go again with "Let It Snow",' the conductor said, also fairly unmoved by my hundredth apology of the morning. Maybe they were used to it. We did it one more time and started on a couple of other songs before we had a break for lunch, and I took the opportunity to chat to the conductor and some of the band properly, feeling more relaxed when we returned for the afternoon session.

The whole time I was working with them, a huge part of me thought these professional musicians would think I wasn't good enough or not taking it seriously. That was a huge motivator for me, but I was always determined to enjoy it. Everyone in the big band helped me so much that day to ensure we all did.

My preconception before I'd started working with the orchestra was that they'd be hoity-toity and a bit snooty and probably look down on me, but of course most of them were football fans. A couple were Leeds supporters and had travelled down from Yorkshire – a bit more successfully than me – and they were all genuinely pleased to see me and be a part of what we were creating. They were lovely.

After lunch, I had to change into my dinner suit because we were filming the recording. Talk about a baptism of fire. It was a whole new, scary world, impossible to compare to football – a totally different kind of pressure, but a good pressure, a nice pressure. I loved it, and it's something I'll never forget. Standing there crooning, in the full black-tie regalia, was a real pinch-me moment.

That whole day is locked carefully away in the memory bank. My memory is definitely getting worse, but there are certain events you never forget in your life, and that day in the studio making a top-ten record is one of them.

★

We started the promo for the record just before its release in November 2019. And again it was great fun. I appeared on *Good Morning Britain* with Shep and was given a choice – sing live to a backing track or mime to the original version. I'd never mimed before and wasn't about to start now. So, reckoning I was much more likely to make a mess of miming, I sang live to the nation at 8.15 a.m.

'You do know not many people sing live on TV, don't you, Kammy?' Shep asked afterwards. I couldn't understand why. I also knew it would be a bigger story to any critics if I'd made a mess of miming.

I did *The One Show*, and a few days later appeared on *Strictly Come Dancing: It Takes Two* with Zoe Ball and Rylan Clark. On that occasion, though, I was really annoyed with myself after the performance. The end of 'Let It Snow' has quite a high note you have to hold for a few seconds, but my voice cracked ever so slightly. Adam said no one else would have noticed – it was the tiniest error in a three-minute appearance – but I knew it had happened and I was angry with myself. We spent an hour in the green room after the show, and in the end Adam had to tell me to stop fretting about the error and shut up. He took me to the pub round the corner to ease my worries. When we walked in, a few people at the bar requested Christmas songs and wanted me to sing. Suddenly, I felt like a proper recording artist and soon forgot about what had happened. In fact, Adam told me people would realize I was singing live because of that little blip. Perfection can be your enemy, and the viewers *would* now be sure I was delivering this stuff live, with no issue remembering the words or the notes, which is more impressive.

I also appeared on *James Martin's Saturday Morning* – recorded on a Wednesday afternoon. James knows me well and is all too aware I haven't got a clue in the kitchen. I've been known to try to change channels on the microwave. He started to make a vegetarian meal for me with celeriac. He turned to me and asked, 'Have you heard of this dish before?'

'No, I thought a celeriac was someone who couldn't drink cider.'

We fell about laughing. Fair enough, I'm not the sharpest knife in the drawer . . . I'm not even the sharpest spoon.

And that wasn't the end of the laughter. Fellow guest Tony Tobin, a top chef, was talking about a dish he'd served to my former Sky colleague George Best. When he'd finished, I said, 'Everyone remembers how he used to drop the shoulder and stick it in from any angle . . . great footballer as well, weren't he?' James and Tony – and the whole studio – burst into laughter.

Despite the promotion going so well, we nearly lost thousands in sales thanks to my old mate Reidy, who'd seen the *GMB* performance and loved it. He texted me immediately afterwards, telling me how brilliant it was and that he'd recorded it on his phone and sent it to a few of the boys. 'They love it, love it, love it,' he said.

I fired a text back – 'Cheers mate. I'll send you a copy of the full album on WhatsApp.'

Within half an hour, I started to get messages congratulating me on the album, and then I received a phone call from an anxious Adam. 'What's going on?' he said. 'Have you uploaded the album somewhere?' I told him I had no idea what he was talking about. Then I remembered Reidy. Turned out he was so impressed with the full album, he'd posted every track on his Twitter account, where his 150,000 followers could listen free of charge. I rang Reidy straight away and asked him to take it down. 'Sorry, Kammy, it's so good I wanted everyone to hear it!' Luckily, no one seemed to notice, and no harm was done to the sales.

We made the front page of the *Daily Star* and *Evening Standard*, and the reviews were amazing. I think some people couldn't believe it was me or that the recording was actually quite good. *The Irish Times* gave it nine out of ten – 'Chris Kamara has delivered a smooth, big-band swing album that is pure class and sounds just like Kammy! And it works.' Wow!

The album even earned me a nomination on the Brits longlist in the Male Solo Artist category with proper stars like Stormzy, Tom Walker, Harry Styles and Mark Ronson – it was great company to be in and felt like a real bonus. I'd have been just as happy to be on the same shopping list.

Robbie Williams also released a Christmas album, one of a number of top-selling performers looking to entice people to buy a stocking-filler that year – Michael Bublé, Celine Dion, André Rieu, even Bing Crosby and the London Symphony Orchestra were competing with me for the top slot, while Westlife, Coldplay and Rod Stewart released new albums, and Take That were pushing a 'live' greatest hits LP.

The positive reaction from the public, which took the album straight to number eight in the charts – convinced Adam and Silva Screen to put plans in place for a thirty-date tour the following year, culminating in a night at the Royal Albert Hall. Then, when the confirmations for the venues were starting to come in, Covid-19 reared its ugly head and the whole tour was cancelled. By then the pandemic had wielded such a shocking impact across the whole world it seemed trivial to miss out on singing a few Christmas songs and telling some funny stories to (with any luck) packed-out venues. But I was still devastated.

Despite this setback, the first album was still a huge hit, so much so that we decided to go ahead and record the second one as planned. Richard Scott and Kelvin Andrews came up with two new songs for the new album: 'And a Happy New Year', which became the title track, and a new ditty called 'Mr Claus' about a lovelorn Casanova looking forward to seeing his wife after a lengthy spell away.

The recording of the second album was much lower key, thanks to Covid and the need for speed. To get the record out for the festive period, I travelled to Richard's studio near Stoke-on-Trent to record ten more tracks – including the two new songs. The social-distancing restrictions after the first lockdown also meant I had to record on my own, but by that point I was comfortable in the studio under Richard's watchful eye. Obviously singing in front of a big band was much more fun, albeit nerve-wracking, but it was important to work quickly and efficiently. Rather than staring out into the pit and seeing twenty-plus musicians, I was in a booth with my headphones on and Richard sticking his thumbs up at me through the window every now and then. It was a much more detached and remote process, but it was still a laugh, even if in the end it was all a bit rushed and the enthusiasm wasn't quite there, mainly thanks to the Covid restrictions.

A highlight was Richard arranging for his pal Roy Wood to contribute to the album with a little cameo on a new version of the Wizzard classic 'I Wish It Could Be Christmas Everyday'. Brilliant! And it was still a good collection of songs – an old number Adam unearthed called 'I Believe in Father Christmas' was particularly enjoyable to sing and allowed me to fulfil another dream – to sing along with just a piano. Elton John eat your heart out! But this time the album only scraped into the top forty, and the critical acclaim and media campaign was much more subdued.

Lockdown was a nightmare for the music industry but did bring me one big singing opportunity. I got the chance to sing with Robbie Williams, albeit not in front of thousands of screaming fans at the 'Home of Football' but on a Zoom call which was watched by nearly half a million people. Danny Jones from McFly invited me to join him and Robbie on an online acoustic singalong version of One Direction's 'History'. Danny strummed along on his guitar at home, Robbie joined in from a desk in his front room, and I was set up in the barn to join in halfway through. It was a bit surreal singing with two legends when we were hundreds of miles apart, and I think it was a surprise to a few people that I was asked – and could hold a tune in such experienced company – but I had sung with the two of them before at Soccer Aid, so it was no shock from my point of view.

I loved my time as a recording artist – a whole different world to football. Since then, my apraxia has unfortunately impacted my singing and the speed of my delivery, but the door is always open for another album, perhaps of slower songs, so we'll see. Sometimes, when I'm alone and having a good morning, I'll turn to Alexa and try to sing Elton John's 'I'm Still Standing'. It feels like a long time since I kept up with the great man's timing, though. I'm nowhere near it. It's not terrible – it's not like Alexa turns herself off – but I'm more of a 'Your Song' man nowadays. I struggle a little bit to keep up with 'Brown Eyed Girl' too. I can't sing it any more – certainly not like I used to – and I can't see me having the courage to get on stage at the Hole in the Wall any time soon.

That wasn't quite the end of my singing career, though. I was asked to take part in the fourth series of *The Masked Singer* in January 2023, and I jumped at the chance, because I knew it would really put a smile on my grandkids' faces. Saturday was the one night of the week when they were allowed to break their bedtime routine and join in with the audience's chant of 'Take it off! Take it off! Take it off!' when the time came to reveal the character beneath the costume.

Like all the guests, I had to keep quiet about my involvement – only Anne knew what I had signed up for. And I wasn't too worried about the singing as long as a suitable song was chosen. My code name was 'Sailor', so I assumed it meant a return to the Navy, but when I was summoned to London for my costume fitting, surprise, surprise, I was 'Ghost' not a sailor.

On the day of filming, I was teamed up with Rhino, Jelly-fish, Phoenix and Otter. They all had elaborate costumes, while I sidled on with a sheet over me. I sang 'Save the Last Dance for Me' by the Drifters, but it wasn't enough to save me from the bottom three. I was joined by Cat and Mouse, who were

What an unbelievable tribute!

Elated as I thank the Boro fans for their massive support at the Riverside Stadium.

Goals on Sunday with Patrick Kluivert and the late Gary Speed, just weeks before his tragic death.

José Mourinho on *Goals on Sunday*, prior to his rant.

James Martin and pals getting together in the *Saturday Kitchen*.

Bake Off time for Sport Relief – with my fellow bakers Victoria Coren Mitchell, Kimberley Walsh and Ed Balls.

Surprising the lovely Lorraine Kelly on her birthday.

Pay attention because this is very confusing . . . for the purposes of
Celebrity Juice (and we all know how crazy that show was), Keith Lemon
and I were the sons of music legend Billy Ocean, making us half-brothers!

Jeff and me in Ireland: just a couple of down-to-earth jet-setters.

No tongues please, Jeff!

The twenty-two-piece band who made me sound decent
for the Christmas album *Here's to Christmas*.

With my poor dance mentor Anya Garnis, given the task for Comic Relief's
Strictly Come Dancing. However did she cope with me and my rubber legs?

Charity night for
Marie Curie with Basil Brush
and 'daft as a brush'.

A proud day for me and the
family. Whatever would Mum
and Dad have thought seeing
me at the castle with royalty?

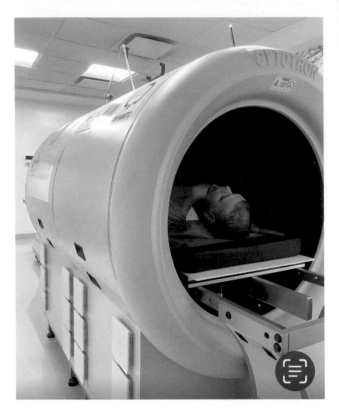

Where I was to be found for
one hour every day in Mexico
for twenty-eight days.

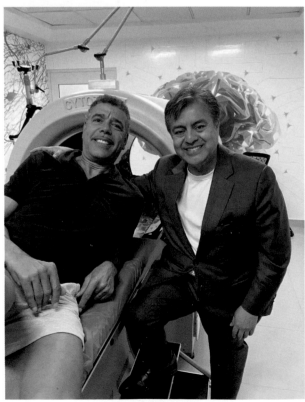

Dr Roberto Trujillo who,
in my opinion, should one
day receive a Nobel Prize.

revealed to be Martin and Shirlie Kemp later in the series, and Knitting, none other than the legendary Lulu.

The panel had to debate which of the three acts would exit the show, and I was the one to go, leaving Jonathan Ross and co. to guess who was about to be unmasked. Jonathan had no idea, and big football fan Mo Gilligan was foxed by my put-on Scottish accent. Rita Ora and Davina McCall were also stumped.

I was disappointed to go out but was looking forward to watching the reveal on TV with the grandkids on New Year's Eve. We arranged for the little ones to have a sleepover, while our friend Marie also came to see us and to share a bite to eat. Marie immediately mentioned that Ghost was wearing a rubbish outfit, and when it was announced that Ghost was the first to go, she said, 'Yeah, get him off, he's useless.' How we stopped ourselves from laughing I don't know.

The kids weren't really interested in the judging process but we told them to get ready for the reveal and to shout 'Take it off! Take it off!' When Ghost removed the sheet, there was a twist – he was wearing a skeleton costume underneath. For the first time on *The Masked Singer*, there was a second chant of 'Take it off! Take it off!' Grandson Sol was perched on my lap while Billie was cuddling up with Marie, and Anne had her phone in hand to record their faces.

As the mask came off, their reactions didn't disappoint – they were genuinely shocked and couldn't stop laughing. 'Grandad!' Sol shouted, while Billie said, in little more than a whisper, 'That's my grandad.' It was pure gold and worth doing the show for that moment alone.

★

Going on *The Masked Singer* was more for the grandkids than me, but I've managed to tick a few things off the bucket list over the years. Near the top of that list was having a chat with my hero Elton. Whenever I was due to cover a Watford game at Vicarage Road, I always told the Hornets press officer in advance and would ask him to let me know if Elton was going to be at the game. It's best to go through the official route – I wanted an interview, not a restraining order! I struck lucky on the day Watford hosted Pep Guardiola's Manchester City in September 2016.

I was near the dressing rooms at the ground about an hour before kick-off, when Sky colleague Tony Gale texted me to say the press officer was looking for me as Elton was in the building. I immediately abandoned my lunch, grabbed my coat and headed down the tunnel towards the boardroom, where I presumed he'd be.

As I reached the end of the tunnel, I bumped into Manchester City boss Pep Guardiola and his assistant Brian Kidd. The pair were coming off the pitch after checking the playing surface. Kiddo and I have got to know each other well over the years from his role as number two to Sir Alex Ferguson at Manchester United, and to several City managers, including Pep.

'Have you met Pep?' Kiddo asked.

'No,' I said, shaking the great man's hand. Pep said he'd watched *Goals on Sunday* many times and really liked the programme – always good to hear from managers, but extra special coming from one of the best. It was lovely to meet him at last and to hear that he was a fan of the show. I was really made up. As much as it was wonderful to chat to one of the great football masterminds of all time, someone I'd normally want to spend as much time with as possible, all I could think was, 'I'm going to miss Elton if I don't hurry up!'

'I'd love to come down to training some time,' I told Kiddo.

Pep jumped in immediately, and said, 'Yeah, come down to training any time you want, Kammy. Have lunch, stay as long as you like, just let Brian know and we'll sort it out.' I was obviously thrilled at that prospect and told Kiddo I'd be in touch. I then wished them good luck for the game ahead and sprinted off to find Elton in the boardroom and directors' suite. But when I got there, and popped my head round a few doors, there was no sign of him.

I headed out to the directors' box and there he was, with his two kids and husband David Furnish. He was pointing up into the stands, and I later found out he was telling his family where he used to stand as a kid watching his beloved Watford. They had their backs to me, and I admit I came across all starstruck. I so wanted to chat with him but as he was with his family I felt I couldn't really shout 'Elton!', so I hovered in the stands above them, looking busy, hoping they might spot me. The TV gantry was in close proximity, so I had that as an excuse if anyone challenged me. Suddenly Elton turned round, spotted me and shouted 'Kammy!' and beckoned me to go down and join them. Nervously, I walked down the steps towards him. I was going to meet two heroes in one day. Heroes are like that. You wait for ages, then two come along at once!

He introduced me to David and their boys and started talking about how much he was looking forward to seeing his team come up against Pep's Manchester City in the Premier League. I had to stop him: 'Elton, how come you know my name?'

'Of course I know you. You played the game, had a great

football career and now, when I'm either home or abroad and can't stream the Watford games, I watch you on *Soccer Saturday*.' So when Elton John is on tour, getting ready to perform to tens of thousands of fans in some far-flung exotic location, he's watching me in the rain at Vicarage Road! I was amazed and made up that Elton John, my hero, knew who I was and what I did.

It was at this point I decided I couldn't possibly tell him that he was my hero because he'd think I was making it up after what he'd so kindly said about me. It blew my mind, and I really didn't know what to say. I did manage to make one request, though: 'Elton, I hate to do this, because I know you've got your kids with you, but can I have a photo, please?'

If he didn't know I was a fan before, he was probably getting some idea by now. 'Yes,' he said, 'but on one condition. That I can have a photo with you.' All I could think was, 'Is he serious?' Then he shouted, 'David, David, come and take this photo of me and Kammy'. He took my phone and passed it to David, who took the picture.

Unbeknown to me, the Sky cameraman in the gantry took a picture of David Furnish taking a picture of me and Elton John on Elton's phone. I don't know if Elton still has the photo David took. Who knows? Maybe Elton John has my face as his wallpaper. And I put my photo out on Twitter immediately.

The Watford directors always invited me into the boardroom after a game, but I only ever went up if they won – and they were thrashed 6–0 by City that day, with Sergio Aguero scoring a brilliant hat-trick. So even though I knew I could get another few moments with my idol, I didn't go hunting round for him a second time. It had been all 'tiaras' earlier. After a 6–0 thumping,

I didn't want to see the 'tantrums'! After I'd interviewed the two managers, I headed out of Vicarage Road to the studio – not knowing that Shep would make sure that the photo of the photo appeared on the show the next morning.

There's an old phrase: never meet your heroes. What a load of rubbish. The more I read about Elton, the more I admire him and think what a great bloke he is. And who knows? Maybe he's reading this! If you are, mate, I'm happy to come out of retirement for that duet of 'Your Song'.

28

Brazil

IF ELTON WAS MY MUSICAL HERO, THERE WAS ONLY EVER one candidate for the football equivalent – Pelé.

The Brazil team of 1970 played the game like I'd never seen it before. In fact, forget me – like the world had never seen before.

The first time I watched Pelé on TV I looked at him and thought, 'Crikey, he's the same colour as me and the same colour as my dad.' I knew also that if ever I could afford to go to Brazil to visit the birthplace of my idol, I was going to do it. That dream became a reality when the World Cup was hosted by Brazil in 2014, with the chance to see England play in the finals thrown into the bargain. I was on a Pelé pilgrimage.

A year before the finals, I had been lucky enough to be invited to the official opening of the new Maracanã Stadium when England played Brazil in a friendly. It was a whistle-stop tour with the FA sponsors and the England contingent, and we barely had any time to see the famous sights around Rio de

Janeiro. We spent most of the time near the ground, watching our hosts sweat about whether the game was going to take place at all. The stadium was still not completely ready when we were given our tour, but thanks to some frantic last-minute building work and a few licks of paint, I saw England play in one of the most iconic venues in the world, drawing 2–2. We were out of there soon after the final whistle and heading home.

My appetite had been whetted, and once the World Cup fixtures were announced, I planned a proper tour of Brazil. I knew it would be easier to make those plans if I had Anne on board, and my stroke of luck was that one of England's warm-up friendlies was to be played in Miami a week before the tournament began. Absolutely perfect. Knowing she'd be able to spend some time with me in the States prior to the World Cup, Anne helped me plan my itinerary – a trip to the Amazon, the iconic Copacabana Beach (Anne drew the line at packing my Speedos), Christ the Redeemer, and Sugarloaf Mountain, you name it, I was heading for it.

And of course the highlight of the adventure – watching another World Cup game at the world-famous Maracanã, home to all the Brazilian greats, from Pelé and the rest of the 1970 team to Zico, Romario, Ronaldo – not 'Fat Ronaldo', as Sir Alex Ferguson once referred to him, but the 'Real Ronaldo' as I call him – Ronaldinho, Kaka and the big star of the current team, Neymar. The Maracanã is also the ground where John Barnes scored his wonder goal in 1984, one of the greatest England goals of all time. It's a stadium every football fan has to visit if they have the opportunity. I couldn't wait to see it again.

Anne and I spent a couple of days in Miami ahead of England's warm-up game against Ecuador. It turned out to be a pretty awful goalless draw in front of a half-empty stadium, but that didn't mean the atmosphere wasn't electric – the highlight of the game was the dramatic lightning storm that delayed the match for nearly half an hour and forced the players off the pitch. That was the moment I really discovered what the phrase 'rain check' means.

My son Ben was flying out to Miami with his fiancée Eve before we watched a couple of games together in Brazil. They were due to arrive in Miami only a couple of hours before the friendly with Ecuador kicked off, and being the dutiful parents that we are, we'd brought their luggage to the States in advance so they could join us with their hand luggage at the match on arrival.

Anne and I endured the journey from hell in our yellow taxi to the Sun Life Stadium in downtown Miami. The driver had obviously been working too hard or had a late night, as we both noticed at virtually the same time that the car was drifting across the freeway. Anne looked in the driver's mirror to see that he was actually fast asleep. She immediately screamed 'Wake up!', which made him jump, and he quickly straightened the wheel. I could see Anne was petrified and that I had to stay strong, even though I was crapping myself on the inside – probably the best place for it. Anne insisted that I engage in conversation with the driver for the rest of the journey. I had to talk rubbish without stopping – luckily, that's my day job. I also think it could have saved our lives.

Ben and Eve arrived at the stadium soon after us, and Anne met them to give them their tickets. Eve, who isn't a big football fan, was out of breath and understandably a little jet-lagged after the ten-hour transatlantic flight. But Anne pointed her in the direction of the wine and the buffet, and she settled in for the afternoon.

Vauxhall, one of the England team's sponsors, had arranged our tickets for the friendly, and joining us as guests in their hospitality box was Southampton's new chairman Ralph Krueger, a Canadian ice hockey coach who had been appointed earlier that year. David Moyes was also at the game. Moyesy and I go back a long way – my first game as Bradford City manager was against Preston North End, who he was playing for at the time. He wished me luck after that game – something I've never forgotten.

I texted him to join us in the box. He was out of work at the time and I thought, 'Let's get him up here to meet Ralph. You never know in this game – a chance meeting with a major player in the Premier League could lead to Moyesy being the next manager of Southampton.' I got a text back from Moyesy to say he was on his way.

Ralph had settled down at the front of the box, presumably so he had a good view of the game, just as Moyesy entered the room.

'Steve,' I bellowed, 'I've got your next manager with me!'

Sadly, 'Steve' didn't acknowledge me. Because he was called Ralph. In my defence, I'm hopeless with names when first meeting people. It tends to go in one ear and out of the other – there's nothing in between to stop it – and once the name 'Steve' was planted in there, I couldn't get it out.

Moyesy was looking for an introduction to one of the Premier League's newest executives and was far from impressed. And I don't think 'Steve' was too chuffed either. Needless to say, there was a tremendous amount of eye-rolling from my family in the box that day – another familiar gaffe from the old man!

When the game started, we settled back in our seats and got a chance to enjoy the hospitality and watch the biblical lightning storm. Eve, who hasn't been to too many matches, asked where David Beckham might be seated if he happened to be at the game. At that time, Becks was in the early stages of setting up a new franchise in Miami to compete in the Major League Soccer (MLS), and the former England captain and his backers were trying to find a stadium to make it all happen. I thought there was a good chance Becks might therefore be here. And so did Anne. 'If he is at the game,' she told Eve, 'he'd be in a box like that one.' She leaned forward and pointed at the box to our left. 'Oh, my God! It's David Beckham!'

Sure enough it was the man in question. 'You're right,' I said. 'It's Becks. It's Golden Bollocks.'

'It's "Golden Balls", Chris,' Anne reminded me. Oh well, at least I didn't call him Steve. One of Becks's party was mouthing, 'It's Kammy!' and gave Becks a nudge, who then looked right at us, gave us the Beckham smile, and a thumbs-up.

We indicated we'd go to see him in his box at half-time. Eve, beside herself with excitement, suddenly announced she needed to go to the ladies. When she came back, her previously dishevelled travel head was a mane of flowing loveliness. She'd put some lipstick on and looked fully glammed up to meet the great man. I'm sure her photo with Becks was on social media within about two minutes. My female fans never seem to be as excited as Eve was. Strange that. It wasn't the first time I'd met David; as ever he was a complete gent, the perfect host, offering us drinks and obliging with the photos that Eve was already using as the new profile picture for her Facebook account.

★

Ben and I left Anne and Eve to enjoy Miami while we headed off to Brazil for England's opening game against Italy in Manaus. I'm so glad we got to spend an incredible day together in the Amazon beforehand. We took a speedboat across the Rio Negro to swim with porpoises, and met an indigenous community for a presentation ritual before they treated us to a tasty lunch. Up until then, the closest I'd ever got to the Amazon was ordering online – but this experience really delivered. Sadly, England couldn't match the delights of that day. We lost 2–1 to Italy, thanks to a Mario Balotelli winner.

I'd been invited by the Football Association to help host pre- and post-match corporate entertainment packages for England supporters who had travelled to Brazil. We'd take over a restaurant or hotel dining room near the stadiums hosting the England matches and I'd tell a few funny stories, have some selfies taken and analyse the games before and after. It wasn't by any means a successful tournament for Roy Hodgson and his team, and it was hard to be positive all the time, but I still had a lot of fun.

After Manaus, we moved on to São Paulo. When I was eight, I couldn't have told you where the Isle of Wight was but I did know the São Paulo region was home to Pelé. I was more than looking forward to visiting his home city and hoped to meet my idol. I was also hoping England would get their first win of the finals against Uruguay. And that is a lot for one man to hope for.

The build-up to the game was all about Luis Suárez, and the former Liverpool striker came to haunt England with two goals to give the South Americans a deserved win. Wayne Rooney gave us some hope with a late equalizer before a delirious Suárez scored the goal to send England home.

Even working for the FA, and being in a venue like São Paulo, it wasn't easy to be upbeat about England that day. I was devastated and felt even worse for the fellow supporters around me, not to mention the players, Roy and his assistant Ray Lewington, and the other coaching staff I knew so well. Ray is an old pal of mine and along with the FA's Adie Bevington occasionally allowed me in to watch training before England's matches.

I became an even bigger England fan after I retired from managing, and following the national team has replaced the passion and desperation I had as a kid to see my clubs, Middlesbrough and Leeds United, win. When you become a professional footballer, the team you play for becomes your focus. As someone who played for ten clubs, three of them twice, my passions moved about like Liz Taylor's. As a result, you do lose a bit of the intensity that you had when you were younger. While I still look for their results, if Boro or Leeds lose it no longer hurts and ruins my weekend. The same can't be said for my former Sky Sports colleague Phil Thompson, who is still Liverpool through and through. Thommo is the most passionate ex-player I have ever met – if Liverpool lose, he still stomps off to bed early. He's just the same as he was when he was a young Scouser growing up near Anfield, dreaming of playing for his beloved hometown club, like I did.

Watching England revived my passion as a supporter, and the desire for England to win can seriously affect my mood. It was certainly challenging that night in São Paulo. To add to my disappointment, I never did get to meet my idol Pelé. Now the great man rests in his beloved Santos following his death in December 2022. I'm simply pleased I managed to spend some time in the place where he played on the streets and where his wonderful career started.

England's last game was against Costa Rica in Belo Horizonte, where I was joined by my brother-in-law Mike Jeans. The mood among the England fans was understandably more sombre than usual. Some had spent their life-savings to get to Brazil, and it must have seemed so pointless to them now. It costs a lot to follow England – the flights, the hotels, the beer to drown your sorrows when they lose – but I tried to lift their spirits, have a good laugh and get them in the mood, promising them England would go out in style with a resounding victory. I have never been more wrong – well, OK, I might have been – but they went out with a whimper and produced probably the worst performance of the tournament in a goalless draw. We'd have struggled against a team from Costa Coffee!

Costa Rica went through, and the two European teams, England and Italy, were out. We re-drowned our sorrows that night with the England fans who'd travelled halfway round the world to see their team. Ninety per cent of them kept reminding me I'd promised England would go out in style. I really couldn't wait to get out of there.

Before the Costa Rica horror show, I wasn't the only one with the difficult task of raising the visiting England fans' spirits. We visited the Minas Tênis Clube sports club in Belo Horizonte, designated as one of the venues for Team GB and Paralympics GB's training camp during the Rio Olympics in 2016. Prince Harry popped in as part of a royal tour of the country to promote the Olympics. The ambassador in Belo Horizonte, Alex Allis, said he hoped we would be able to meet the prince afterwards, but there were simply too many people trying to get a piece of him.

After meeting some athletes and playing in goal in a kickabout with a few local kids, the prince gave a speech. He'd just started when he spotted me in the audience. He looked over at me with recognition and mouthed, 'It's Kammy!', and started smiling. I burst out laughing and gave him the thumbs-up. I'm not sure if that's royal protocol. If I ever get knighted, I'll give it a go. When he'd finished his speech, Prince Harry headed down the opposite side of the stage from where Mike and I were standing. He was absolutely mobbed before he was escorted out of the room, so sadly we never did get to formally meet him.

I later discovered that during his student and Army years, the prince and his mates were huge *Soccer Saturday* fans. Like so many of his generation, he was more than familiar with my face and my onscreen antics around England's football grounds. He might have even played the 'Unbelievable, Jeff' drinking game on one or two occasions.

The following morning, Mike and I went to the check-in desk for our flight to Rio, to continue enjoying our trip even without our team. We put our luggage on the conveyor belt and handed over our tickets. I was about to give the assistant our passports when she said, 'You do know you are twenty-four hours early?' Another twenty-four hours in Belo Horizonte would not have been a problem under normal circumstances, but we had two penthouse suites overlooking Copacabana Beach with our names on them waiting in Rio de Janeiro!

The rooms at the Golden Tulip Hotel had been booked by the English FA for the duration of the tournament. They came into our possession because the hotel had been unable to sell them on to another nation following England's World Cup exit. They'd been paid for in advance and as they were going to be free for the next two weeks anyway, Keith Michaels, the head of Vauxhall, asked me if I wanted them, as he knew we were staying for the rest of the tournament. Did I want them?! Wow! Keeping my cool, I reluctantly said, 'Oh go on, then. But we'll only need the one suite.'

'You might as well have both,' he said. So we were both looking forward to staying on in true luxury for the final – if the hosts made it that far.

There was no way we could stay in Belo Horizonte just to catch the flights Anne had booked for the following day. Not with Copacabana Beach and the luxury suites waiting for us. I spotted a car outside the airport and saw that, while it wasn't marked as a taxi, the passengers were paying the driver in cash. We asked the driver how long and how much to Rio. He explained it was a seven-hour journey and he'd do it for 1,200 Brazilian real – about £200. That was probably about a week's wages to him, although he did face the prospect of a fourteen-hour round trip to earn it. Mike and I looked at each other and nodded – a hundred quid each for a night of luxury. Sold!

He told us we'd have to accompany him to his home first while he told his wife, plus he also needed some money upfront to pay for petrol. We agreed, put our luggage in the boot, got in the car and set off for his home. Even though we were two grown men who could look after ourselves, going up the hill in his taxi towards the favelas in Belo Horizonte was still a daunting prospect. It took nearly twenty minutes to get up that big incline, past the thousands of shacks and small homes built on the slopes.

Our driver parked his car and invited us to come with him to his home. We walked through the alleys, passing people drinking, playing music and enjoying themselves in what we thought were bars. I asked our driver if his family were happy living in the favelas. He promptly put me in my place. 'This is our community,' he said.

He introduced us to his wife and three young kids, who stared at us across the tiny front room. He tried to explain to her why he'd brought two complete strangers into their home, before going upstairs to get changed into some fresh clobber. We just kept smiling and nodding until he was ready to hit the road, head back down that hill, and on to Rio.

We were heading to luxury beyond our wildest dreams, but the seven-hour journey in a clapped-out cab could not have been more basic and eye-opening. It was 272 miles, less than the distance from Middlesbrough to Portsmouth, and the 157 miles of motorway were fine. The rural areas, though, were a pain in the rear – literally. Some of the roads were simply unfinished, riddled with potholes. Hit one and it shook your bones and dislodged a few brain cells – bad news if I'd had any in the first place. If this was how the England team were getting about it might explain the results! Having reached Rio, our poor driver had to endure the reverse journey back home to the favela. We saw him off outside the Golden Tulip Hotel with an extra few quid. He'd earned every real.

It took a bit of persuading to convince the receptionist that we were representing the English FA and their sponsors in our crumpled state, but eventually we made it to the penthouse rooms. They were far too big and posh for the likes of us, and in the end we hardly spent any time in them because there was so much to do on the streets and beaches below. The views to Copacabana had me singing the Barry Manilow song, while the sunsets and sunrises were magical and will live with me forever.

★

I've done a few advertising campaigns over the years, and they usually involved shouting the word 'Unbelievable!' at some point. I've chased Jermain Defoe and Peter Crouch around a park pitch on a Sunday morning for an FA campaign, ridden a rollercoaster in Amsterdam with England manager Gareth Southgate and Robbie Fowler to flog some Danish lager, and even dressed up as a Cadbury's Creme Egg. And no, I don't want to know how you eat yours. But I don't think anything will be as important – or as scary – as the public information video I unwittingly did for the British Consulate in Brazil after my brother-in-law Mike was mugged, and I escaped death or what might have been serious injury.

Our hotel was close to the media centre, which had been specially constructed close to Copacabana Beach to offer background pictures of the iconic sands to viewers across the globe. One evening I spotted Gordon Strachan in one of the booths, working for the BBC. I gave him a wave and told him to give me a ring.

He called later to say that he was coaching some kids on Ipanema Beach the following day with Adrian Chiles, the BBC presenter, tagging along. 'He's going to collect the balls,' Strach said, 'but I'm not letting him anywhere near the coaching. You and I can do that. Do you fancy it?'

'Yeah, I'd love to. I've got my brother-in-law Mike with me. He can collect some balls as well!' We agreed to be there for midday.

We set off at eleven the following morning, walking slowly across the seafront. Immediately we spotted UEFA president Michel Platini jogging bare-chested on the beach. Mike took his shirt off too; I didn't mention that he looked nothing like the former France captain! We never thought about it at the time, but Mike had a gold chain round his neck, and it was very exposed now that he had his T-shirt off. Two young men, about twenty-five years of age – one muscly, the other much skinnier – started walking alongside us. One of them then asked the time in English. I found out later that this was to establish if we were locals or World Cup visitors.

I told them it was five to twelve, then mentioned to Mike that we'd better hurry or we'd be late to help Strach with his coaching session. Suddenly, the bigger lad came in between us, hooked his finger into Mike's gold chain, yanked it off him, and ran off. To this day, I don't know why – whether it was instinct or a moment of utter madness (knowing me, it was a bit of both) – but I ran after him. He headed across the road, back towards Copacabana Beach. My chasing him, however, forced him to change his direction of escape. The police said later that switch probably saved my life – there was a very good chance an accomplice would have been hiding at the beach, ready to stab or shoot anyone pursuing his partner in crime.

I was oblivious to any such danger. I kept running after the mugger – 'Stop thief! Stop thief!' I was fifty-seven, he was about half my age, but every time he looked back he knew I was catching him. He headed towards a large hotel, with me getting ever closer, shouting like a maniac, when a security guard suddenly appeared from nowhere and just stood in front of him, sending him to the pavement as if he'd run into a brick wall. I was there within seconds and started grappling with the bloke on the ground. The security guard asked me what he'd done. The robber was trying to break free but as soon as I explained the situation, the guard put him in a headlock. I sat on his back. After all that running, a sit-down was exactly what I needed!

The police were there within minutes. They were on virtually every street corner trying to make sure this type of thing didn't happen and if it did were able to react instantly. An officer tried to handcuff the thief while the security guard asked me if I'd got the chain back. When I said no, he turned to the wriggling robber, with the policeman still trying to put the handcuffs on, and shouted at him in Portuguese. He then stood up and kicked him in the face. I was horrified to almost feel the crunch when he planted his boot. There was blood everywhere. With that, the guard reached into the robber's trouser pocket and pulled out the necklace. 'Your chain,' he said.

Once cuffed, the lad was pulled to his feet and a police officer pulled his vest over his head. I asked why. He said it was because tourists would take photos. Also, if he tried to run, he'd end up either under a car or going face first into a brick wall. I told the police that as far as I was concerned that was the end of it – I was still hoping to make the coaching session and not let my mate Strach down. The cops were having none of it. They told me I had to go with them to the police station to make a statement. If I didn't, the assailant would be free to go. They didn't seem to be leaving me with much choice in the matter.

Right then, Mike, the Robin to my Batman, arrived. 'Where is he?' he panted, before lunging at the half-naked handcuffed man hidden underneath a vest. I started laughing and pulled Mike away. 'It's under control, mate.' A police car came to take the crook away, and I thanked the security guard for his intervention, leaving a little cash tip in his hand. 'No problem,' he said. 'Any time.' Hopefully, the next time would be never.

We got in another police car and headed to the station. We were a few minutes into the journey when the copper driving us looked in his rear-view mirror. 'You know when the hotel security guard kicked him in the face? You didn't see anything, did you?'

Mike, who hadn't even been there, replied, 'Oh yeah, we did.'

The copper frowned – 'No, I mean, you didn't *see* anything, did you?'

We both looked at each other – 'No, no, we didn't see a thing.'

It was a short journey to the nearest cop shop and we were taken to a reception area with two settees. We settled into one of them, Mike still seething that he'd been robbed. The robber was then bundled in, still cuffed, hands behind his back, with his vest still wrapped around his head – and made to sit on the vacant sofa opposite us! Mike and I looked at each other, eyes wide open. They kept us waiting there for twenty of the longest minutes of our lives. Finally, they took him away, coincidentally just as Mike found his voice again. 'Let me at him! Let me at him!' he shouted – once the robber was a good distance away.

An officer came to take my statement, which was immediately typed out and presented to me. It might as well have been in a foreign language. In fact, it was – Portuguese. We'd been in the police station for more than two hours at this point and simply wanted to get out of there, so to this day I have absolutely no idea what I signed. I could have confessed to JFK, Shergar and the *Marie Celeste*.

Before he let us leave, the officer told us in no uncertain terms that we were lucky to be alive and to have avoided being stabbed or shot. And to think I was feeling sorry for the mugger when he was being kicked by the security guard a couple of hours earlier.

When we eventually emerged from the police station, British Embassy staff were waiting outside with cameras in the background. A well-dressed gentleman, who turned out to be the British deputy head of mission, Jonathan Dunn, walked up to us. Jonathan was working for the British Diplomatic Mission during the finals, and later at the 2016 Olympics in Rio, by which time he was consul general. He was there for any crisis that might occur. The good news is I was pretty much the biggest incident he had to deal with during those two major sporting events. 'Well done, Chris,' he said, shaking my hand, 'but I need you to go on camera and tell people what a stupid idiot you've been and how lucky you are.' He sounded exactly like my producer on *Soccer Saturday*.

'Why?' I said, baffled. 'I acted on instinct and got him.'

'Not many people get to tell the story you're going to tell. Other tourists taking a leaf out of your book might not be as lucky as you. They could be killed. How much is the chain worth?'

I wasn't sure – 'Probably about £200.'

'So you lose your life for a 200-quid chain. You're so lucky to be alive. Please get on that camera and say your bit.' I took his advice, went on camera, and put it out there.

In all honesty, I was oblivious to the danger I might have been in when I ran after that mugger. I'd been in Brazil for three weeks by then and never felt in any danger. I'd neither seen nor heard of any trouble involving friends, colleagues or other

England fans – not a thing. I was definitely lucky to get away with my actions, and the story of our close escape went everywhere on TV and social media.

Strach, meanwhile, thought I'd let him down. We headed back to Ipanema Beach, but he'd gone. I did send him a message, saying he wouldn't believe what happened – and I was pretty sure he wouldn't. But as he said when we met a few days later and I told him the whole tale, how could you make something like that up?

With England out of the tournament, Mike and I made the most of our stay. We visited the most famous landmark in Brazil, Christ the Redeemer, or *Cristo Redentor* in native Portuguese, heading up to the top of Mount Corcovado with the hordes of tourists. As a one-time practising Catholic and ex-altar boy, seeing one of the most famous icons of Christianity close up took me back to my childhood. It was well worth visiting.

We also took the cable car that runs between the peaks of Sugarloaf Mountain and the adjacent Morro da Urca. We'd seen the sun setting many times from our hotel rooms, but it was even more spectacular from so high.

I got my chance to revisit the Maracanã when we took in Colombia's 2–0 win over Uruguay in the last sixteen. Uruguay were without their talisman Luis Suárez after his record nine-match FIFA ban after biting Giorgio Chiellini in the group game against Italy, and I've got a great picture of Mike as we're walking into the ground coming up behind a Uruguayan fan in his Suárez shirt, pretending to bite his neck. It was amazing to visit one of the most famous stadiums in the world again, evoking memories of that wonderful 1970 team. It's just a shame the team in yellow that day was Colombian, not Brazilian.

The plan was to stay on for the final, as we'd lined up a couple of the FA's allocation of tickets. We decided to watch the Brazil–Germany semi-final in a fan zone in the city. We got there a couple of hours before kick-off to find a huge street party, with thousands of people dancing and drinking beneath the yellow and green streamers, bunting and balloons that stretched across the streets from apartment block to apartment block. The locals were already sinking their beers and spirits long before the game started – to be shown on huge TV screens scattered around the place – looking forward to one more match before the much-anticipated, and expected, grand final: Brazil v. Argentina or the Netherlands. The mood soon turned sour. The hosts were battered 7–1, and it was hard to enjoy the game among those passionate locals as their team embarrassingly disintegrated in front of us. Without the injured Neymar, they were five goals down within the first twenty-five minutes. There was no trouble, but the atmosphere among the Brazil supporters changed very quickly from a wonderful street party to celebrate the beautiful game and Brazil's progress to the final to a sombre wake among shell-shocked, tear-stained fans.

Brazil's loss broke their thirty-nine-year unbeaten home record in sixty-two competitive games and was seen as a 'national humiliation'. It was also the end of Brazil's World Cup. And ours. We didn't fancy watching a final in the Maracanã without Brazil. It was time to head back to Miami.

The following day we packed our bags and flew to Miami so Mike could enjoy a few days savouring the sights and attractions. As he is Anne's brother, we had got the all-important seal of approval to extend our trip a bit further rather than flying straight home.

Kammy

I was stopped when we got to passport control in Florida. The bloke kept looking at my passport, then he looked at me, then the passport, then me again. He frowned, checked my photo and my face one last time, then picked up my passport and disappeared without saying a single word. The look on his face didn't look like good news for me. Do I look like a drug smuggler? I don't think so. Do I act like I'm on something? OK, don't answer that one.

I was left on my own for about fifteen minutes – it felt like a lifetime. Mike had already gone through passport control at this point and stood waiting for me within my eyeline, putting his hands out to ask what was going on. I had no idea. Had the statement written in Portuguese that I'd signed in the police station in Rio after the mugging come back to haunt me?

The passport officer came back with a mate, and, much to my surprise, they were both full of smiles. Before I knew it, they were asking for a photo.

'We know you,' the first one said, as we posed for the picture and he handed back my passport. 'We saw you on Fox News last week. You're the guy who caught the mugger in Brazil! Welcome to Miami, man.' And they waved me through. Told you! Kammy, international crimefighter!

29

Animals

BRAZIL WAS THE EPITOME OF NOISE, CARNIVAL, FULL-ON in-your-face atmosphere. But I am at heart, believe it or not, a quiet man. And animals especially have been vital in giving me the escape from the hustle and bustle I've always needed.

It doesn't matter whether it's wandering in the fields at home with the sheep and horses or on safari in Africa with Anne, I've always had this passion. I had dogs when I was young, and luckily my son Jack shares my love and has turned our smallholding into a home for rescued sheep and chickens. We're never surprised when he pulls up in his van and beckons us excitedly to come and see the new addition to our animal family.

One of life's small joys during lockdown was spending time with my grandkids. Connie, Sol and I spent hours with our sheep and horses. We have six woolly friends now: Howard, Cookie Bear, Ben, Rudy, Ivy and Bramble. They're all incredible – such cute, friendly creatures. I love going to see them every morning and chatting to them while they're feeding. If it wasn't for the crapping everywhere, I'd have them indoors like house pets! Howard and Ben do pop in regularly for a nosy around when we let them, and Cookie Bear is occasionally brave enough. Jack often walks them through the village, and if the schoolkids spot them, they're always excited to see our sheep pals, offering them treats and lots of petting.

After years of listening to Jack, who is vegan, I changed to a vegetarian diet six years ago when we got the sheep. Once I saw how much character they had, I just couldn't bring myself to eat meat again. We also keep chickens, so KFC is off the menu too. As a Boro lad, I was always a big fan of a chicken parmo – the legendary local delicacy. I did try the veggie option in a takeaway when I visited Middlesbrough for Channel 5's *There's No Place Like Home*, and it was surprisingly tasty. I enjoyed it as much as the chicken version.

Anne and I also love nothing more than seeing animals in their natural habitats. As fun as it is to have Howard and Ben in the house, I know enough about zoology to realize that the living room is not a sheep's natural environment. We are always planning our next trip and have been lucky enough to enjoy some incredible journeys to the jungles and plains of Africa, experiencing all kinds of beautiful animals up close in the wild. Sometimes a little too close!

We've fed giraffes in Kenya, watching them emerge elegantly from the bush. And on another safari with Mike and our nephews Ollie and Brad, we were treated to a rare sight when a hyena came into camp looking for leftovers from our sumptuous outdoor banquet. We didn't hear it laugh. Maybe it had been listening to my anecdotes over dinner. Shrieks from the staff and other campers alerted us to the animal peering from behind the table as it searched for tasty titbits.

We're huge fans of big cats and loved walking with lions, which was one of our craziest experiences. We were in Zambia for a few days, visiting the magnificent Victoria Falls and taking in the wildlife, including hippo spotting on the Zambezi, elephant trekking along the riverbanks, and one encounter we hadn't expected, walking with the kings of the jungle. We simply couldn't say no to that and signed up – including the waiver form, of course. I checked to see if they were providing lunch. Then checked again to see if it was for us or the lions.

When we arrived at the right spot, the guides sat us down and gave us the safety briefing. And a stick. They had guns while all we got was a flimsy bit of wood! What were we supposed to do? Point it and shout 'Bang!'?

Our guides explained that, whatever happened, the lions were to be kept in front of us. If a lion turned around and came towards us, we were to stand still.

'What about the stick?' I asked.

'That's to beat them off!' the guide replied, nonchalantly. I think he also had a little smile on his face, a suspicion that was later confirmed when he told us we'd really be using the sticks to indicate to the lions where they should go and also, remarkably, play with them. We got to do that when they climbed into the lower branches of the trees and we stretched out our sticks for them to swat away, similar to what we now do with our own cat in our garden at home.

Walking with lions was one of the most exhilarating experiences of my life. When they stopped, we managed to stroke one of them as he wandered among us. Thankfully they were having a veggie day, and Kammy burgers were off the menu. The video is a wonderful memory to have.

On a safari in South Africa, meanwhile, we were taken to a lion sanctuary caring for abandoned cubs before their return to the wild. They were so unbelievably cute I could have taken them home, although I expect the sheep would probably have had something to say about that. They were also quite hungry. The lovely guides offered us one of the cubs to hold. I said I'd video the experience while Anne took the first turn with the big ball of fur. He was six months old, rather heavy and quite lively. As he started chewing on Anne's arm, he drew blood and she let out a shriek. The young cub had to be gently pulled away from what he thought was his next dinner, and Anne had failed her audition for *Tarzan*. 'Your turn now,' Anne said, with blood dripping from her wound. I 'politely' declined, even though I really wanted to hold it up in the air and sing 'Circle of Life'. Anne often tells the grandkids that she was once bitten by a lion – she just forgets to mention it was a baby one. To be fair, I don't mention the bit about how brave Grandad hid behind the camera and refused to go anywhere near those razor-sharp teeth.

We also did a day of trekking in the Ugandan jungle to see chimpanzees. The idea was to enter the jungle and find a chimp family, which was in fact quite easy, as you could hear their chattering and calling and rustling as they swung from tree to tree. One cheeky little chap definitely had a bit of fun with us. As we were quietly watching him, he suddenly ran screaming towards us – as if he was on the attack. At the last possible second, he leaped into the air and swung off into the bushes and trees, shrieking as he went – we only felt the slightest brush of his fur on our heads as he passed. The guides said they do it all the time for their own amusement. Our home video of the chimps' antics is one of our eldest grandson's favourites – he often asks Anne to show it to him, as he imitates the chimp's noises and laughs at our screams.

But of all the African adventures, nothing could beat pretending to be David Attenborough, Anne's absolute hero, and meeting gorillas close up in Uganda – even if I nearly died at the hands of a great silverback, much to the amusement of my loving wife.

A number of mountain gorillas inhabit the Virunga Mountains National Park straddling the border between Rwanda, Uganda and the Democratic Republic of Congo. Dedicated trackers take you to meet these precious primates in their natural environment. Ours took Anne and me plus two other couples through the jungle. And I mean real jungle. It was so demanding – walking for miles in draining heat, across really rough terrain, up and down massive hills, through streams and dense trees, to get to the gorillas, who move on and build a new nest each night. It was quite tough for Anne and some of the others, but worth every step, because seeing them was so rewarding.

The gorilla families have been painstakingly educated over a long period of time to accept humans being around them in the jungle. Taking tourists to observe them is how the local trackers make their living, and helps with the gorillas' preservation.

The gorillas accept the presence of humans, but every tour group must go through the important ritual of meeting and being accepted by the silverback leader of the group. You must not approach any member of his family without his permission or he's likely to attack you. The guide was telling us all this as we took in the enormous silverback sitting in the middle of the clearing with baby gorillas and young adults playing and lazing about close by.

'Whatever you do, turn off the flashes on your cameras,' the guide warned. An Italian couple moved to the front of our silent group, and we all shuffled to within about twelve feet of the alpha gorilla. This wasn't near enough for the Italians, so they discreetly shuffled even closer to the mighty primate. I wanted in on the action myself, and as no one had said we couldn't do the same, walked forward to join them, smiling smugly at Anne as she stayed back beside our guide. As I turned to take in the unique silverback experience, the Italian woman took a picture of the gorilla – with the flash still on. This giant ape went absolutely . . . well, ape. I turned to see him stand up, let out a mighty roar and head towards me. The Italians were off, and he came hurtling in my direction. Within seconds he was right in front of me. He was gigantic. His nails were as long as my fingers. I made a move to run. 'Stop! Stand still! Stand still!' shouted the guides.

My initial thought was, 'You're joking!' but I did as they said. This massive gorilla was inches from me. And he let out another enormous roar that nearly blew my head off.

The guards sprang into action – 'Don't run! Stay calm! Stand very still!'. Eventually, the silverback turned and walked away. 'He'll be fine now,' one of the guards explained. Trembling from head to toe, I turned back to the group. All I could see was Anne doubled over and crying with laughter. She explained that a guide had quietly assured her that it was 'OK, no panic – he's just showing his authority'. She'd actually enjoyed the horror on my face while I wondered how I'd get out of this one alive!

From then on the guides kept telling me, 'No flashes! No

flashes!' and shaking their heads – and I kept trying to tell them it wasn't me who'd upset the gorilla in the first place!

Once our mighty leader had relaxed and given his unorthodox thumbs-up, we had a wonderful hour or so with the rest of the gorilla family, observing the adults playing with their babies and watching the youngsters as they ran around like naughty little kids. The old silverback sat chilling as we had one of the best days of our lives. Somehow, trekking back out of the jungle and up and down the tree plantation hills wasn't quite as hard as our entry into it. We were completely shattered but buzzing from the excitement of our unique day – and my relief at not being torn apart! Anne says her one regret is, while doubled over with laughter, she didn't capture a video of my face to share and show (and laugh about *again*) with the family back home.

Stepping back from my TV commitments will allow me to do more trips to see animals in the wild in the future, rather than just the sheep in my field. And I'm sure there'll be plenty more laughs – and hopefully no more confrontations – along the way.

30

Royalty

Ladies' Day at Royal Ascot has to be seen to be believed. It's full of exclusive, well-groomed breeding stock worth millions – all there to watch the horses. There's the pomp and ceremony when the royal procession arrives, and every gent is in top hat and tails and the ladies in the most glorious and beautiful high-fashion outfits.

The meeting is steeped in history and tradition, and so to be asked to present the trophy to the winning owner, jockey and groom of the Hampton Court Stakes in June 2022 was a huge honour. I'd only been to Royal Ascot once before, with Steve Gibson, but for horse-lovers it's up there with the greatest events on the sporting calendar. Just a wonderful day. To be invited into the royal enclosure, and have a chance of meeting the Queen, was like a dream. The invitation extended to four, so Anne, Mike and Netti were on board too. Mike in particular loves racing as much as I do, and we usually go to the Cheltenham Festival together.

That morning the sun was shining and everything was perfect as we pondered the prospect of meeting the Queen. We didn't know if she'd actually be there, as she'd not attended the meeting for either of the previous two days, having not been well in recent weeks. Knowing how much our Queen loved her race meetings, and Ascot in particular, we were hoping she'd make it on Ladies' Day.

Having stayed in a hotel the night before, we enjoyed our breakfast together, watching the early morning paddleboarders on the Thames, before wandering outside to the riverbank for our own little photoshoot, marking the start of our day. We were intercepted by the hotel concierge who had come to tell us that our car – a red limousine with the Royal Ascot emblem emblazoned on the side – was waiting. Holding the door open was a smart chauffeur in suit and cap. We were really being spoiled. I expected to see a tray in the back full of Ferrero Rocher. We took our seats in the limo, to the envy of the coachload of punters who were being collected from the same hotel. I hope we didn't spoil their day – they'd been quite happy with the coach until they saw us getting the VIP treatment!

The limousine took us to Ascot, and then through the crowds like royalty to the main entrance, where we received our access-all-areas passes to one of the most exclusive places to watch horse racing in the world. This was incredible – we were buzzing.

Our box was right next to the royals and we were greeted by Her Majesty's representative at Ascot, Sir Francis Brooke, who had been designated to look after us all day. We had a meal with the other guests, including former boxing and snooker promoter

Barry Hearn and his wife, and Judge Robert Rinder and his lovely mum, who told me she was a huge fan.

Sir Francis gave a speech paying tribute to everyone there, including me. I could hardly take it in – this was the head of Ascot, the Queen's representative of this magnificent race-course, and he was talking about me. I sat there smiling, trying to take it all in – so humbling.

Before the first race, Sir Francis asked us if we'd like to go into the saddling enclosure and see the horses and grooms. He explained we'd have to pick the best turned-out horse for the Hampton Court Stakes, and it would give us an idea of what to expect and look out for. Mike and I couldn't wait to get into the inner sanctum of Royal Ascot.

As we headed through the eager racegoers, we found it diffi-cult to move on as swiftly as we needed to because I was in such demand for selfies. This is something I never mind, and Anne is used to it, but even she was panicking. I guess this is why they don't let you take selfies with the King or Queen. They'd never get anywhere! In racing terms, I was a straggler, coming in well behind the pack.

Beforehand, we'd been taken down through the crowds to experience the arrival of the royal procession, loving the regalia, the horse-drawn carriages and the cheering crowds. Unfortu-nately, the Queen didn't make it that day, and although we were disappointed, we were excited to see Princess Anne and her family in the procession. I had previously worked with her son-in-law Mike Tindall and was looking forward to catching up with him and his lovely wife Zara. Also part of the royal entourage was Sophie, Countess of Wessex, Prince Edward's wife, who was so down to earth. She made her way to the royal box through our room, right past our table on the terrace. I nearly dropped my bread roll. She probably got a ticking off for ignoring royal protocol and security.

Back in our box, we settled into our afternoon of living the high life with only a security guard between us and the royals. Our table on the outside terrace had been carefully bagged by Anne and Netti because of its position right next to the royal box. Anne, by her own admission, isn't the most athletic person, but the speed she travelled to ensure we had the prime spot right next to where the Queen might be sitting was worthy of a gold medal in the 100 metres – if anyone was going to rub shoulders with Her Majesty that day it was going to be us.

The Hampton Court Stakes was the fifth race of the afternoon. By then, Anne, Mike, Netti and I were absolutely lapping up the atmosphere. I had to pinch myself to believe I was there at Ascot, judging the best turned-out horse and, after the race, presenting the winning owner and trainer with their trophy. We had plenty of time to mingle around the saddling enclosure and, unbeknown to me, Sir Francis had arranged for us to meet Princess Anne.

'Lovely to meet you,' I said, mentioning that we'd met once before actually, many years ago, at Wakefield Riding for the Disabled, one of her charities.

'How's your mum?' I asked, much to the dismay of my wife – I'm not sure you're meant to come straight out with stuff like that. Anne replied along the lines that she was fine – just not up to the very hot weather.

'Chris is presenting the trophy for this race,' her security guard told her. 'The Queen's horse is the favourite.'

And she simply came out with it. 'Oh, interesting. Well, then, if it *does* win, you must take the trophy to Windsor Castle and present it to the Queen yourself.'

I could see all the bods in security thinking, 'Flipping heck, how are we going to pull that off?' Now, I needed Frankie Dettori to win on the Queen's horse, odds-on favourite Reach for the Moon – come on, you beauty!

As the princess moved on, the security guy came back to me and shook my hand. 'It's great to meet you, Kammy,' he said. 'I'm a big Leeds fan. I've been a supporter for a long time. I know all about your career.'

I went back to our group – 'Crikey, the bodyguard is a big Leeds fan.' I pointed to the tall bloke rejoining the royal party.

'That's not her bodyguard,' Anne told me. 'That's Timothy Laurence, her husband. Really, you are so ignorant.' And she was right, I was ignorant – I made a note to brief myself properly for any such occasions in the future. If ever I was invited back!

After my chat with my new pal the princess, I saw Mike Tindall heading over from the other side of the enclosure. With the others now keeping an eye on me and warning me to behave and remember where I was, I threatened to shout 'Tinders' as he strode nearer. It's my usual form of greeting, and I knew he wouldn't have minded – he's such a good lad. I toned it down, though, and we had a man hug and a good laugh about two Yorkshire lads scrubbing up for Royal Ascot before he went back to his mother-in-law and his quite well-known family.

Next, I met the one and only Frankie, again someone I'd known for a long time. 'You've got to win,' I told him, explaining how a trip to Windsor Castle was on the cards if the result was right.

He shot his arms into the air and covered his ears, screaming,

'Aaaargh, don't jinx it, don't jinx it!' To be honest, his mount was the heavy favourite and I couldn't see him losing.

It was time to judge the magnificent beasts in all their finery. These horses get the very best of treatment. OK, they don't get me singing Christmas songs at them, but everything else is great. We all agreed that Claymore, which was to be ridden by Adam Kirby, was best turned-out. It was to be an omen.

We didn't have time to go back to the box and so we watched on the big screen in the enclosure.

Reach for the Moon was second to Claymore virtually all the way round. The crowd cheered, I tutted, and whoever organizes visits to Windsor Castle breathed a sigh of relief.

Truth is, I didn't back a single winner all afternoon, but our royal experience was the best day I've had at the races – one of the best days I've experienced anywhere.

And in fact, while I might not have made it to Windsor Castle that time, a visit to the great royal residence wasn't too far away.

★

The email said it was from the Ceremonial Officer at the Cabinet Office. You might think someone like me gets emails asking for advice from the government all the time: 'Kammy, what do we do about the environment? What do we do about fiscal policy?' But, surprisingly, you'd be wrong. Like many people, we've been scammed in the past, and we are always wary about opening emails from unlikely sources. And they don't get much more unlikely than the Cabinet Office.

Anne, who deals with a lot of my emails, ignored it initially, but when Ben, the family IT expert, called round later, her curiosity got the better of her, and she thought she'd run it by him to see if it was authentic. Ben took a quick look and announced excitedly that it was indeed genuine. It was the news that I was to be awarded an MBE for services to football, anti-racism and charity in the King's 2023 New Year's Honours list. Anne and Ben quickly phoned Jack, who wouldn't have to come far to witness my reaction to the news because he lives next door. It turned out he was travelling home from London, but he told Anne to video my reaction so he could see it.

When my granddaughter Billie handed me a printout of the email, my wife and son, beaming as they looked on, must have been so disappointed by my reaction – nothing! Totally under-whelmed. There was my family, so excited for me, and expecting me to share in that excitement, but it felt a bit strange, not real, not right. In my mind, MBEs are awarded to people for out-standing achievements and for changing the lives of others for the better, and I wasn't sure I fitted that mould.

I had so far served forty-nine years in football, from player to manager to pundit to presenter, and I'd loved every minute of it. How could I be honoured for that? I had the privilege of using my platform in the public eye to support several chari-ties, mainly Marie Curie, but the fundraising I've been involved in has given me so much personal satisfaction – so why was I being honoured for it? And anti-racism is something I have been involved with for many years through Show Racism the Red Card, but I would always support the cause, so no award was needed. But these were the three reasons the MBE was being given to me. I couldn't have been more doubtful if they'd awarded it based on my naval career.

I could see my family were chuffed for me, and they couldn't understand my muted reaction. I told them of my reservations – they dismissed them instantly. They convinced me that all my work, be it for charity or not, had been recognized due to all the hard graft I had put in. I listened to them and agreed to accept the MBE but was still dubious about what others would have to say. Would some be jealous? Not knowing what I do aside from football, would some be thinking I was only being awarded the MBE because I had come out publicly about my illness?

I needn't have worried – all the positive reactions I did get were very reassuring. I deserved it, apparently.

The next challenge was keeping the MBE quiet until the New Year's Honours List was announced. Over the years, keeping quiet hasn't been my strong point. You always know when I'm keeping a secret – I've told you it. However, I had just finished recording *The Masked Singer* as 'Ghost', and that had called for me to keep schtum until it had aired a couple of months later. The security around Buckingham Palace is almost as tight as the security around ITV's reality shows.

When news of all the awardees was announced, the deluge of congratulations poured in – by text, email, phone, social media, the lot. The messages were so heart-warming and came from people I had never even met, from people I had not heard from for years, and also some from people in high places. I even got a letter of congratulation in the post from His Royal Highness Prince William. What?! I asked Ben Shephard if he thought it was usual to get a letter from the royals in these circumstances. He said that he wasn't sure but could easily check it out with a pal of his who had received an MBE. He came back saying that no royal letter had been forthcoming for his mate. Perhaps things had changed under King Charles's watchful eye.

It was still crazy to me, but after receiving all these good wishes I was getting in the swing of it, especially when Anne told me I should stop being so negative and accept the MBE as the great honour it is.

We learned that my MBE investiture would be held in March at Windsor Castle. The invitation did not provide an answer to the big question: who would be presenting the award? You don't find out until you turn up on the big day.

I only have two sons, so my plus-three invitation was a no-brainer: Anne, Ben and Jack. Anne is fiercely camera shy and shuns much of the showbiz life I have somehow fallen into. However, she was soon pulling out her glad rags in anticipation of the right royal day ahead. Funnily enough, she'd done the same when I'd been asked to present the Duke of Edinburgh Awards at St James's Palace in early 2020. She's very selective – in some areas.

We booked into the Castle Hotel right opposite the gates to Windsor after travelling from home the day before the investiture. As we were checking in, I turned to see a familiar face doing the same – it was Richard Bevan, CEO of the League Managers' Association. I was surprised to see him in the hotel and asked why he was there. Richard said he was there to receive an OBE, so, delighted for him and his wife, I congratulated him and let him know that I thought it was well deserved. With the mystery of the Prince William letter still niggling me, I jumped on the opportunity to ask Richard if he had received a similar royal message. 'No,' he replied, 'unfortunately, I don't enjoy the same status as you, Kammy.'

We completed our hotel check-in and went to drop our luggage in the room. Immediately upon closing the door, Anne turned to me. 'Why the hell did you have to ask Richard about receiving the same kind of message as you? It looked like you were gloating – a positive case of one-upmanship.' I was devastated that Richard might have thought that – my lasting curiosity over the letter had got the better of me. I'd thought I had a chance to solve the mystery – I had in no way intended to gloat.

The four of us had a lovely meal that night in the shadow of the castle, all of us anticipating the momentous day ahead. We could hardly talk about anything else. Would it be the King I'd be meeting? Would it be HRH Princess Anne? Or William, indeed, who'd sent me the congratulations letter? Should I bow or shake hands? Should I curtsy? Could I look them in the eye? Did I have to walk backwards? What if I tripped over a corgi? It was a good job I wasn't getting a knighthood – if I'd had to kneel, I'm not sure I'd have been able to get up. 'Arise, Sir Kammy' would very soon lead to 'For God's sake get up, there's others waiting for their big moment, too, you know . . .' I lost count of the times Anne reminded me that night to not forget my manners. And under no circumstances was I to call our king 'Chaz'.

It had been a drizzly start to the morning, but luckily it was dry as we walked into Windsor Castle. I had originally hoped for Buckingham Palace, but Anne was happy with our venue. We had lived around there when Ben was a baby, and Anne loved the place and was pleased to be back. It took me no time to warm to the castle, the sheer splendour of our surroundings, the friendly staff ushering us along and offering their best wishes – everything was perfect, and we were determined to enjoy being in such a historic building. I felt a surge of immense pride as I walked along, my wife and sons by my side, fussing over me and doing all they could to help make this day special.

I thought back to my mum and dad, and Anne's parents too, sadly all no longer with us, and could only imagine what they would have made of this amazing day had they still been here to share it with us. Dad with his oversized three-piece suit (oversized because it was usually one of my cast-offs – I never had the heart to tell him they weren't a great fit when he'd been so chuffed to get his hands on them), and Mum in her twin set, carefully selected with help from her sisters (Grattan's catalogue would have been her first choice). Anne's dad Roy would have had a battle with her mum about buying a new suit – why did he need a new one when the one he wore to our wedding forty years earlier was still in perfect nick? My mother-in-law Sylvia would have dragged Anne out to help with buying her outfit, insisting she looked silly in a hat. One thing is sure – they would all have been as proud as Punch, as they would have said, and I hoped they were all watching over the four of us as we made our way into Windsor Castle.

We were shown through various state rooms, chatting to fellow award recipients and their proud families as we went. We were in awe of the magnificent artwork draped around each room. There was a bit of nervousness floating around, but after spending so long chatting and socializing, the tension eased, and everyone vowed just to enjoy the day.

Word had gone round by this time that it was Prince William who would, literally, be doing the honours. My family and I were more than happy with that, and I looked forward to chatting to him, knowing he was a footie fan. Maybe I'd get to the bottom of the letter at last.

Jack spotted Liverpool ace James Milner, who was also there to receive an MBE. James's career has always been of interest to me, with him being a Leeds lad, and I've followed his journey all the way from Elland Road to Anfield. It was lovely to talk with him and his wife Amy about how well his career had gone and how he'd served the game so well. I joked about his time at Aston Villa, bearing in mind Prince William is a Villa fan. James, laughing, said he thought he'd done OK. 'I think you did more than OK,' I said.

The organization of the awards is done with military precision – nothing is left to chance. I was briefed on where I had to stand, what I had to do and, thankfully, not on what I had to say. It was too many instructions for me, but Anne managed to fire some of her own warnings out of the corner of her mouth, telling me to make sure I bowed and called him 'Sir', etc. I needn't have worried – I think I got through it all right. The rest of the family had been told where they should stand so they had a prime view of me and William – or Wills as I threatened to call him. Anne said she welled up when the military ensemble sitting in the corner of the room started playing Elton John's 'Can You Feel the Love Tonight'. This, she was convinced, was fate. As you know, I love Elton's music, and her favourite Disney film is *The Lion King* from which that song comes. Fate, indeed.

I duly moved forward when my name was called. It had been made clear that I didn't have to bow in front of Prince William, but, out of respect, I did so anyway. William was pinning the MBE on me before I realized I'd managed to pick up a few nervous vibes after all, but they were soon dispersed when we began chatting. He said my award was well deserved, and that, as a football fan, he had grown up following my career on screen. Because I knew he was an Aston Villa supporter, I asked him how that had come about. He said he'd wanted to be different to his pals, who were all fans of Manchester United, Liverpool and various other big clubs, and he had managed to get to Villa games in his youth, with a beanie hat pulled down to hide his face. I was surprised when he asked how I was and about my current health issues. Such attention to detail and concern for me – from our future king.

Before our chat was over, I told him I was pleased he'd been handed the role this particular day because it gave me the opportunity to thank him for his letter of congratulations on my MBE. He said the award was well earned and long overdue. And there was me thinking I was not worthy.

I moved back to my family, with a huge beam from ear to ear. We had a quick hug before we were ushered into another magnificent room for the official photos. None of us could stop smiling. We headed back outside for a few words to the waiting TV cameras.

Yorkshire TV were so pleased for me and told me my investiture would be the first item that same evening on *Calendar*, the regional news programme in our area. They also asked to speak to Anne, but she swiftly handed them over to Ben and Jack. My sons had a couple of minutes in front of the camera, saying how pleased they were for me and how proud they were that their dad had been recognized.

BBC's *Look North* were the next cameras in line, followed by *Sky Sports News*. I felt this chat with Sky was my way of saying 'thank you' to them for the platform they had provided me the past twenty-four years – they were part of the reason I was at Windsor Castle to collect my medal in the first place.

Anne had a talk with Prince William's PA, who told her that the prince had been very excited that I was to be there. I guess that was backed up later when someone messaged me to say that there was a tweet on the Prince and Princess of Wales's account that read, 'We're off to Windsor Castle where there's been an MBE but for who @chris_kammy?' Who would have believed that this Boro lad would end up at Windsor Castle with an MBE being pinned to his chest by the future king? To top the big day, the royal family were even making fun of me for missing that red card all those years before. On reflection, even I find it hard to believe what I've packed into my life. To coin a phrase, it's been unbelievable.

★

I was left similarly nonplussed when I was hoodwinked into accepting the Contribution to League Football Award at a ceremony in London.

I've always enjoyed a good relationship with the Football League and done a lot of work and campaigns with them. So I thought nothing of it when the EFL invited me to their annual awards at the Grosvenor House Hotel in London in March 2023 and was happy to accept. After all, a free meal is a free meal.

Shep was first choice for my 'plus-one', but he was going to be away with his family so couldn't make it. Amazingly, he wouldn't cancel a family holiday for a night out with me . . . I know, crazy! At that point I thought about cancelling and making my excuses. 'Don't worry about it,' I texted. 'You don't have to come back. I'm not sure about going anyway.'

He texted me straight back: 'Don't cancel. I might be able to make it. Keep it open 'til the last minute.'

Unbeknown to me, Shep had filmed a video in my honour, as part of a secret presentation – and I had sent him into a blind panic by saying I might not come. Luckily, by the time he cried off, I'd arranged a replacement in Sean Cooney, who handled all the PR for the Christmas albums.

As soon as we walked in, I was swamped by some great friends: Jeff and Bianca Westwood were the first to greet me, and Sean and I were sitting on the Sky table, including three of the *Goals on Sunday* producers, who I hadn't seen in years. As we took our seats, Sean spotted the table next to us was empty – 'Maybe they've decided not to turn up,' he noted, 'or they're all stuck in traffic somewhere.'

After a couple of early awards, the MC, David Prutton, announced the 'most prestigious award the Football League can hand out, the Contribution to League Football Award, and here to present it is – Jeff Stelling.' To a big round of applause, Jeff left the table, but I was still none the wiser about what was going on.

'You know this fella pretty well,' said David as he handed the microphone to Jeff. And then it dawned on me what was happening, and I realized I only had a few minutes to think of something to say. It was daunting and suddenly rather nerve-wracking – all I could think was that the old me would have relished every minute of it.

I was called up to the stage after they showed a video tribute that included Jeff, Mark Schwarzer, the keeper I signed for Bradford City from Germany, and, of course, Shep. I managed to say a few words of thanks, but it wasn't great.

After Jeff and Rick Parry had handed over the award, David Prutton said, 'And we have one last surprise.' And on walked my family and some friends, which was certainly a shock. Ben and Jack were there, my brother-in-law Mike and his sons Olly and

Brad, and good friends like Christine Matthews, who I have known for many years. But the biggest surprise was seeing Anne, who had dropped me off at the station only a few hours earlier.

The EFL had arranged everything, even the timings of the presentation so we could fill that empty table and have a brilliant night together. How the EFL managed to organize it, and just about keep it all secret, is one of the great mysteries. It was a special way to celebrate my long-standing relationship with the EFL, and I felt incredibly honoured to receive such a remarkable recognition.

31

Giving Back

I'VE SAID IT BEFORE AND I'LL SAY IT AGAIN, MY MUM IRENE was my world. 'Mam' – which is what we all call our mums in Middlesbrough – protected me and my brother and sister when we were growing up. All she ever wanted was for me to be happy – and she supported me in everything. I have many happy memories and will never forget her beautiful smile and laugh. Whenever I hear Tina Turner's 'The Best', it makes me smile and I always think of her. She would say that in her eyes the title referred to me, and she loved to dance when it came on. Mum had a walking stick in later years due to thrombosis, but once a couple of milk stouts had been downed and Tina Turner was blasting out, she'd throw that stick away and hit the dance floor like a *Strictly* professional.

We'd speak every day, no matter where I was in the world, and I always told Mum when I was going to be on TV, even though Sky Sports was on most of the time in her house in case

I made an appearance. She loved seeing me on the telly, and I know she would have enjoyed watching me on Saturday night primetime shows like *Ninja Warrior* and Ant and Dec's *Saturday Night Takeaway*.

My biggest regret is that I wasn't there the night she died in 2003. Mum was diagnosed with terminal breast cancer during my early days on *Goals on Sunday*, and I was busy as an established part of *Soccer Saturday* and *Soccer AM*. I got my priorities all wrong.

I spoke to Mum before covering a game on Easter Saturday. We knew she was close to the end, but I told her not to worry – I was coming home after *Goals on Sunday* and would see her on Easter Monday. Condo then called me after the Sunday show and asked me if I'd cover QPR v. Notts County the following day as a favour. I turned him down at first, because I was planning to go to Middlesbrough, as promised, to see Mum. 'Don't worry about it,' he said.

Like an idiot, I changed my mind. 'No, wait. It's fine. I'll do it.' What was I thinking?

I phoned Mum and told her I'd be up the day after instead. She just let out a deflated 'Oh'.

'What do you mean?'

'Oh dear. Oh well, no, it's fine, it's fine.'

I went home to Wakefield after the QPR game, only to get a call from Mum's sister, my Auntie Doreen, at seven o'clock the next morning to tell me she'd passed away. I'd missed the chance to say goodbye. I should have been with her and I have beaten myself up for that over the years. Those feelings of regret are still with me. Nothing has helped me to make peace with it, although someone once said to me that a mum loves you unconditionally. That's always stuck with me. Mum knew how much I loved her, which has been at least some consolation for missing her at the end.

Marie Curie nurses provided Mum with great care, and she was able to pass away, as she wished, at home. One nurse in particular did her shopping, cleaning and cooking and was a friend to her during her final few weeks.

After Mum died, I made it a personal mission to raise as much money as possible for Marie Curie in her memory. Nothing would take away the guilt, but I wanted to show my personal gratitude to them for being there for her, and for hundreds of thousands of other families. Until I got involved with the charity, I'd never spoken about Mum's death and I always find it emotional recalling her last few days, whether I'm talking live to Lorraine Kelly, to a newspaper journalist or at a Marie Curie event with a few hundred people. But I take great solace that they were there for her and I'm doing my bit in her memory.

My involvement with Marie Curie, which has hospices up and down the country to look after people with life-limiting illnesses, started with a golf tournament in Tenerife, where Anne and I have an apartment. My friends Greg James and Fergal Flaherty from the Hole in the Wall in Playa de las Americas agreed to support Marie Curie at their annual fundraising event – and a few of the lads from Sky flew in for it. Jeff Stelling, Paul Merson, Phil Thompson, Alan McInally and Charlie Nicholas all came over, and we had a brilliant turn-out. The people of Tenerife were so welcoming, the local radio station Oasis FM promoted it, and a timeshare company donated rooms to me and my guests. They also put on meals and drinks for the boys – you can imagine the festivities! We raised tens of thousands of pounds

and even managed to play a bit of decent golf. I was still swinging the sticks at that time, and I loved it.

Over the years, Niall Quinn has come over to Tenerife to
play, as did the late Cyrille Regis MBE, Steve Howey, Dean
Windass and boxer Ricky Hatton, a one-time neighbour on
the island and a big supporter of the fundraising week. Singer
Daniel O'Donnell, a frequent visitor to the island and friend of
mine, has also turned up to support my cause, and as word went
around, the number of teams wanting to join the fun just grew
and grew. Iain Dowie and journalist Max Rushden swelled the
numbers one year, while former Blackpool boss Michael Apple-
ton, who was staying in Tenerife, rang me to ask if he could
take part along with all his mates. The last tournament attracted
seventeen teams and we have now raised more than £100,000.

As well as the golf tournament, I agreed to become a national
Marie Curie celebrity ambassador in 2010. One of my first roles
was to launch the national campaign for Marie Curie's Charity
of the Season partnership with the Football League. Fans across
the country got involved, and the campaign raised more than
£500,000. Not a bad start. Managers and players from Football League clubs got involved too, and it has now extended to
the Premier League. I think one of my proudest achievements
as a Marie Curie ambassador is seeing virtually every manager
wearing the yellow daffodil pin badge leading up to the charity's
National Day of Reflection on 23 March. Shep and I talked on
an episode of *Goals on Sunday* about the wonderful work Marie
Curie do, and why people should fundraise for the charity and
wear our daffodil pins. I even persuaded the studio crew to wear
them – all helping to raise awareness of the charity. Everyone

in football and TV I have asked to support Marie Curie in this way has always said yes.

We've come up with some ingenious ideas over the years, including the Christmas-themed photoshoot 'All Chris wants for Christmas is you', casting light on the crucial work Marie Curie nurses carry out over the festive period. Hotter Shoes made me a bespoke pair of daffodil shoes to raise money, while we also launched 'Kammy's Hot Sauce' online, with a recipe in honour of my dad. I even went all arty and designed a daffodil sculpture for an installation in Paternoster Square, near St Paul's Cathedral in central London.

I've also appeared on every charity quiz going – *The Chase*, *The Wall*, *Catchphrase*, you name it, admittedly not always getting the right answer. When I appeared on *The Chase*, Bradley Walsh asked me, 'The extinct volcano Shira forms part of what Tanzanian mountain?'

In a panic, I said, 'Newcastle United?' All I'd heard was the Shira bit, and I went straight to footballer Alan Shearer.

Poor Bradders couldn't keep it together. Thankfully it was the last question, the buzzer went, and he managed to regain his composure. 'Shearer? It's Kilimanjaro.'

Despite my rocky start, I got through to the final chase, which I was really pleased with, but took away only a consolation £1,000 for Marie Curie. 'Given that your persona is one of uncontrolled anarchy at times,' the chaser, 'The Sinnerman' Paul Sinha, told me, 'you really focused there and gave a performance you can be really proud of.' How come none of my schoolteachers ever gave me such a glowing report?!

I've enjoyed most of the quiz shows I've been on, even though the fact there's charity money at stake adds extra jeopardy.

In particular, my appearance on *Who Wants to Be a Millionaire?* in October 2022 turned out to be a bittersweet affair. When I was asked to join Jeremy Clarkson to do a charity episode of the show, I had no hesitation. It would be an honour to take part and a great chance to fill the coffers of Marie Curie. I didn't expect to walk away with £1 million – I mean, I could have, but only if I'd had ten lifelines and nine of them were 'you can google it'. I still hoped I would be able to come away with a respectable amount of cash.

I'd asked Jeff and Shep if they would each be a 'phone a friend', but they were both busy, so I asked Steph McGovern, who said she'd love to do it. My other phone-a-friend was Andy Smith, my long-term pal who was also my chief scout at Bradford City. You don't have to be clever to be on this show, but you do have to have at least two friends.

I felt nervous, which wasn't like me. There was serious money at stake and I wasn't having a good day speaking-wise. I'd never met Jeremy Clarkson before, but he said he'd never seen me so quiet. However, even though I wasn't my former chatty self, I surprised myself. Contestants always say it's more difficult in the hotseat than watching at home – and it was. A couple of answers I would have stuck by at home had me doubting myself. This was real money, and I didn't want to lose it. I wasn't helped by Jeremy telling me that Harry Redknapp had gone out without a bean, not even reaching the £1,000 mark, with all lifelines used. No pressure there then, Clarkson!

I was pleased I did a bit better than Harry. Somehow, I got through the £32,000 question and had the chance to play for £64,000 with one lifeline left. It was on Formula One – not my strongest subject – and I had used Jeremy as a lifeline in an earlier round. I was gutted. And so was Jeremy, who of course knew the answer. My only remaining lifeline was to phone Steph or Andy. I knew the people from *Who Wants to Be a Millionaire?* were at Steph's house, keeping a watchful eye on her, making sure she wasn't quickly going online for the answer. I decided I should ask her, feeling guilty that she'd given up her time for me. I wasn't that bothered about Andy – I knew he would understand, although he told me later it was intense having someone there watching him and waiting in anticipation for a call. My appearance on the show only amounted to twenty minutes in the final edit, but I was on the floor in the studio for over an hour. Throughout that time, Andy said he was allowed to have his phone switched on but couldn't touch it until word came through to his minder that we'd finished.

I couldn't have let Steph go all through that and not get the call. Even though I didn't think she would know the answer, I chose her. Massive mistake. Of course, she had no idea – but Andy did.

Question: Since 2000 the Formula One Championship has not been won by a driver from which one of these countries – Finland, Spain, Netherlands and Brazil?
Answer: Brazil.

I rang Andy the following day to thank him for his time and apologize because he hadn't been needed. He then told me he'd become quite a big fan of Formula One over the previous five years – but he'd never thought to mention it to me. Poor Steph was distraught when her stab at the answer failed. I consoled her and let her know I was sure Marie Curie would be more than delighted with £32,000.

The charity estimates we've raised more than £3 million from the various launches, dinners, events, functions, the Great Daffodil Appeal and the Marie Curie Keepy-Uppy Challenge, which raised nearly a million on its own. My keepy-uppies are definitely better than my quizzing.

In February 2023, I went to Downing Street to hand in a petition with more than 166,000 signatures pleading with Prime Minister Rishi Sunak and his government to allow terminally ill people early access to state pensions so they don't die in poverty. I'd agreed to appear with Shep on *Good Morning Britain* earlier that day to highlight the reason behind my visit to Number 10, and Sam Royston, the policy and research director at Marie Curie, was kind enough to come with me and, literally, hold my hand through the interview. Sam was there for me in case I started to struggle to get the message across, but, as it turned out, I felt fine and got the words out. Just. Having Shep guiding me through it and relaxing me, asking me about my illness first, helped, of course, but I won't forget Sam's support.

Before handing in the petition at Number 10, I met up with Cheryl Whittaker and her husband Mark, and Tammy Prescott and her husband Lintyn. Both women had stopped work due to their terminal illnesses and knew first-hand how difficult it was to make ends meet at such a tough time, their husbands having also given up work to help care for them. They were campaigning so that others in the same position would not suffer similar hardship. It was so inspiring to walk side by side with these two lovely ladies, and I was more than happy to help spread the word in the hope that the government would consider making the necessary changes.

We had to show our identity documents when we arrived at the entrance to Downing Street. Once cleared – which for me was just an 'All right, Kammy?' – Cheryl, Tammy and I were ushered forward to knock on the famous black door and deliver the box of names supporting our petition. We didn't get to see Prime Minister Rishi Sunak on the day, but I truly hope he got to see the evidence of our efforts and seriously considered increasing financial support available for families living through terminal illness. I was so saddened to hear that Tammy passed away a couple of months later.

★

After the loss of a close friend, Jeff Stelling has worked incredibly hard for a charity close to his own heart, Prostate Cancer UK. Over the years, I've answered the call to participate in Jeff's fantastic March for Men charity walks on a number of occasions. Jeff has now raised more than £1.4 million since his first walk in 2016, highlighting an illness that affects one in eight men and on average kills one every forty-five minutes. The figures are worse for black men, whose odds of contracting the disease are one in four. Jeff always used to invite the lads from the show along and, over the years, Merse, Thommo, Charlie Nicholas, Matt Le Tissier, plenty of the production crew, and I have walked with him and his fellow fundraisers from various football grounds across the UK. It's always a pleasure to spend time with Jeff, whether it's a few minutes on screen laughing at each other on *Soccer Saturday* or out on the road.

Jeff's first walk was 262 miles from his beloved Hartlepool

United's Victoria Park to Wembley Stadium – ten marathon distances across ten days. I don't know if that official figure includes the extra eight miles we did on the second day because we managed to get lost around Leeds. And before you say it, I wasn't in charge of the directions. If I had been, we'd still be there!

I'd joined the group in York to walk from Bootham Crescent, then home of York City, to Leeds United's Elland Road. The hours on the road flew by because we walked in small groups and chatted. Everyone taking part had a reason to be there – they were living with someone with prostate cancer, knew someone who had it, or had lost someone to the disease. It wasn't all doom and gloom. The walks were a good chance to share laughter as well as experiences. I enjoyed trying to keep people's spirits up and the laughter going.

On that particular leg, the leading pack went off at quite a pace, led by the late Chelsea legend Ray Wilkins. I was behind with Jeff and a couple more members of the party, a little bit delayed because we'd stopped to do radio interviews en route. Even though I know Leeds pretty well from my playing days and frequent visits to the city, I had no idea where we were or where we were heading. Neither did Jeff or the rest of our group. Unfortunately, when we came to a junction just outside the city, we went left instead of right and got lost.

To say Jeff was seething as we trudged those extra miles to Elland Road would be an understatement. I, on the other hand, was enjoying myself, and the extra miles were no problem. I continued in my usual jovial manner, but struggled to get a laugh out of Jeff as he came to terms with the unnecessary extra mileage and the prospect of eight more days on his feet before reaching Wembley. Safe to say the navigation has now been perfected.

To date, Jeff has visited 104 football clubs and trekked 864 miles – a wonderful achievement. He's also had to put up with his fair share of blisters, aching limbs, cold baths and horrible days of walking through typically rain-soaked British summer weather. He always manages to do it with a smile on his face – as long as he's not been taken on a wild Kammy chase – and along the way has gathered some fantastic support from the world of football, and other sports stars like Sir Ian Botham, to raise funds and awareness of a cause which means so much to him.

A couple of years ago, our good mate Ray Clemence died of prostate cancer, and it was lovely to see three generations of the former Liverpool, Spurs and England keeper's family and his wife Vee join Jeff on various stages of his 2021 walk. Prostate Cancer UK's mantra is 'Men, we are with you', and joining Jeff for his marches sums that up perfectly.

★

Charity work is often as inspiring as it is moving. In 2012, I was contacted by Joanne Wright from When You Wish Upon a Star, an incredible organization which has a simple mission – to grant the wishes of children living with a life-threatening illness. Joanne asked if I'd meet a young lad called Mikey who was very poorly with a life-limiting illness.

Mikey had three wishes: to be driven in a Ferrari, to have a big birthday party, and to meet his hero – me! Thanks to the charity, Mikey had been granted his first two wishes, and Joanne got in touch to ask if I'd meet him, spending the afternoon with him, playing football in his back garden and games in the living room. We had fun the whole time.

As I was leaving, Joanne invited me to join a When You Wish

Upon a Star trip to Lapland the following Christmas. I jumped at the chance. Putting on a Christmas jumper and woolly hat for such a great cause was always going to grab me. It was the first of five trips I made with the kids to see Father Christmas in his magical kingdom near the North Pole, and I threw myself into every expedition. I wanted to spend as much time with everybody – the kids, their mums, dads and siblings, and the volunteers – as I could, singing Christmas songs and keeping spirits up on what was a long and difficult trip for some. I was there to entertain and play Kammy to his absolute maximum, and that's exactly what I did. Everywhere I went, the kids came with me like the Pied Piper. I loved every minute. At the same time, the trips were so humbling and heart-rending that I'd be emotionally drained when I got home and would think 'never again'. Of course, as soon as I got the next call from Joanne, I'd be off again. It doesn't matter how many times you witness it, when the kids see Santa for the first time, it takes your breath away.

Joanne went on to set up a new charity in Grimsby, Sunflowers Children's Action Group, and continues to arrange Christmas parties for children who suffer from life-limiting or life-threatening conditions. Every year she invites me along to an incredible occasion where hundreds of children and their families have one day where they can simply relax and enjoy themselves. Joanne is such an incredible person and doesn't get enough recognition for the work she does. Her daughter Rebecca requires constant care, but somehow, over twenty-five years, Joanne has found the time to help so many other children and their families. The work that Joanne and charity workers like her do is so inspiring to me, and now I have my own health issues I'm even more committed to following their lead and helping more people in the future.

32

A Mountain to Climb

IN 2011, MARIE CURIE ASKED ME IF I'D LEAD A GROUP UP
Mount Kilimanjaro in Tanzania, with the aim of raising
£400,000. I've taken on some tough challenges in the name of
charity, but climbing Kili, the largest free-standing mountain in
the world, proved to be one of the most gruelling, exhausting
and mentally demanding experiences I've ever had.

The expedition was to be carried out in conjunction with the
Football League. Any chairman, manager, ex-player, journalist
or footie fan who wanted to help us raise funds for the charity
could join us on the trip, as long as they were doing it in memory
of a loved one or for a terminally ill person. It therefore wasn't
difficult to fill the thirty-one spaces available – we could easily
have doubled that number.

I was head of the team, joined by, among others, my boy
Jack, old pal Steve Gibson, his brother Dave, Brendan Rodgers,
who had just won promotion via the play-offs to the Premier

League with Swansea, Coventry manager Aidy Boothroyd, and journalists Mark Clemmit and Des Kelly. We all boarded the plane from Heathrow in summer 2011. The biggest surprise was seeing Brendan at the departure gate when we all met up. He had to plan for Swansea's return to the big time. 'I wouldn't let you down,' he said, 'and most of all I'm doing this for my mum.'

After a two-hour journey by coach from our hotel, we reached the foot of Kilimanjaro and set off for the summit from the north of the mountain on the Rongai route, with our support staff of doctors, chefs, porters and guides in tow. I put on my easy-to-spot headgear, a fedora hat, which stayed on for the entire trip, and if I looked a prat, nobody mentioned it. We trekked through dusty fields, heathlands and pine forests, with the odd black-and-white Colobus monkey curiously observing us. It was quite a gentle climb, and as we went along the camaraderie built up among the group of strangers, all with their own cancer-related tale to tell. The team spirit was brilliant from the moment we set off, and it grew across that first day as we mingled and helped each other. My son Jack was the cameraman for the journey and recorded the official film for the Football League and Marie Curie.

We set up camp late afternoon to prepare for a bigger ascent the next day. So far this was easy-peasy, a stroll in the park. Brendan's promotion to the Premier League ten days earlier was on my mind when I asked him if our first day of the climb was as good as leading a team out at Wembley. 'It feels better,' he said.

'Careful,' I replied. 'The chairman might be watching!' It summed up how good that first day on the trek felt. Nothing could prepare us for what was ahead.

We were paired randomly in tents, which were tucked tightly

together across the small camp – ideal for singing round the campfire; less ideal when we were surrounded by heavy snorers. It was a difficult night for some, not helped by some very unpleasant aromas inside the tents. We had a nine-hour trek ahead of us, up some very steep inclines in the searing sun.

About half a dozen of the party started to feel the serious effects of sickness and diarrhoea early on. Brendan was among them; he had a tough second day and needed a long chat with the doctor to make sure he was OK. It turned out he'd picked up a debilitating bug that affected him all week, and he could easily have been forced to pull out. It was a miracle he made it anywhere near the top. I was being quite sensible about what I ate. I didn't fancy the prospect of using the camp toilet, which was basically a hole in the ground.

The highlight of the day was arriving at camp for the night and being treated by the porters and guides to a welcome song-and-dance show which had us all in good spirits for the night and day ahead, although Mark Clemmit made a bad start to day three when he fell and sprained his ankle before we'd even set off. After months of training and getting in the right condition, fellow Boro lad Clem nearly had to abandon after Aidy Boothroyd failed to catch him when he went in for a man hug and he ended up in a heap on the ground. As team leader, I had to ban all physical contact – Sergeant Kammy needed his army over the line in its entirety. Thankfully, Clem was able to continue, so we still had our full contingent at the halfway point.

The steep climbs to our next camp at Mawenzi Tarn took more than five hours, but they were worth every effort – the views across the valley were spectacular. Despite this, the whole team felt exhaustion and pain at some point. Me? I was loving every minute of it, and hardly felt any physical difficulties. Was there something wrong with me? My fellow trekkers kept talking about the altitude and lack of air, whereas I felt there was more air, if anything – my lungs were as good as ever.

The peaks seemed never-ending, and every time we hit a new one, I would go from the back of the group to the front, passing everyone to make sure they were all good and up for the climb ahead. Again, that team spirit among a group of men and women who had barely known each other a few days before pushed us through.

I caught up with Steve Gibson on camera during another delightful lunch. 'Steve, you've eaten in some of the best restaurants in the world, how does this compare?' I asked.

'Well,' he reflected, 'considering we're at 14,000 feet, that meal is exactly what we needed after our five-hour hike. We are all more than pleased with it. The red wine will have to wait 'til next week.'

Fine dining and expensive wines seemed a million miles from that bitterly cold mountainside. I'm sure the two of us ate much worse as kids when we were growing up. Steve's main concern wasn't the food. It was that he was walking on only one good knee and didn't know if he would make it to the top.

After lunch, we were led on a three-hour acclimatization walk by the porters, which involved scaling another thousand feet or so and then coming back down. It was designed to give our bodies a sample of the tests to come. That evening, as we recovered, our expedition leader Chris Hill mapped out the plan for the next two gruelling days. We hadn't even started the hard stuff yet.

The drop in temperature at night was remarkable. Once the

sun went down, it fell below freezing. Fewer male members of the party were prepared to take a midnight pee, that's for sure. We set off at six in the morning and walked a barren and seemingly endless track across an alpine desert towards the top of the mountain.

We suffered our first casualty when Aileen Trew, wife of Notts County chairman Ray, was forced to give up. As we headed across the desert paths, she fainted and fell. She tried to carry on, but she started to vomit violently, and our doctor, Megan, had to persuade her to call it a day. Poor Aileen was devastated.

The final climb to that night's camp was one of the hardest parts of the ascent, but, Aileen aside, we all made it. There was another small 'meal' waiting for us, and we had only a couple of hours' sleep in the falling temperatures before a midnight bid for the summit.

We woke at 11 p.m. and made the final preparations for the last stretch – wrapped up in layers of thermals, fleeces, waterproofs, arctic gloves, balaclavas and woolly hats. The fedora was back on my head, and I had a gallon of water in my backpack. The first climb that night was tough and painful at times for me, and must have been hard work for some of the others too. My head was hammering due to the altitude. A couple of steps felt like a marathon, I was struggling so badly for my breath. I'd reach for my secret Salbutamol inhaler, take a blast to clear the lungs, and then I was back. I've been asthmatic all my life. I had tuberculosis when I was eight and when that cleared I was diagnosed with asthma. I used an inhaler from that point on but never told one of the football clubs I played for. The condition is worse in the summer and when my immune system is down,

resulting in wheeziness. Ironically for an animal-lover, I'm particularly affected by cat, dog and horse hairs.

For the first time on the trip, the altitude had started to affect
me, but I certainly didn't want the rest to know it, especially
when others started to reach their limit. Two people were led
away, showing signs of pulmonary and cerebral oedema, fluid-
retention conditions which can be critical and seriously impact
a person at high altitude.

These were definitely abnormal conditions for the human
body. At the top of Kilimanjaro, the atmospheric pressure is
half that at sea level, and a normal blood oxygen reading, which
might be around 97 per cent, can dip to the mid-70s. Somehow
the brilliant Doctor Megan managed to run between us all and
check everyone was able to continue.

At various points, as well as medical assistance, we all needed
a bit of extra encouragement. As the leader of the group, the
last section was particularly difficult for me because it really
was everyone for themselves. We were walking on narrow paths
and, with the porters keen for us to keep moving, I couldn't keep
going backwards and forwards through the group. I just had to
trust that everyone would make it. I found out later that Clem
had a wobble on that last stage and was certain he wouldn't be
able to continue, but Brendan was there for him with words of
encouragement. 'Quitters never win. Winners never quit,' the
former Leicester manager kept saying.

We pushed on and on, with many of us suffering hallucina-
tions, sickness, fainting and mini panic attacks. It was strange
how some people's bodies reacted to being so high up and
exposed to the elements. Nearly five hours after we'd set off, we
clambered over one last rock to reach Gilman's Point, the end

of the scree slopes and the beginning of the crater rim and trail to the summit. The Gibson brothers, Brendan, Aidy, Clem, Des and Jack all made it over the top to huge cheers. As did Lucy from Liverpool, who arrived with blood running from her nose and tears streaming down her face.

People then had the choice to head back down or continue to the Uhuru peak, an additional three-hour round trip and another 1,000 feet up and around. I was the group's leader and felt fine, so of course I wanted to keep going. In the meantime, I rested, took on some energy bars and water, and congratulated my fellow walkers on reaching Gilman's Point. I was oblivious to the fact that Jack wasn't resting properly – or at all – because he was so busy filming everyone so they'd have a record of reaching that important first summit and the famous wooden Gilman's Point sign that marks the spot. It took about twenty-five minutes for the last of the troop to arrive. I announced we'd have another fifteen-minute break before heading off for the last climb to Uhuru, Kilimanjaro's peak. That's when Jack finally put his camera down. I encouraged him to get a couple of energy bars down his neck. But when Jack stood up, he fainted into my arms. Porters and guides came straight over to help me, and Jack sat down for a couple of minutes before declaring he was fit to go. The guides' warning was stark. They told us Jack had to go back down because he could suffer a brain haemorrhage if he continued. Chris Hill also told him to quit, but Jack was having none of it.

'I'm fine, Dad. Let me go up.'

'But it's not worth it, Jack. What if something terrible happens? I could never forgive myself.'

He was adamant: 'I am going on. Either you help me or you don't.'

I went for another conflab with the guides and Chris Hill, and Chris told me that as I was leader, I got the final decision on whether Jack should continue. What a choice. My son's life in my hands.

I understood Jack's desperation to complete the task and get to the very top, but I don't think he fully understood the risks. After his continuous pleading, I agreed we'd walk slowly together – I'd be with him every step of the way. That meant I had to abandon the rest of the group for the final leg. They understood and vowed to push each other on. My priority now was Jack. Sometimes he'd fall asleep as I held him, the porters on hand with sledges ready to whisk him off if anything untoward happened. And so we walked slowly but surely to the top. All the time I was making sure I got a reaction from Jack when his eyes closed, otherwise those porters would spring into action and Jack would be 'blue lighted' to the lower levels where the air was thicker.

I wasn't enjoying this any more – the trip had turned into a nightmare. This final trek seemed to take an eternity but somehow we all made it to the top. And when we got there, Jack suddenly had a new lease of life. It was like a miracle. He picked up the camera and started filming the group as if nothing had happened. What a relief! We posed for a few pictures at the Uhuru sign – 'Congratulations, you are now at Uhuru Peak at 5,895 m' – and had a final chat to the camera for Jack.

'That is the worst pre-season I have ever had,' said Aidy. 'Ten pre-seasons in one.'

Des had a word too. I told him I hadn't had him down as one

who'd make it. 'At least we made it,' he replied, 'and we're here to tell the tale and bore everyone until the end of time about it.'

'You're boring us now, Des,' I told him.

When Jack had finished filming, we took in the spectacular views, Tanzania and Kenya stretched out below us. We congratulated and hugged each other as we took in our achievements.

I was still keeping a close eye on Jack. After about ten minutes he collapsed right next to me. Within seconds, the porters had him on a stretcher. They told me they needed to get him down to breathe in normal air, but that he'd be OK. Two guys held the sides of the stretcher and one guy took the front and they set off like Usain Bolt. I abandoned the group and raced like a mad man after them. All I could think as I chased behind them was, 'What have I done? How could I allow my son to continue against the advice of the experts? What kind of father am I?'

The minutes it took to get down felt like hours, with all kinds of horrific outcomes running through my head. We reached a lower camp in no time, though, and Jack quickly got the oxygen and medical attention he needed. He was soon up and about but taking it very steady and leaving the filming to someone else. I was taking no more chances with my son's well-being – I was so relieved he was OK – and ordered him to take it easy and get as much rest as possible. We had more than enough photographic evidence of our task!

In all, twenty of us reached Gilman's Point, nine made it to Uhuru and three were ruled out due to illness.

'Would you do it again?' I asked Dave Gibson.

'Err . . . once in a lifetime,' he replied. I think we all felt the same.

Back at base camp, we spent some time re-acclimatizing before heading back to our hotel for some proper rest and relaxation and a good night's sleep. We stopped at a mud hut off-licence for some refreshments for the night ahead, and broke into an impromptu sing-song on the bus. It was a great atmosphere, and the sense of achievement and pride among the group was fantastic. Our hotel was not the most salubrious but no one cared. At the bottom of Kilimanjaro, luxury is not the top priority. After six days and nights on Africa's largest mountain, all any of us wanted was a shower! It was also the first time we'd had a phone signal for nearly a week.

While the rest of us got our first feel of hot water for days, Steve was on his phone, catching up with news from the outside world and his business affairs. I was in the room next to him, and as I headed down to the bar for the evening, he suddenly appeared in the corridor, towel wrapped round his midriff, heading to reception. Unfortunately, all the hot water had been used and the Middlesbrough chairman, still filthy from his exploits on the mountain, was not a happy man. Worse was to follow. Steve trudged disconsolately back to his room for a cold shower, and I headed back a few minutes later to check he was OK. I got as far as his door when I heard swearing and cursing from his room. A pipe in his bathroom had burst and a deluge of sewage had exploded across the floor and into the bedroom. Of all the people for this to happen to, it had to be Steve. As the head of the group, I had to plead with the hotel manager to find Steve an alternative room for the night after he turned down my very kind offer to sleep on my floor.

In the wake of the trip, I received the Above & Beyond in Memory of Sir Bill Cotton Award – Bill was a vice-president of Marie Curie as well as a landmark figure in the broadcasting world. That trip will always live long in the memory, as will everyone who battled so hard to raise that money for such an incredible charity.

Of course, it was some time before I told Anne what had happened with Jack at the top of the mountain. In fact I don't think I ever did! I think in the end she read about it in an interview. If ever there was a time to be covering a game at Plymouth, that was it!

33

Mexico

Truth is, while I might have stood on top of the world – well, almost – I still have my own mountain to climb. Recently, though, I feel as if I have been given a huge boost in my quest for the summit.

When I finally announced the details of my health problems, specifically through the Steven Bartlett podcast, I was inundated with offers of help. Far too many to follow up. There were people telling me of their own similar experiences, husbands and wives, mothers and fathers, grandparents, medics, specialists, faith healers, therapists – people from all walks of life.

There were also people telling me I should never give up – should always carry on being me, doing what I'm good at. One such was none other than Sir Alex Ferguson. He was beaming as he came over to say hello when we met behind the royal box at the League Cup final between Manchester United and

Newcastle in 2023. 'Don't you retire, son,' he told me. 'Whatever you do, don't you retire.'

Sir Alex has been through his own health issues in the past few years, but I couldn't believe he knew I had problems too, and that he was kind enough to say something so encouraging. If Sir Alex – a man who'd worked at the very top of the game until he was seventy-one – was telling me not to give up, then maybe I should listen. When Sir Alex Ferguson tells you to do something, you tend to do it.

When it came to practical help, there were far too many kind offers to follow up. And then a doctor, Rohit Kulkarni, contacted me from his office in Wales. He explained he was involved in groundbreaking treatment which could possibly reverse my condition. I did respond, thanking him for his interest, but it was a full five months before I contacted him again to confirm that I would like to take up his offer of help. In the meantime I'd tried various alternative health regimes and, while I felt great from the wholesome food I was putting into my body, it did nothing for my speech or my dwindling strength. My brain was simply not sending the signals to where they were needed, no matter how hard I tried. Believe me, the desire was so strong, but the brain was rejecting any attempt to overcome the problems I had.

I reconnected with Rohit after I'd appeared on *GMB* for Marie Curie, along with Ben Shephard and Kate Garraway. For a few weeks Ben had been urging me to chat to Kate about the treatment which Rohit had mentioned. Kate was keen to help me. Her husband Derek had undergone the experimental treatment himself in Mexico following his well-documented recovery from Covid which left him with numerous health issues. Although Derek was not fully recovered, Kate assured me that the method had, indeed, worked wonders for him, and she was hopeful further treatment would result in more amazing improvements. Kate urged me to speak with the people behind the prototype scanner which had given her, Derek and their family so much hope. A Zoom meeting was arranged with the scientist behind this exciting lifeline, Dr Roberto Trujillo. It took no time for me to be convinced I had nothing to lose. I'd exhausted all other avenues, which were few, so Anne and I immediately began our search for flights and accommodation – we were both bound for Monterrey, where the treatment was based, for the whole of the month of June.

The couple of months leading up to our departure passed quite quickly. I had a few work commitments to fulfil, some of which were just about possible; others, due to my uncertain speech, I had to cancel. Despite our anticipation, our immediate family were cautious. 'Are you sure about this?' 'Have you really checked these people out?' 'There's lots of untrustworthy folk out there, ready to rip you off'. The warnings were many, and we could totally understand the concerns. But Kate had done a good job assuring us the whole set-up in Monterrey would surprise us, very professional, using cutting-edge technology, with incredible results – so good, in fact, that it could maybe change the face of treatment for neurological conditions across the globe.

We managed to reassure the family that, although there were no guarantees, we were very hopeful that we'd eventually be returning home having made some kind of positive progress. They agreed it was a nothing ventured, nothing gained situation.

Anne and I were due to leave Heathrow Airport early in the morning. I'd been invited to the League Managers' Association

Awards dinner the night before, held in the Grosvenor Hotel, London, and, although Anne was with me, Ben Shephard was my plus-one for the evening. Anne and I would have plenty of time together, after all. Ben and I had a great night, met lots of old acquaintances, and all the while I was hoping that the next time I was in this kind of situation I'd be back to my old self, speaking clearly and confidently. I couldn't wait to get on that plane to Mexico in a few hours' time.

Anne had become used to being the packhorse of our partnership during the past couple of years, which had been an embarrassment to me, but I had had to get used to that. So, once again, she duly stepped up to the mark and swiftly got us to the check-in desk.

The journey to Monterrey was smooth and restful – at least to start with. At Dallas, the passport control officer welcomed us with a broad smile – 'You look familiar, do I know you?' This wasn't unusual territory. We asked if he had watched British soccer, maybe *Ninja Warrior UK*, but that wasn't ringing any bells. We were about to give up when realization dawned on his face – 'Got it! You were in *Ted Lasso*! It's a big favourite of my wife and I. In fact, we're planning on watching the last ever episode tonight!'

We'd now been with the bloke a while and were worried the queue behind us would be growing impatient.

'OK, Chris,' Anne said, 'we'd better move on. This man has work to do.'

'Are you kidding?' the officer replied. 'I'm the guy with the gun. If I want to chat to you, I will! I just wish I had my cell with me to take a picture!' Unbelievable!

I arrived in Monterrey airport very tired, a little bruised

after my fall on the way to the gate at Dallas, but relieved to be there. We were met by the support team of Neurocytonix, the medical people who were going to be taking good care of us for the length of our stay. We were left to unpack and prepare for the start of my treatment the next day. Neither of us relished the challenge of adjusting to the seven-hour time difference between our temporary home and the UK, now far behind us. Nevertheless, we looked forward with excitement to getting on with the job in hand.

Next morning we were picked up at 8 a.m., the time we'd chosen for my treatment for the following twenty-eight days. Our reasoning was that we'd then have the remainder of the day for sightseeing. Sadly, we were soon to learn that, although a lovely city, there was not that much to occupy us as far as day trips were concerned, and everything was limited due to the heatwave the area was experiencing – we were going to be melting in 40-plus-degree heat for most of our stay. This was not one bit daunting to me, I love those temperatures, but Anne was horrified – she baulks at heat over about 15 degrees. I could see this was going to be uncomfortable for her. The one saving grace was that our hotel was built into one of the largest shopping centres I have ever seen. We could step straight out of our hotel room, into the lift, and be deposited right on the ground floor of the mall with shops, restaurants, snack outlets, entertainment stretching right out before us. It wasn't a healthy thought but, if Anne didn't want to, she had no need to step out of this air-conditioned heaven for the duration of our stay.

Our first day at Neurocytonix was as busy as it was interesting. We were driven to the clinic, where we met the numerous people who were going to be looking after me. I had various tests, which included taking blood, and checking my memory, and was also asked to perform several small moves with my hands and feet to test my dwindling coordination before being whisked for an MRI scan of my brain. While I was occupied with the scan, the neurologist, Dr Leonel Adrian Cantu Martinez – thankfully shortened to Leo! – had a chat with Anne about my current health issues and how they had developed. Later we both admitted to each other that during various conversations between doctors, conducted in Spanish, we heard the word 'Parkinson's'. Although previous scans had cleared me of the disease, it was definitely on our minds until the next day when we were assured my brain wasn't so bad for my age, maybe just a bit of damage to my neural pathways, probably due to concussions during my footballing career.

The next day, I began the first of twenty-eight one-hour sessions in the 'wonder' machine. Day one showed us the routine we'd adhere to on a daily basis. First up was a little chat with the English-speaking doctors about my previous day – what I'd done, how much sleep I'd had, how much I'd eaten, how much water I'd managed to drink, how much exercise I'd performed, if I'd been tired, had a headache, taken a nap and, the ever awkward question, had I pooped and peed OK? While this was going on there was always a nurse taking my blood pressure, heart rate and temperature, the results of which the doctor reported to me before I was shown into the room housing the machine which I so hoped would change my life for the better. Similar to an MRI scanner, in front of me was basically a tube with two open ends which transmits radio frequency and magnetic fields into the body as the patient lies inside. Unlike an MRI scanner, though, there is no noise, to the extent you are actually left wondering exactly what is happening for the hour you're in there! I was helped inside, jiggled around until I was in the correct position for the machine to do its work, and so started the first hour of relaxation. To pass the time I'd listen to music – eighties hits, since you ask – and chat with Anne as she sat by my head, checking out emails and messages which had come in overnight.

The sophisticated equipment was primarily programmed to target my brain, but after chatting with me about my past medical history, the doctors decided my back, knees and neck also needed attention to aid my balance, strength and coordination. Being an ex-footballer, I'd been suffering with terrible back pain for many years, during which time I'd had to throw away the golf clubs as a bad job because the pain and strain on my spine was too great. Attempting to fix my whole body was too good to be true, I thought. In the past, and in addition to having steroid injections to my lower back, I'd had MRI scans on my spine which showed that my neck was riddled with arthritis. I was very sceptical about this fix-all machine coming up with the goods. However, here I was, with a willing and enthusiastic team of medics who were absolutely confident I'd soon be seeing positive results.

Afterwards, we headed back to the mall, specifically the Starbucks, where we'd sit and plan our day. As a dedicated tea-drinker all my life I began to suspect my treatment was even changing my taste-buds. I discovered coffee and looked forward to it every morning, although Anne said I was getting above my station when I insisted on a caramel macchiato for my daily fix. Good job Starbucks isn't so close to home in the UK – I'd soon be putting on the pounds! We'd video call the family from there before the grandkids went to bed, which was lovely, and kept us going, especially in the first week or so when the days seemed to stretch out in front of us forever. One thing we mentioned was the fact we'd not seen or heard another person from our part of the world. The family couldn't get their heads round this. 'Wherever you go, Dad, someone always recognizes you! You'll definitely be recognized during this trip.' Anne and I weren't so sure. Monterrey isn't exactly a tourist destination. I'd imagine few Brits venture there, unless it's for business. So I decided to put my money where my mouth was and predicted it wouldn't happen. The wager was on.

Later, after a rest at the hotel, we'd get our daily step-count up before choosing somewhere to eat. There was no end of food outlets. From tacos to sandwiches, Chinese to Italian, the choice was amazing, apart from, to my dismay, not a single restaurant in sight serving Indian food – shameful!

After a few days, Dr Leo advised that it was important for a person of my age to keep up my body strength as best I could, so I decided to visit the hotel gym. Of late, working out had proved impossible for me. My heart was willing, but my body wasn't getting the signal from my brain to perform the tasks I so wanted to do. My first session on day five triggered the will and desire I'd hoped to arouse, and I was secretly pleased with the hour or so I spent there. It was like stepping back in time and I was full of enthusiasm, mainly because I'd detected small changes in my strength and coordination which were making the tasks no longer impossible. I was wary of jumping the gun so was reserved when Anne asked how it went, but confirmed I'd be making it part of my daily routine.

After a week of groundhog days, Dr Roberto Trujillo arrived

from the USA and invited us to join him for dinner. Finally a bit of excitement! At last we were meeting him face to face, as well as the patients he brought along, many of whom were children with cerebral palsy. Anne and I sat next to Dr Roberto as he carefully and patiently explained everything and enthused over the predicted outcome of my month of treatment. He was adamant I'd return home so much better than I'd arrived. His reassurance was music to my ears and really set me in a positive frame of mind. Anne couldn't sleep, she was so excited and overwhelmed by this enthusiastic, clever man and his scientific invention which could potentially put me on the road to recovery.

By day eight, I'd slipped into the habit of taking a daily walk to a park around a mile away, where I began testing my balance to see if there was any improvement. Anne was amazed when I returned to show her that I was able to stand on my left foot and raise my right off the floor, holding the position for thirty seconds or so. A small feat for most, but a real breakthrough for me. I was totally made up. It meant my brain was sending the signal out, and, at last, my body was responding. I began to drive Anne crazy by standing on one leg at every opportunity – in the hotel room, waiting outside the lift, inside the lift, in a queue – I missed no chance to practise my balance. If I looked slightly odd I didn't care. Nobody knew me, after all, and I was just delighted to be able to do something that had been lost to me for so long.

By day ten – get this! – not only could I stand on one leg, I could actually hop! I could get my body off the ground and perform seven hops! Although I did tend to veer off sideways after about the second one. Nonetheless, I was ecstatic. It felt like the breakthrough I'd been hoping for, the one the doctors here told me would come but I hadn't dared pin my hopes on. It felt like I could look ahead to not falling over, to regaining my fitness, playing footie with the grandkids. We didn't want to get carried away, but this was an amazing leap (or hop) forward and we were buzzing for the rest of the day. Of course, Anne posted it immediately on the family WhatsApp group chat and the response was both emotional and uplifting. Eighteen treatments to go and I was definitely a believer!

Day twelve brought another revelation. Not only was my body leaving the floor according to what the brain was ordering, the pain in my back had eased. I was working out in the gym, bending and stretching, and suddenly there was no discomfort. All those years of wearing back braces, of osteopaths, chiropractors, even steroid injections to get me through a match or over a spasm, and here I was, pain free. This was definitely the stuff dreams are made of – and I proved it to Anne with a showing of several star jumps, again performed by the pool. So now I was able to touch the ground, formerly impossible due to the condition of my back, and then jump off the ground in a star shape, several times in a row. There I now was, hopping and jumping poolside – luckily it was not well frequented! But, again, I didn't care! I had something to get my teeth into and improve upon.

Day fifteen, just over the halfway mark, brought great news for Anne – I was able to open a jar of olives! For the past couple of years I'd handed all jars straight over to her, knowing my failing strength would not allow me to unscrew the lids, but here I now was relieving her of that task. I began to imagine that, at this rate, and not satisfied with this small show of strength, she'd even be calling on me to carry the luggage on the return journey to the UK – maybe I should slow down this progress lark!

My only concern was that, while all the strength and balance improvement was taking place – by now I could bend and touch my toes, something I hadn't been able to do since I was forty – only a small change was happening with my speech. On the video calls back home I was being told I was sounding clearer and faster, backed up by some of the clinical staff, but me being me, it's fair to say my ideal scenario would have been perfect, clear, fast speech from day one. So, although I was pleased to hear that changes were being recognized, I was far from certain that I was being cured of the apraxia.

On day twenty-one, Dr Roberto came back to Monterrey and, once again, we were invited out to dinner. This was a much smaller gathering, only a couple of us patients and some of the staff. The highlight of the evening, for me, was when Dr Roberto invited each of us to take a few minutes to tell everyone a little about ourselves. I delivered the longest and most concise impromptu speech I had managed in two, maybe three, years. I surprised myself to the extent I'm sure the others around the table thought I was a bit too keen on the subject of myself! But the truth was I was just amazed. I couldn't believe the clarity of my voice and fluency of the words coming out of my mouth.

A couple of days later, we arrived back at the hotel around 9.30 a.m. as usual and headed straight for Starbucks. I'd perfected my Spanish to the extent I'd become the one designated to get the order while Anne waited at the table outside. When she heard a commotion from inside, she jumped up immediately and started recording on her phone. Immediately she posted the video on the family WhatsApp group – 'OMG, it's happened! It appears, not only do these people know him but, amazingly, Dad seems to know them too! From this distance I've no idea who they are myself but I'm sure I'll soon find out . . .'

Inside Starbucks, I'd been minding my own business, waiting in the queue to be served, but became aware that four guys who'd sauntered in behind me appeared to be staring at me. When I looked round I was flabbergasted. At the same time as a stream of inappropriate words left my lips, I was hearing an equally surprised, 'Kammy, what the hell are you doing here?' I couldn't believe it – standing there beside me were the Westlife boys, Nicky Byrne and Shane Filan, along with their security man Basil and an interpreter. Nicky, who had been at Leeds United like me, way back before his Westlife days, is someone I've known for a long while, and to meet Shane as well was such a pleasure. We all moved outside, where the guys introduced themselves to Anne.

'We hope you don't mind Westlife,' they told her, 'because you're coming to the concert tonight.'

'Hold on, lads,' I thought, 'I need to consult the diary. Oh, hang on, tonight's the same as the past three weeks!'

'You'll be doing a bit of dancing tonight to "Uptown Girl",' Nicky told Anne. We were excited for the rest of the day – an event at last!

On day twenty-six I woke feeling a bit fuzzy. Though not particularly late, we'd stayed out longer the night before and not adhered to our usual early eating routine. Never mind, a gym session later would get me going in the right direction. At the end of my hour in the 'tube', and as I got myself upright and on to my feet, I noticed something different. I immediately mentioned it to Anne. I couldn't put my finger on what felt different but, in the car back to the hotel, I said I didn't feel quite so disorientated. I hadn't needed the usual few minutes to adjust, my legs didn't have their usual, very slightly, jelly-like feel about them. I decided to try out my hopping and was overjoyed when I performed sixty on my left leg, a new PB, and was immediately able to change feet and complete forty-two on my right. And on each foot I'd told myself to stop, not wanting to overdo it. Great progress – I was well pleased.

And that's something else that's changed. I'm able to think of apraxia with a smile on my face. Tony Gale, for instance, still rings me regularly and says, 'You got a minute, Kammy?' Then, light-heartedly, 'No, sorry, have you got twenty minutes?' If you can't laugh about these things, you might as well give up. Laughter has always been one of my greatest releases. There have been times when I've wondered if I'd ever smile again. Those times are gone.

Day twenty-eight was soon here. It felt very strange when Anne and I woke up, knowing we were off to the clinic for the last time and I was about to complete my very last hour with the machine. We had mixed feelings about not seeing the doctors again. After all, we'd been on this journey together and they were so attentive and interested in my progress. We'd also had a chuckle together each day when they asked me about my pooping and peeing routine – Anne assured them she wouldn't be doing the same while helping with my aftercare when we were back home.

My last sixty minutes in the machine came and went, after which I had several tests to compare with those I'd had twenty-eight days earlier – my gait, reflexes, etc. Next day I returned for blood tests, brain scans and cognitive tests, again to be compared with those I'd had at the start of the treatment.

Later in the afternoon, while we were having our farewell trek through the mall, I had a call from Dr Trujillo. He'd received the scans and was calling to talk me through the results. He was so excited to tell me that my brain had reacted to the treatment to the extent that I now had 2,000-plus more neural pathways (the bundles of fibres which connect one area of the nervous system to another) than when I'd arrived in Monterrey. His elation was evident – and very infectious. Anne and I were jumping for joy. Of course, we knew I was so much better, but to see the scans, the evidence in pictures, was amazing. We were on cloud nine as we enjoyed our last celebration Mexican meal that night.

We arrived home two days later, reunited, at last, with our family. It was so good to see them – like we'd been away five months instead of five weeks. The grandkids were excited to get the gifts we'd brought home for them and, when they eventually left us to it, we still had enough energy to tidy up all the debris they left behind – Anne and I looked at each other and agreed it was like we'd never been away!

★

Forty-eight hours later, I was on the road again for a trip to Sofia in Bulgaria to work on an ad for male grooming company Manscaped. When I'd been approached a few months earlier, I wasn't sure I'd be able to fulfil the commitment due to the state of my voice. It was on my mind during the first two or three weeks in Monterrey and I'd promised myself I'd pull out of the engagement if there was no improvement. As I did feel better, here I was on my way, although I remained a little apprehensive.

My job was to act as a commentator on a football match, in particular a streaker running full length of the pitch, regarding whether he could benefit from being treated and trimmed by

Manscaped products. After a few rehearsals we felt ready for the proper take the next day.

I spent a few anxious hours that night wondering if my voice would really carry me through the filming. Though more fluent than a month ago, my speech was still susceptible to setbacks, slower at some times than others, although not as slow as it had been before treatment. I realized I was still in that will it/won't it perform situation, and it was getting to me. I managed to sleep in the end but decided the next morning to adopt a positive attitude. Instead of wondering if I could get through it, I told myself I *would* get through it.

After breakfast I went for a walk around Sofia with one of the ad guys. After admiring the sights we headed back to the hotel. Around a hundred metres from the entrance we were stopped at a makeshift barrier by police. They were swarming all over the area. They asked where we were going and, when we showed them our key cards, allowed us through. When finally we got to the hotel, there were two more police officers with rifles and also an airport-style X-ray machine. Puzzling, and also a little worrying – following my treatment in Monterrey, I wasn't permitted to go through an X-ray of any kind. I'd had to show an official letter to this effect at airports during the past few days. 'This is too odd for words,' I said to the ad guy. 'Who gets X-rayed to go into a hotel?' Mystified, I made it past the security check and headed to my room to collect my gym gear.

By the time I went back to the reception area en route to the gym, there were many more police officers. They were very intimidating and their presence began to worry me. I decided to ask the hotel staff what was going on. The receptionist refused to divulge any information. This only heightened my gathering fear and I insisted that, as a hotel guest, I should be told of any danger I might be in. The desk staff relented – 'It's President Zelenskyy, he's here from Ukraine and has stopped over to freshen up before meeting with the Bulgarian president.' So that answered my question – certainly not what I'd expected to hear.

Later, in the recording studio, I began with a few nerves but, as the words began to flow, and I realized they were fluent, I began to relax, giving the sentences intonation and clarity, near to how the old me would have performed. The Manscaped bosses were more than happy with how it was going, but the director asked if I could go a little faster. This could have had me panicking, but instead I was relaxed, buoyed by how well my voice was doing. 'This is as good as it gets, I'm afraid,' I explained. He didn't ask again. We continued with no hiccups, and everyone was very pleased.

During breaks in recording, I'd called Anne, knowing she too would be nervous as to whether I'd get through it OK. I was able to tell her the good news. We couldn't help but get emotional when we thought about how far I'd come in a month.

I returned home marvelling at the new me – full of confidence, more concise, and definitely much fitter. All in all, I was 75 per cent of how I used to be. They tell me I'll continue to improve over the coming months. If that's the case, bring it on! I'll certainly be giving regular updates – just not from the gantry at Fratton Park!

34

Extra Time

AND SO THERE WE ARE. THAT'S IT – THAT'S WHERE KAMMY is right now. It's been a long, emotional and bumpy road but I do feel I have found him again. I do feel that when I look in the mirror I'm no longer searching for the person I want to be, but am seeing the person I am. And I'm happy with that. Yes, there will always be part of me that yearns to be 100 per cent Kammy – the *Soccer Saturday* motormouth delivering a report from a far-flung ground while self-inflicted mayhem lurks, ready to spring, at any moment. I'm back on track, though. No longer am I reaching for words. They are there. And no longer is a lucid, uninterrupted sentence an insurmountable hurdle. I say what I want to say. Maybe not at a million miles an hour. But I say it.

That's ultimately what this book is – me saying what I want to say. There have been times when people have tried to silence me. But I never let prejudice get to me and I won't allow apraxia to close me down either. I know that I have a great life, packed with amazing friends, surrounded by beautiful family. I have a lot to live for. And I'll forever be in the thick of that life, smile on my face. A genuine smile – not one that I think people want to see.

I have learned a lot in the past three years. The main thing being that clamming up and pretending to be OK is never a good idea. Not sharing is destructive and will only push you lower. If I can achieve one thing with this book it will be that one person reading it, whatever issue they are struggling with, reaches out for help. Because I can guarantee that person will only experience the best of surprises – there is always someone out there, known or unknown, who will offer them a welcome embrace.

I hope in some ways, through these pages, I have offered that embrace. I'm glad I've shared. Glad I've written a book that is more than recollections of goals scored, fun times shared. I always wanted this book to matter in some way. It matters to me because it's the truth. I hope it matters to other people because it offers a glimpse of a shared reality – we are all great in some ways, but we are all vulnerable in others. I have laid that vulnerability bare.

Unbelievable? Actually, no. Because this, now, is the real Kammy. The real me.

Acknowledgements

This book was never going to be a simple piece of work.

Regardless of the problems I have had to endure over the past couple of years due to whatever might be going on in my brain, it has to be said that my memory has *never* been great. Everyone who has helped me and contributed to bringing *My Unbelievable Life* to completion is witness to the struggles I endure to recall specific details. If you've happened to have a strange text or call from me recently asking about a certain incident/date/person/venue/event etc., it would have been all in the cause of bringing this book together – and to the many of you involved in this way, I would like to take this opportunity to thank you sincerely.

My sympathy lies with Colin Young for spending endless hours with me, often painstakingly extracting details about my life, only to produce a very small amount of material with which to work. Those sessions were interminable and probably very frustrating for him, although he wouldn't admit it to me. But we

Acknowledgements

also had fun along the way! Thank you, mate; we both know I wouldn't have done it without you onboard.

Much gratitude to John Woodhouse for agreeing to lend his expertise by structuring the book superbly. Special nods to Chris Harvey and Adam Bostock, who both added their own flavours to the final result. Cheers, chaps.

At a time when I was certain I did not want to write this book and that nobody would want to read it anyway, my publishers at Pan Macmillan believed in me and urged me to give it a go. They were there throughout to allay any concerns and to offer support, and they did not give up on me. My immense appreciation goes to them.

Finally, it has to be said that, without the unwavering support of my wife, Anne, I definitely would not have waded my way through the experience of working on this book while also coping with other distractions in my life. I attribute my sanity, such as it is, to my sons, Ben and Jack, and their partners, Eve and Perdie, producing the absolute loves of my life. It is my privilege to be called Grandad by Sol, Connie, Billie and Morgan.

I love you all.

Picture Acknowledgements

1. Chris Kamara
2. Chris Kamara
3. Chris Kamara
4. Chris Kamara
5. Mike Walker via Alamy
6. Copyright unknown
7. Copyright unknown
8. *Yorkshire Evening Post*
9. Peter Hatter, PA Images via Alamy
10. Tony Harris, PA Images via Alamy
11. Chris Kamara
12. Chris Kamara
13. Matthew Ashton, PA Images via Alamy
14. Adam Davy, PA Images via Alamy
15. Sean Dempsey, PA Images via Alamy
16. Chris Kamara
17. News Images Ltd via Alamy

Picture Acknowledgements

18. Boro Twitter on behalf of Middlesbrough FC
19. Chris Kamara
20. Chris Kamara
21. Chris Kamara
22. Comic Relief via Getty Images
23. Chris Kamara
24. Chris Kamara
25. Seb Daly via Sportsfile
26. Chris Kamara
27. Chris Kamara
28. Chris Kamara
29. Chris Kamara
30. Jonathan Brady, PA Images via Alamy
31. Chris Kamara
32. Chris Kamara